NATURAL LAW IN JUDAISM

This book presents a new theory of natural law, significant for the study of Judaism, philosophy, and comparative ethics. It demonstrates that the assumption that Judaism has no natural law theory to speak of, held by the vast majority of scholars, is simply wrong. The book shows how natural law theory, using a variety of different terms for itself throughout the ages, has been a constant element in Jewish thought. The book sorts out the varieties of Jewish natural law theory, illuminating their strengths and weaknesses. It also presents a case for utilizing natural law theory in order to deal with current theological and philosophical questions in Judaism's ongoing reflection on its own meaning and its meaning for the wider world. David Novak combines great erudition in the Jewish tradition the history of philosophy and law, and the imagination to argue for Judaism in the context of current debates, both theoretical and practical.

DAVID NOVAK holds the J. Richard and Dorothy Shiff Chair of Jewish Studies at the University of Toronto, where he has been since January 1997. He previously held the Edgar M. Bronfman Chair of Modern Judaic Studies at the University of Virginia. His many publications include *Jewish–Christian Dialogue* (Oxford University Press, 1989), *Jewish Social Ethics* (Oxford University Press, 1992) and *The Election of Israel* (Cambridge University Press, 1995).

NATURAL LAW IN JUDAISM

DAVID NOVAK

CAMBRIDGE
UNIVERSITY PRESS

PUBLISHED BY THE PRESS SYNDICATE OF THE UNIVERSITY OF CAMBRIDGE
The Pitt Building, Trumpington Street, Cambridge CB2 1RP, United Kingdom

CAMBRIDGE UNIVERSITY PRESS
The Edinburgh Building, Cambridge CB2 2RU, United Kingdom
40 West 20th Street, New York, NY 10011–4211, USA
10 Stamford Road, Oakleigh, Melbourne 3166, Australia

First published 1998

Printed and bound in Great Britain by Biddles Ltd, Guildford and King's Lynn

Typeset in 11/12.5pt Baskerville   [CE]

A catalogue record for this book is available from the British Library

Library of congress cataloguing in publication data
Novak, David, 1941–
Natural law in Judaism / David Novak.
p.   cm.
Includes bibliographical references and index.
ISBN 0 521 63170 X
1. Jewish law – Philisophy.
2. Natural law.
3. Ethics, Jewish.
1. Title.
BM520.6.N69   1998
296.3'6 – dc21   97–50609   CIP

ISBN 0 521 63170 X hardback

To Zehavya Tzipora

May you see your children's children. Peace on Israel!
Psalms 128:6

Contents

Preface

This book began in 1995, when I was invited to deliver the Lancaster-Yarnton Lectures for 1996. Four lectures were to be delivered, first at the University of Oxford under the auspices of the Oxford Centre for Hebrew and Jewish Studies, and then at Lancaster University under the auspices of the Department of Religious Studies. Being free to choose any topic relating to Judaism, I decided these lectures would provide a good opportunity to bring together in a more coherent conceptual presentation the question of natural law, a question that has concerned me since my student days. And it has been a *leitmotif* throughout my work for twenty-five years or so. Indeed, to a great extent, this book is stimulated by a challenge directed to me by a perceptive reviewer of a collection of essays of mine, *Jewish Social Ethics* (New York: Oxford University Press, 1992). Writing in the journal *First Things* (no. 34, June/July 1993, p. 48), Edward Oakes expressed his "high hopes for what David Novak can accomplish in the future in a more consistently theoretical work." Oakes' challenge gave me the hope that there was more to be said on natural law in Judaism than had been said in my previous work, and that there are people who might be interested to hear it. I cannot really think of any better reason to write a book.

What are now chapters 1, 3, 5, and 6, were initially written during the summer of 1995. They were then delivered in Oxford and afterwards in Lancaster in February of 1996. An abridged version of chapter 1 appeared in *First Things* (no. 60, February 1996) as "Law of Moses, Law of Nature." An original version of chapter 3 appeared in the *Journal of Jewish Thought and Philosophy* (vol. 5, 1996). I am grateful for the marvelous hospitality of the Oxford Centre during the month I lived at Yarnton Manor. Special thanks are due to Professor Martin Goodman, the Acting President, and to my old friends Dr. Norman Solomon of the Centre, and his wife, Mrs. Devora Solomon, who always provide me with a home-away-from-home when I am visiting in England. In Lancaster, my stay was greatly enhanced by the kindnesses shown me by the Department of Religious Studies under the chairmanship of Professor John Clayton, and, especially, by Dr. Linda Woodhead, Dr. Robert Segal, and Dr. Paul Morris.

Chapter 2 is an expanded English version of a lecture, "Das Naturrecht und die jüdische Theologie," which I delivered at the Protestant Theological Faculty of the University of Munich in February 1996. I am grateful for the invitation and solicitude of Professor Gunter Wenz, and for the hospitality and insightful conversations shared with the great theologian Professor Wolfhart Pannenberg, and his wife, Frau Hilke Pannenberg.

Chapter 4 on Maimonides was written for this volume. Parts of it are reworkings of two previously published articles: "Maimonides and the Science of the Law" (*Jewish Law Association Studies* IV, 1990), and "Maimonides' Concept of Practical Reason" (*Rashi 1040– 1990: Hommage à Ephraim E. Urbach*, Paris, 1993).

Books should begin in conversations about ideas with one's friends, and this book is no exception. In putting this book together, I recall conversations at the University of Virginia, where I taught from 1989 through 1996 with: Robert Wilken, Daniel Westberg (now of the Memorial University of Newfoundland), James Childress, and Gary Anderson (now of the Harvard Divinity School). There I learned much from the students in the seminar on "Natural Law in Judaism and Christianity" that Daniel Westberg and I taught together on two separate occasions. Gary Anderson was also very helpful in looking over chapter 2 on "scriptural foundations." He saved me from numerous scholarly errors, even though he is by no means responsible for any of my conclusions. Here at the University of Toronto, my new academic home since January of 1997, I have benefitted from conversations with my colleagues in University College: Kenneth Green and Robert Gibbs, as well as from students in the seminar on "Natural Law in Judaism and Christianity" that I am now teaching here in the Centre for the Study of Religion.

Natural Law is the overall topic of the ongoing "Ramsey Colloquium" of the Institute on Religion and Public Life of which I have been a participant from the outset about seven years ago. I am grateful to Richard John Neuhaus, the President of the Institute, for his friendship in general, and his leadership of the Colloquium in particular. Significant conversations have been held there with such friends as Hadley Arkes, Robert George, Mary Ann Glendon, Russell Hittinger, Gilbert Meilaender, George Weigel, and others. And finally, as always, I thank David Weiss Halivni of Columbia University for being ever willing to share his unequaled talmudic learning and insight with me whenever I approached him, and Lenn Goodman of Vanderbilt University for his philosophical perspicacity on the questions that have regularly concerned us both for almost twenty years.

It is an honor to now publish a second book with Cambridge University Press. I am grateful for the care of my editor Ruth Parr and her most competent colleagues at the Press.

Finally, the dedication. Zehavya Tzipora Stadlan is our first grandchild, the firstborn of our beloved children, Marianne and Noam. My wife and I see in her young life and upbringing many of the things we have held sacred in our life together. All thanks be to God.

Abbreviations

B.	Talmud Bavli (Babylonian Talmud)
M.	Mishnah
R.	Rabbi, Rabbenu or Rav
T.	Tosefta
Tos.	Tosafot
Y.	Talmud Yerushalmi (Palestinian Talmud)

CHAPTER I

The challenge of modern secularity

How do we sing the Lord's song on strange soil?
(Psalms 137:4)

THE HISTORICAL LOCATION OF THE QUESTION

Any normative question asked by contemporary Jews must be seen in the context of Jewish modernity. Jewish modernity has been largely determined by three momentous experiences: (1) the acquisition of citizenship by Jews as individuals in modern, secular nation-states; (2) the destruction of one third of Jewry in the Holocaust; (3) the establishment of the State of Israel. If natural law be initially defined as those norms of human conduct that are universally valid and discernible by all rational persons, then the question of "natural law," by whatever name it happens to be called, is inherently involved in all three of these momentous experiences. That is because all three of them are essentially political, and the question of natural law is essential to political thought.

The acquisition of citizenship by Jews as individuals in modern, secular nation-states has been a seismic change from the political situation of Jews in the Middle Ages. During the Middle Ages, Jews were members of a semi-independent polity within a larger polity. The political status of the Jewish communities was determined by some sort of contract with the larger, host societies by which they were allowed to live, as it were, as *imperium in imperio*.[1] Since these larger, host societies, being either Christian or Muslim, were religiously constituted just as

[1] See Jacob Katz, *Tradition and Crisis* (New York, 1971), 11ff.

I

the Jewish community was, the relationship of the Jewish communities with them was largely determined by religious criteria. Since Judaism, Christianity and Islam are religions of revelation, religious criteria for each of them are necessarily grounded in each of their respective revelations.

For the Christian or Muslim hosts, their task was to find some sort of religiously tolerated status for a community of nonbelievers living in their midst. For the Jewish guests in these societies, the task was to find some sort of religiously tolerated status for a society of non-Jews under whose general rule Jews had to live. The task was made somewhat easier for both sides by the fact that Jews are not an ordinary group of nonbelievers in the eyes of Christianity and Islam, and Christians and Muslims are not ordinary gentiles in the eyes of Judaism.[2]

Ordinary nonbelievers in the eyes of Christianity and Islam are pagans, as are ordinary gentiles in the eyes of Judaism. But Christians could not regard Jews as ordinary nonbelievers because they affirm that they and the Jews worship the same God and are bound by the same revelation of that God in the same book – the Bible – however much they differ in their forms of worship of that God and their ways of reading that same book.[3] Muslims too could not regard Jews as ordinary nonbelievers because they affirm that they and the Jews worship the same God. And even though Muslims do not see themselves bound by the Bible as do Christians in common with Jews, they regard the Bible as a valid revelation, although suffering from a flawed transmission. In fact, it was the Muslims who named the Jews "people of the Book," meaning a community having a valid revelation, one which Muslims must respect.[4] Therefore, the interrelationship, despite its many tensions and even its periodic breakdowns, was possible, none-

---

[2] See D. Novak, "The Treatment of Islam and Muslims in the Legal Writings of Maimonides" in *Studies in Islamic and Judaic Traditions*, ed. W. M. Brinner and S. D. Ricks (Atlanta, 1986), 233ff.; *Jewish–Christian Dialogue* (New York, 1989), esp. chs. 1–2.

[3] See "Declaration on the Relationship of the Church to Non-Christian Religions" in *The Documents of Vatican II*, ed. W. M. Abbott, trans. J. Gallagher *et al.* (London and Dublin, 1966), 663ff.

[4] See *Quran* 2:88, 106.

theless, because there was at least some commonality between the respective revelations of all three faith communities. At this level, the terms of the relationship between the Christian or Muslim hosts and the Jewish guests were largely theological and historical.

They were theological inasmuch as the presence of Jews in larger, foreign societies had to be justified by the criteria of revelation, which enabled Christians or Muslims to regard Jews as a community somewhere in-between the believers totally inside sacred space and the nonbelievers totally outside sacred space. Jews had to justify their presence in these societies to themselves by quite similar criteria. And all of this too was constituted by both sides against an eschatological horizon. This meant that the present political relationship was only tentative, and that it would be ultimately subsumed in a world totally redeemed. That redemption would be in a time un-ending, when sacred space would encompass all, when all of the outsiders would finally and permanently find themselves either in that space or nowhere at all.

Although the theological constitution of that relationship in general was seen by both sides from the revealed perspective of God, its specifics were negotiated very much within the histor-ical situation at hand. Usually, those historical specifics that determined the terms of the relationship between Jewish guests and their gentile hosts were the most ephemeral of all; they were largely economic. Jewish presence in these societies was usually justified at this level of *Realpolitik* by their economic usefulness to their hosts.[5]

To be sure, the question of natural law did enter into these negotiations but, for the most part, they were conducted either at the level of God's revealed law or human-made law. (Natural law, as we shall see in due course, is the idea of a reality that is less exalted than direct divine revelation and more exalted than merely local human arrangements.) This is largely the case because the parties to these relationships could confine their self-definition to the more historically immediate categories of

[5] See Katz, *Tradition and Crisis*, 51ff.

Jew, Christian, or Muslim, and had to rely much less on the more abstract category of "human person," with which natural law is concerned.

However, all of this changed with the breakdown of the *ancien régime*. For with the new self-constitution of European society into nation-states, the issue of natural law directly entered the picture in the form of natural rights. The view of society that came in the wake of the social contract theorists of the sixteenth and seventeenth centuries was one that posited in one way or another the notion that human beings qua human beings have constructed society *de novo* with certain rights already in hand. Unlike what pertained in the older pre-modern societies, the individual human did not come *from* society; rather he (and later she) came *to* it. The task of society, then, was to constitute itself in order to facilitate the exercise of the rights of these human beings which they brought from nature.[6] In this view, all human beings began from zero, so to speak, and everyone entered society (in theory anyway) at the same point in time and space.

This new notion of human personhood and human society had antecedents to be sure, but they functioned far more as partial contributors to its emergence than as its actual causes. Furthermore, and for our purposes here most important, this provided the necessary theoretical conditions for the political emancipation of the Jews into European society and culture.[7] But here the concessions from both sides required for this new relationship were far more radical than the theological inter-pretations and economic adjustments required by the medieval relationship. Here both sides had, in effect, to assume a primary and public identity as rational, ahistorical human beings, and reserve their secondary and private identity as Jews or Christians for more domestic spheres. (At this point in history, the Jewish–Muslim relationship becomes quite different than the Jewish–Christian one.) The attitude of Jews who

[6] See Leo Strauss, *Natural Right and History* (Chicago, 1953), 165ff.
[7] This became the basis of Moses Mendelssohn's arguments for Jewish emancipation in his 1783 book *Jerusalem*. See Alexander Altmann's introduction to Allan Arkush's English translation of this work (Hanover, N.H., and London, 1983).

accepted this new situation was most famously expressed by the nineteenth-century Jewish Enlightenment poet Judah Leib Gordon, who coined the slogan (in Hebrew): "Be a Jew in your tent and a human being (*ben adam*) when you go out of it."[8] What is most important to bear in mind is that the new relationship between Jews and the larger world was negotiated by philosophical, not theological, means.

At least in theory, Jews were now offered their admission ticket to European society and culture; and, seemingly, it did not require that they abandon their Judaism by any detour through Christianity, as had been the case in the past. It is little wonder, then, that the vast majority of European Jews (and, later, Jews in the New World) regarded this as a very good offer whenever it was made to them, or promised to them, or even hinted at. And, although this process of admission took various forms and had various levels of success, at the theoretical level at least, it required Jews to justify their political presence by the criteria of natural law, especially in its modern version as "natural rights," which became better known as "human rights" (*droits de l'homme*). Indeed, much of Jewish thought, from Baruch Spinoza in the seventeenth century to Moses Mendelssohn in the eighteenth century to Hermann Cohen in the late nineteenth and early twentieth centuries, was a Jewish justification of human rights and liberal society based on them. This still explains the persistent loyalty of large numbers of Jews in Europe and North America to quite stringent notions of secular social space as an absolute desideratum. And in justifying their own admission to a larger society, these Jewish thinkers had to constitute an opening for Judaism on the horizon of a new universal order. That was the case whether Judaism was to be deconstructed as Spinoza suggested, or to be tolerated as Mendelssohn asserted, or to be the historical source of true universalism as Cohen speculated.[9]

---

[8] This is from Gordon's 1863 Hebrew poem "Awake My People." See M. Stanislawski, *For Whom Do I Toil? Judah Leib Gordon and the Crisis of Russian Jewry* (New York and Oxford, 1988), 50ff.

[9] For Spinoza and Cohen on this issue, see D. Novak, *The Election of Israel* (Cambridge, 1995), chs. 1–2. For Mendelssohn on this issue, see Alexander Altmann, *Moses Mendelssohn* (University, Ala., 1973), ch. 6.

The second momentous experience that has determined Jewish modernity is the Holocaust. Here the question of natural law enters the discussion either by its affirmation or by its denial. For the great debate among Jews who ponder the Holocaust is whether it is to be interpreted along general or singular lines.

For those who argue that its significance is singular, the introduction of any universal element into the discussion only serves to dilute the Holocaust as a uniquely Jewish tragedy. For these thinkers, to explain the Holocaust in universal terms, even universal moral terms, is to ultimately explain it away.[10] However, if this view is carried to its logical conclusion, and any universal point of reference is eliminated, the tragedy of the Jews can only be presented to the larger world as the tragedy of a super-human species, a race of angels rather than a human people. Accordingly, the connection with these victims has to be more one of fantastic projection than reasoning about persons with whom any other human shares certain universal commonalities. (Of course, isn't it easier to turn a super-human species, with whom one shares nothing essential in common, into a sub-human species, with whom one is equally remote, than it is to relate to fellow humans with whom one does share something essential in common? Are not romanticization and demonization too similar not to be troublesome?) In other words, the explicit elimination of a natural law perspective makes any reasoned attempt to come to grips with the Holocaust harder in the world.

The slogan that has emerged after the Holocaust – "Never again!" – implies that the Holocaust has a universal moral meaning, which if properly learned, can provide at least a theoretical prophylactic against its repetition in the world – against *anyone*. Ideas do indeed have practical consequences, as modern ideologies have so vividly demonstrated in this century especially.

At this point, I would also argue that to present the Holocaust as a human, moral tragedy no more dilutes its

---

[10] See Emil Fackenheim's introduction to Yehuda Bauer's *The Jewish Emergence from Powerlessness* (Toronto, 1979).

unique sorrow for the Jews than does one's demanding that the
murderer of his or her own child be tried before a general
tribunal. For that in no way lessens the need of the bereaved
parents to mourn their unique loss in the most intimate way.
The deeper need for mourning and ultimate consolation does
not eclipse the more general and immediate need for justice,
either the justice of retribution or the justice of prevention.
Indeed, the proper resolution of both spheres of concern
requires that the respective phenomenality of each sphere be
kept separate.

Despite a tendency of contemporary Jewish thought about
the Holocaust to take the anti-natural law line in making its
claims upon the world, another tendency, equally strong I
think, takes a natural law line (whether it is aware of its
philosophic underpinnings or not). This line of thought
(whether consciously or unconsciously) is surely what is behind
contemporary Jewish interest in the whole issue of human
rights in the world, and which makes itself manifest in such
attempts as the international drive against racism and ter-
rorism, to which many Jews have been so dedicated. In these
attempts, Jews have had to present their own victimhood
against a universal horizon. In other words, Jewish suffering as
epitomized by the Holocaust has had to be presented as the
most poignant example of the violation of human personhood
and its essential rights.[11] When such presentations rise from the
level of special pleading to the level of truly rational reflection
and argument, the perspective of natural law must make an
essential entrance into the discussion.

The third momentous experience that has determined
Jewish modernity is the establishment of the State of Israel.
Here the question of natural law has entered into the discussion
by way of the debates about what sort of a polity the new
Jewish state is to be. These debates began with the very
inception of modern Zionism at the end of the nineteenth
century, and they have continued unabated both before and
after the actual reestablishment of Jewish sovereignty in the

[11] See Hannah Arendt, *Eichmann in Jerusalem*, rev. edn (New York, 1965), epilogue.

land of Israel in 1948. And as has been the case with contemporary Jewish thought about the Holocaust, natural law has
entered the discussion both by affirmation and by denial.

For those who have envisioned the State of Israel to be a
democracy, which although primarily a Jewish polity for Jews is
one in which non-Jews can become citizens and enjoy equal
civil rights with the Jewish majority, the question of natural law
is enunciated in the question of human rights.[12] Because Israel
has from her inception allied herself with the West, and this for
a variety of reasons both theoretical and practical, she has had
to justify her existence to the West (primarily the United States)
on the grounds of her being a constitutional democracy.
Especially on the issues of guarantees of personal liberty and
the protection of minorities, there has had to be some sort of
affirmation of natural law thinking by those Zionists who have
advocated this type of polity out of conviction and not just as a
rhetorical ploy to satisfy both the powerful American Jewish
community in particular and American public opinion in
general.

However, as in the case of contemporary Jewish thought
about the Holocaust, there has also been what might be called
a revisionary type of Zionism, one that is based on a denial of
natural law, that is, when viewed philosophically. In this view,
which has both secularist and religious advocates, the sole
purpose of the State of Israel is to enhance the power of the
Jewish people.[13] There is no attempt in this school of Jewish
thought to constitute any sort of *modus vivendi* with non-Jews
based on the idea of common humanity rooted in common
human nature.

Culturally, this type of Zionism has argued for the maximal
isolation of the Jewish people from the larger western civilization in which they find themselves and with which they have
had to cast their lot, like it or not. And politically, where such

[12] For an important discussion of what might be termed the universal significance of
both the Holocaust and the reestablishment of the Jewish state in the land of Israel,
see A. B. Yehoshua, *Between Right and Right*, trans. A. Schwartz (Garden City, N.Y.,
1981), 6ff.
[13] See C. S. Liebman and E. Don-Yehiya, *Civil Religion in Israel* (Berkeley, Calif., 1983),
66, 229.

isolation is less and less of a possibility in our increasingly interconnected world, the *modus operandi* has been one of strict *Realpolitik*. The only points in common with the non-Jewish world are based on questions of common interest of the most specific, and ephemeral, kind. In fact, advocates of this position are not only not interested in pursuing more philosophical discussions of commonality, they are more often than not actually hostile to them. For such discussions would force them to admit that there is some sort of commonality deeper than that of momentary interests, and that is something they really deny. Occasionally, most often at moments of great political stress, less sophisticated Jewish elements, both inside and even outside the State of Israel, will actually deny any common humanity between Jews and non-Jews. Such denials are most often explicit, dramatic, and vehement. Because of their sensationalism, these outbursts will frequently attract wide media attention. In response to the obvious questions they raise, embarrassed cohorts of those who have made them will usually utter some sort of half-hearted denials.[14] However, this embarassment is more rhetorical than philosophical. It almost always comes from those who have to deal more regularly with the larger world and who realize that the fact of such outbursts – not their actual content and truth value – will make diplomacy in that larger world more difficult.

THE PHILOSOPHICAL LOCATION OF THE QUESTION

In thinking about the three determining experiences of Jewish modernity, the invocation of natural law type concepts has largely presupposed the historical value of the Enlightenment. The political emancipation of the Jews from the confines of the ghetto is seen as philosophical liberation; the Holocaust is seen as a denial of Enlightenment values of liberty and equality;

---

[14] Thus the response of many Religious Zionists and secularist nationalists to the massacre of twenty-nine Arabs in a Hebron mosque by the Religious Zionist, West bank settler Dr. Baruch Goldstein on Purim 5754 (29 February 1994) was one of either covert sympathy or tepid disapproval. The disapproval impressed many as being quite disingenuous.

and the State of Israel is seen as the great historical opportunity for the Jewish people to be constituted as a western type
democracy.

Nevertheless, all of this has been attacked, since the time of
the Enlightenment itself, but especially since the Holocaust, as
being a betrayal of the true reality of the Jewish people. As we
have already seen, as regards the Holocaust and the State of
Israel, this attack has been conducted on the grounds of
Realpolitik. The Holocaust and what is perceived as the continuing political isolation and vulnerability of the State of Israel
are supposed to have taught us that the Jews have been asked
to give far more than they have received from western civilization. And this has been used to argue, retroactively, that the
Enlightenment itself, at least as regards the interests of the
Jews, and maybe in and of itself, has been a failure. And since
almost all modern Jewish thinkers who have dealt with the
question of natural law have assumed that it is identical with
the modern idea of human rights, any assault on the value of
post-Enlightenment modernity would seem to entail the elimination of the question of natural law from contemporary Jewish
thought.

Even if one does not hold such a negative view of the value
of the Enlightenment in general and for Jews particularly, the
question of natural law as it has been raised for modern
Judaism is nonetheless a great problem. For the universality
essential to the very idea of natural law seems to imply that
Judaism itself must be justified by the criteria of something
greater than itself. And even if that greater universe and its
nature do not totally deconstruct Judaism beyond all recognizable continuity with its past, Judaism seems to have to play a
secondary role in this whole scheme of things. But how can a
tradition like Judaism do any such thing in good faith? Whatever role the tradition has allowed universal human reason to
play in its own thought processes, it has been unwilling to allow
any such guest in its house to undermine that house's foundation in revelation. For commitment to the truth of the Jewish
tradition forces one to admit that revelation presents truth that
human reason cannot uncover by itself. Natural law has usually

been seen as the objective correlate of human reason. In chapter 5 I shall return to this question, one that constitutes the border between theology and philosophy for Judaism.

At this point in history, it seems as though a Jewish thinker has one of two options when it comes to the question of natural law. One can either affirm natural law and seemingly allow Judaism to be swallowed up by something greater and more universal than itself, or one can deny natural law and leave all issues of the relations of Jews with the non-Jewish world on the level of pure power politics, that is, on that level of human interaction where concern for truth is precluded. In the next two chapters, I shall present a theological way out of this conundrum. Here I shall suggest a philosophical way out of it. The difference between these solutions is that the theological way out is constituted from within the sources of the Jewish tradition; the philosophical solution is constituted by a way of looking at the world outside. Furthermore, I maintain that these two solutions complement each other, and neither is satisfactory without help from the other.

The philosophical solution requires radical criticism of the key political idea of the Enlightenment, one whose roots lie in social contract theory. This idea is that human beings can construct their own primary society autonomously. It is an idea running from Locke to Kant to Rawls to Habermas, but one having philosophical opposition running from Burke to Hegel to Gadamer to MacIntyre – *mutatis mutandis*.[15] Thus if one sides with the former group of philosophers, the true human condition and its fundamental task, will not allow anything else to usurp its primacy. Indeed, such a task seems to require nothing less than the radical preclusion of prior commitments of any

---

[15] See John Locke, *Second Treatise of Government*, ch. 5; Immanuel Kant, *Groundwork of the Metaphysic of Morals*, trans. H. J. Paton (New York, 1964), 98ff.; John Rawls, *A Theory of Justice* (Cambridge, Mass., 1971), 255f.; Jürgen Habermas, *Moral Consciousness and Communicative Action*, trans. C. Lenhardt and S. W. Nicholsen (Cambridge, Mass., 1990), 207ff. Cf. P. J. Stanlis, *Edmund Burke and the Natural Law* (Ann Arbor, Mich., 1965), 125ff.; G. W. F. Hegel, *Phenomenology of Spirit*, trans. A. V. Miller (Oxford, 1977), 266ff.; Hans-Georg Gadamer, *Truth and Method*, trans. G. Barden and J. Cumming (New York, 1982), 482ff.; Alasdair MacIntyre, *Whose Justice? Which Rationality?* (Notre Dame, Ind., 1988), 349ff.

kind, and certainly commitments to a tradition grounded in a revelation of the transcendent God.

The view I need to overcome has been most recently presented to me by a well-known contemporary "autonomist," the philosopher Richard Rorty. Now Rorty had been my colleague at the University of Virginia, and in the fall of 1994 he and I engaged in a public discussion there. (Because of its cordiality, I hesitate to call it a "debate" due to the hostile connotations of that word.) The discussion was essentially an exchange over Rorty's assertion that anyone who invokes God's will in a democratic conversation is unavoidably a "conversation-stopper."[16] As someone who believes in the authority of God's will as I believe it to have been revealed to the Jewish people, and as someone who is convinced that there are no acceptable alternatives to democracy in the world today, certainly for Jews, especially because of its emphasis on and enforcement of human rights, I could not allow myself to leave such a challenge unanswered. The success of this effort depends on more precise answers to the following questions: (1) Must democracy be one's primary community if it is to function well or function at all? (2) How does "God's will" function for a Jewish believer? (3) Is God's will the only basis for a normative relationship with God?

COMMUNITIES AND SOCIETY

One could very well define modern democracy as a secular society presupposing the natural or human rights of its members and basing its operations on the fulfillment of those prior rights. Accordingly, it is clear that democracy cannot be based on revelation inasmuch as revelation is a historical not a natural phenomenon. Moreover, revelation's historicity means that it is revelation to a singular community within humankind, a community that has been uniquely elected for that purpose.[17] The identity of human rights and history would require a universal human history, something that for Jews at least is a

---

[16] See "Religion as Conversation-Stopper," *Common Knowledge* 3 (1994), 1–6.
[17] See Novak, *The Election of Israel*, 10ff.

matter of humanly irretrievable antiquity or the humanly unattainable *eschaton*: the end of history itself. At any point in between these two unreachable temporal limits, nature is constituted generally and revelation singularly. The question, therefore, is whether those who base their morality on a revelation and its tradition can be members of any such modern democracy in good faith, that is, by an affirmation of truth as distinct from a mere accommodation for purposes of political and economic expediency.

As we have seen, many have thought the answer to this question to be necessarily "no." However, that denial has presupposed that democracy must be one's primary community in order to function well or function at all. Nevertheless, it can be argued that democracy actually functions better when it is not one's primary community but, rather, one's secondary community. If this can demonstrated, then those committed to a revelation and its tradition, like religious Jews, can indeed be members of any such modern democracy in good faith.

At this point, it might be useful to invoke the famous thesis proposed by a pioneering modern sociologist, Ferdinand Tönnies, namely, his distinction between society as *Gemeinschaft* and society as *Gesellschaft*. *Gemeinschaft* designates societies that many have termed "folk cultures," that is, human communities that are not rational constructs but which have imperceptible historical roots extending back to hoary antiquity.[18] The essential feature of such communities is that one's presence in them is not a matter of free choice, that is, one does not decide at a particular point in time to join such a community, even hypothetically. Human relationships in such communities are constituted more along the lines of status than contract, status inevitably being a matter of kinship.[19] *Gesellschaft*, on the other hand, which in modern German is the word for a "corporation," designates societies that are rational constructs, societies that can date their origins, like the United States, for example, which calls itself on its great seal, *novus ordo seclorum*, "a new

[18] See *Community and Society*, ed. and trans. C. P. Loomis (East Lansing, Mich., 1957), 34f.
[19] See Sir Henry Maine, *Ancient Law* (Oxford, 1931), 140f.

order of the ages." Along the lines of this sociological distinction, something like the traditional, religious Jewish community
is certainly a *Gemeinschaft* not a *Gesellschaft*. For the sake of
English-speaking precision, let us call a *Gemeinschaft* a "community" and a *Gesellschaft* a "society."

Because "communities" have usually been studied by
modern social scientists committed to "society" as their
primary human association, there has been a tendency to see
society as transcending community in the way the universal
transcends the particular. Democracy has been seen by many of
this frame of mind as being the epitome of society, and
traditional religions, such as Judaism, as being examples of
communities. The concept that usually links society and community is that of "culture." Culture is seen as something that
develops from being a matter of historical custom to becoming
more and more a matter of rational organization and tech-
nique. Here one recalls the social philosophy of that quintes-
sential American apostle of democracy and its own culture,
John Dewey.[20] In such a scheme of things, traditional religions
like Judaism can only be seen as something to be deconstructed
by criteria that are ultimately secular. If they persist in their
integrity, let alone flourish, however, this is usually seen as some
sort of temporary inversion of the inevitable progress of human
rationality.

But the point lost in much of this thinking is that the very
word "culture" comes from the word *cultus*. And the "cult" is
not regarded by its adherents as something "quaint" or
particular at all; they regard it as the *axis mundi*, the very
connection between God and the world, and that which gives
humans their true place in the cosmos.[21] To call them "folk
cultures" as that term usually is used to designate something
like "native crafts" is to avoid any phenomenological integrity
at all. Indeed, such communities, which are inevitably religiously constituted, operate at a deeper level of human exist-

---

[20] See *A Common Faith* (New Haven, 1934), 49f.; also S. C. Rockefeller, *John Dewey* (New York, 1991), 445ff.
[21] See Mircea Eliade, *The Sacred and the Profane*, trans. W. R. Trask (New York, 1961), 36ff.

ence than any society possibly could. For they deal with the most profound of all human questions: What is my true place in the universal order of things? That is *the* ontological/existential question. A society like a modern democracy can at best only deal with the question: What is my proper role in an association based on the rights of various, disparate wills? That is only *a* procedural question.

Of course, one can dismiss the former question as being the result of irrational fantasy, something modern rationality can overcome, as Freud argued many times.[22] However, the repression of this question has proved no more successful than the repression of sexuality Freud found so unsuccessful. In fact, one could argue, moreover, that the repression of this question is at least as harmful to human well being as the repression of one's erotic quest. Such fundamental human questions simply refuse to allow themselves to be reduced to anything else. Furthermore, in their attempt to deconstruct traditional religious traditions as "mythological," modern thinkers like Freud inevitably construct their own mythologies to replace them. Indeed, as we shall soon see, the idea of a "social contract" in the modern sense is every bit as much a mythology as is, for example, Freud's idea of the original Oedipal situation.[23] If "mythologies" are what might be termed "primal stories" (*Urgeschichte*), then they function far more effectively for human existence when they are received (*traditio*) rather than made-up (*fictio*). For one can actually believe a tradition's narrative to be true, however much metaphor it might contain. But one knows by definition that a fiction is false, however much truth it might suggest.

At this point in our inquiry, we must see whether a religious tradition like Judaism, that is, a community concerned with the most profound of all human questions, can handle the participation of its members in the more mundane questions of a

[22] See esp. *Civilization and Its Discontents*, trans. J. Riviere (Garden City, N.Y., 1958), ch. 1.
[23] Along these lines, see George Bernard Shaw, *Saint Joan* (Baltimore, 1951), preface, esp. 20ff.

democratic polity, without their having to live some sort of schizoid life.

GOD'S WILL AND GOD'S WISDOM

Richard Rorty is right about the invocation of God's will being a "conversation-stopper," that is, in a conversation conducted within the confines of a democratic society and observant of its criteria of discourse. For God's will only has meaning, let alone truth, in a community explictly related to that God. Only there can it be a "conversation-stimulator." There it continues to stimulate the ongoing exegetical conversation that is essential to the very life of the community's active transmission of revelation and its content.[24] For Jews, that is a historically real covenant with God, a covenant whose law has the ultimate authority of being God's will. Being a co-relationship, however, this covenant does include the will of its human participants as well, albeit secondarily. Conversely, in a democratic society, there is only the interplay of human wills. For God to be a participant in such a polity would require the admission of the political primacy of revelation for that society, an admission that we have already seen is impossible. Furthermore, democratic thinking quickly eliminated the Deistic notion that the natural order itself, which it presupposes (however sketchily), requires positing the will of a primordial being to explain its own origins. When taken as a rational construct, such a society requires no such primordial origin at all. Natural rights do not need natural theology. (In chapter 5 I shall argue that natural law does not need natural theology either.)

So, if God's will were all that religious persons had to bring to democratic society, there would be no opening there for such a gift. But God's will is not all that religious persons have to say about their God. They also speak of the wisdom of God.[25] And the assertion of the wisdom of God can be shown to have a public significance in secular, democratic space that the assertion of the will of God cannot and should not have there. Here

---

[24] See B. Kiddushin 66a; Menahot 29b.
[25] See Maimonides, *Guide of the Perplexed*, 3.26, 49.

is where Jews are going to have to retrieve the conceptuality of natural law from within our own tradition and not just rely on the modern idea of human rights, as I hope to show in the next two chapters. This need arises from the question of origins, which, as we have seen, is basically inadequate when God's will is asserted in Deistic fashion, and is basically irrelevant when God's will is asserted covenantally, in a democratic context.

If a Jew who is religiously committed to his or her tradition is going to be able to participate in a democratic conversation, he or she will have to speak of the wisdom of God. But what is the difference between speaking of the will of God and the wisdom of God? The difference is one between statements formulated out of a theology of creation as distinct from statements formulated out of a theology of revelation. (And as we shall see in chapter 3, Jewish theologians who reduce revelation to creation constitute natural law improperly for Judaism.)

To speak of the will of God, when "will" functions as a transitive verb, is to speak of an object which cannot be separated from its subject at any time, even conceptually. Thus, to say, for example, "The Lord spoke to Moses and Aaron saying unto them to speak to the Israelites as follows: . . . and the pig . . . from its flesh you shall not eat . . ." (Leviticus 11:1–12, 7) is to assert that the very meaning of the prohibition of eating pork is a direct response to the will of God as revealed in the Torah. Whatever wisdom we perceive in this commandment is phenomenologically subsequent to our obedience to it.[26]

But to speak of the wisdom of God, when "wisdom" functions as a predicate, is to speak of a state which can be spoken of, at least initially, apart from the subject of whom it is predicated. For when we speak of something as being the product of the wisdom of God, we can see its meaning, at least initially, in and of itself. Thus, for example, we can appreciate the wisdom of the commandment "you shall not murder" (Exodus 20:13) before we eventually understand that its prescription is part of God's wisdom as creator of the universe and

---

[26] See D. Novak, *Jewish Social Ethics* (New York, 1992), 26f.

its nature in which moral law is an inherent ingredient.[27] All of this, to refer to the respective examples just cited, is why Jews can speak persuasively in secular public space about the prohibition of murder in a way we cannot (and should not) speak about the prohibition of eating pork there. And that is why the prohibition of murder is taken to be immediately universal, that is, rationally perceivable by all normal human persons capable of hearing it through nature. The prohibition of eating pork, conversely, is not immediately universal and requires, therefore, special revelation to a singular community in history.

Nevertheless, this argument as presented heretofore has one more major objection to overcome. That objection is as old as Plato. The objection, often called the "Euthyphro Problem," which roughly paraphrased for our context here is as follows: If God has willed something because it is wise, and if that wisdom is accessible to any rational person, then what difference does it make *who* has willed it? Is it not something that is *always to be willed by anyone*?[28] Is not the predicate "wisdom" prior to anyone of whom it may be predicated? In modern times, the same sort of critical logic has been at work in one of the most basic methodological rules applied to scientific theory, namely, what is called "Ockham's Razor." This rule states that the sufficient explanation of any phenomenon with the fewest required premises is always to be preferred. In short, in our context, why can't the assertion of practical wisdom on any moral issue in secular, public space eliminate the requirement that it be ultimately predicated of God? What does "of God" add to the discussion? Is it not a distraction after all?

The answer to this question depends on the distinction made above between "community" and "society." If society is our primary locus of human association, then even mention of God's wisdom has no meaningful point of reference here. It should be remembered that even for Aristotle, who frequently gets invoked by various critics of modern sociality, the gods are

---

[27] See Maimonides, *Mishneh Torah*: Rotseah, 4.9.
[28] See Plato, *Euthyphro*, 10 Aff. For an analysis of why there is no such insurmountable problem for a covenantal theology, see Novak, *Jewish–Christian Dialogue*, 152ff.

not constituents of the *polis*. Theology – "god-talk" – is either part of the traditional domestic sphere, which is beneath the *polis*, or it is the epitome of the contemplative sphere, which is beyond the *polis*.[29] If this is even the case for Aristotle with his natural view of human society, how much more is it the case for modern political thinkers with their more technical view of human sociality? Indeed, these moderns refuse any intelligible role to either the domestic or the contemplative sphere, thus denying any place to god-talk at all.

But what if community not society is the primary locus of our human sociality? And what if this communal space includes a cosmic dimension beyond the interest of the secular polity, a cosmic dimension that cannot be relegated to an inferior "particularistic" role? If this is the case, which indeed it must be for traditional Jews (and for members of the other two traditional communities constituted by revelation: Christianity and Islam), then the relation between the language of community and the language of society is similar to the relation between historical and technical languages that has been at the heart of much of linguistically oriented philosophy in the last half of this century. As Wittgenstein saw with such great insight, technical languages are the "suburbs" of historical languages, that is, they are built onto them. The clear implication of his striking metaphor is that these "suburbs" (*Vorstädte*) cannot subsume the city onto which they have been "incorporated" (*einverleibt wurden*), and if they attempt to do so they destroy the larger human context in which they themselves must find their deeper meaning.[30] One cannot technically construct an all-encompassing metalanguage any more than one can construct an all-encompassing metaculture.

Conversely, the same philosophical trend that saw the subordination of community to society manifested itself in the attempt to subordinate historical languages to artificial ones. In this trend, one sees a line of thought extending from Locke to Kant to Carnap.[31] The technical thinking of *homo faber* is what

[29] See *Nicomachean Ethics*, 1179a22–29; *Politics*, 1252b22–29.
[30] *Philosophical Investigations*, 2nd edn, trans. G. E. M. Anscombe (New York, 1958), 1.18.
[31] See Rudolf Carnap, *The Logical Structure of the World*, trans. R. A. George (Berkeley

makes society as Kant asserts, or language as Carnap asserts.
That which has been inherited is only intelligible when it can
be postulated by this technical thinking, that is, deduced from
it. Along these lines, one should think of the very artificial
"God" postulated (that is constructed) by Kant for pure
practical reason, a God whom no Jew, Christian or Muslim
could possibly live or die for.[32]

But when we assume that historical languages are always
prior in human social existence, technical languages are, then,
abstractions *from* these prior historical languages, not the
transcendental ground *of* them. They are abstractions designed
to function in particular areas where condensed precision is
called for. This is like being aware that the use of the word
"tree" in the historically constituted world of full human
association (what Husserl called the *Lebenswelt*) is far more rich
and subtle than its use in the technically constructed language
of botany.[33] When we need to perform precise operations
involving trees, we defer to the language of botany and
temporarily bracket the function of "tree" in the richer language of the historical community. But, in this century
especially, we have surely seen what happens to technology
when it is elevated above the larger human context from which
it emerged and which it was originally designed to serve.[34]

Following this analogy, we can now see how one can speak of
the *wisdom of God* in a social context in which only *wisdom* is
immediately intelligible. For to assert any wisdom is ultimately,
for Jews, the wisdom by which God creates, structures, and
sustains the world.[35] Even if the assertion that this wisdom is
God's might not have immediate meaning in a democratic
conversation, it can, minimally, be asserted in that context as a
statement of where one is *coming from*. That statement of origin

and Los Angeles, 1967). esp. 89f.; Hannah Arendt, *The Human Condition* (Garden
     City, N.Y., 1959), 136f.
[32] See Hermann Cohen, *Der Begriff der Religion im System der Philosophie* (Giessen, 1915),
     51.
[33] See *The Crisis of European Sciences and Transcendental Phenomenology*, trans. D. Carr
     (Evanston, Ill., 1970), 103ff.
[34] See Jacques Ellul, *The Technological System*, trans. J. Neugroschel (New York, 1980),
     256f.
[35] See *Beresheet Rabbah* 1.1 re Prov. 8:22.

is only irrelevant when one is required to affirm society as the primary locus of one's human association. Such an assertion, however, ultimately requires that one speak as if he or she were an atheist. But that price is simply too high to pay for any member of a traditional religious community, whatever the benefits of democratic society happen to be.[36] "There is no wisdom (*hokhmah*), there is no understanding, and there is no counsel that can be set up against the Lord" (Proverbs 21:30). But, that price is only required by the questionable assumption that democracy itself must be both one's society and one's community. It is based on the erroneous notion that democracy must create it own culture rather than drawing upon the practical wisdom of more primary cultures, cultures like Judaism that inevitably trace their wisdom back to the God who has created all and who has revealed himself to its adherents. As so much of the modern secularist attempt to create culture has shown, it finally leaves the soul impoverished. To use the term popularized by the contemporary American anthropologist Clifford Geertz, it is simply too "thin."[37]

The issue is whether one is required to be a *secularist* in order to be a participant in *secular* space. And here is where the religious have a clear advantage over the secularists in a

[36] One of the truly important questions of public philosophy today is whether democratic theory can admit proposals based on religious premises or not. Are religions only to be tolerated as purely private concerns, which for any adherent of a religion of historical revelation is a *contradictio in adjectu*? Or, can religious voices be participants in democratic conversation as such? For many, the debate has been focused around the thought of the leading democratic theorist today, John Rawls. For the view that Rawls' theory does not preclude religious voices in democratic public discourse, see Paul J. Weithman, "Rawlsian Liberalism and the Privitization of Religion: Three Theological Objections Considered," *Journal of Religious Ethics* 22 (1994), 3ff. For a contrary view, see Timothy P. Jackson, "Love in a Liberal Society: A Response to Paul J. Weithman," *ibid.*, 29ff.
[37] See *The Interpretation of Cultures* (New York, 1973), 5ff. Along these lines, note Michael Walzer, who, speaking of "moral minimalism" as "thin" in Geertz's sense of the term writes in *Thick and Thin* (Notre Dame, Ind., 1994), 7: "they mean that the rule serves no particular interest, expresses no particular culture, regulates everyone's behavior in a universally advantageous or clearly correct way . . . a kind of moral Esperanto. But this hope is misbegotten, for minimalism is neither objective nor unexpressive. It is reiteratively particularistic and locally significant, intimately bound up with the maximal moralities created here and here and here, in specific times and places." Along similar lines, also see MacIntyre, *Whose Justice? Which Rationality?*, 326ff.

democratic conversation. For the religious are actually better able to constitute the secular as an abstraction from out of their own traditions of revelation than the secularists are able to postulate religion by deduction from a transcendental base. That constitution of the secular by the religious includes such attractive modern institutions as natural science and human rights based jurisprudence – in all their own integrity. But even when the secularists postulate "religion" rather than their more usual attempts to destroy it, they can never do that in a way that anyone would recognize the "religion" they have so constructed. That is because they must remove the cosmic dimension of any such religion. But a religion like Judaism without its cosmic dimension is quickly unrecognizable. Thus Jewish secularists, who often call themselves "cultural Jews," that is, Jews who want some of the substance of Jewish life (often called "Jewishness") without its form (better called "Judaism;" best called *Torah*), not only distort the meaning of Jewish life, they also distort the meaning of culture. In the deepest sense, there is no "secular culture." I know of no historically transmitted culture which when probed deeply enough does not invoke some transcendent reality as its source. Conversely, a phenomenology of secularity (as opposed to secularist ideology) would show that the very constitution of the secular sphere merely brackets all cosmic questions. But secularism as an ideology either attempts to usurp these cosmic questions unto itself, or it attempts to repress them altogether.

Finally, here is the point where the idea of natural law must replace the idea of human rights, at least in its modern version. For the idea of human rights has usually assumed that these rights can simply be posited without the enunciation of any ontology underlying them, that they create themselves as it were. This is done by the most systematic of the secularist thinkers, from the beginnings of modernity to this very day, by the construction of a elaborate fiction, originally called the "social contract." This is the artificial notion that society can be seen as the agreement between self-constituted individual persons, who come to it from a fictitous "state of nature" or "original position." Of course, the argument is circular inasmuch as a contract presupposes a social context already in place in the same way that every artificial language presupposes a matrix in a historical language. Hence it is one thing to see how various fictions or hypothetical situations can be constructed *within* an existing community for various reasons (for example, a *fictio juris*), but quite another thing to see human sociality itself grounded *by* a fiction.

However, if persons are seen as existing in traditional communities founded by revelations, then the social contract need not be an artificial construct at all. Society is founded when members of various communities have to come together in order to live in justice and peace. Let it be emphaszied, though, that they come as real bearers of older cultures (whether everyone can admit that or not), not as hypothetical individuals without a history, beginning from nowhere as it were.[38] That society is best worked out when demands for totality are not placed upon it, but when the members of the respective communities can affirm the finite value of the social arrangement they have contracted, and are always allowed to affirm the homeland from which they come and to which they must ever return. They cannot be expected to live like *Marranos*.[39] In John Rawls' helpful term, such inter-cultural political discourse and its practical results are "overlapping consensuses."[40]

To be sure, such overlapping consensuses between members

[38] Thus the seminal rabbinic principle "the law of the kingdom is the law" (*dina de-malkhuta dina* – B. Baba Batra 54b and parallels) is a recognition of a real social/historical situation where Jews must participate in a civil society with others, a civil society not of their own patrimony. See D. Novak, *The Image of the Non-Jew in Judaism* (New York and Toronto, 1983), 65ff.

[39] *Marranos* is the name for those Jews who openly converted to Christianity when faced with the choice of conversion or expulsion (as in Spain in 1492 and in Portugal in 1497), but who secretly attempted to retain Jewish faith and as much of Jewish practice as they possibly could. They are to be distinguished from those Jews who refused to maintain such a schizoid existence and, therefore, departed from those societies in which they could no longer live openly as Jews. For the classic study of this historical phenomenon, see Cecil Roth, *A History of the Marranos* (Philadelphia, 1932).

[40] Although he uses the term in his 1971 work *A Theory of Justice* (see 387f.), Rawls seems to be more committed to its pluralistic meaning in his later work. See *Political Liberalism* (New York, 1993), 35ff. Especially as used in his later work, "overlapping consensus" is a helpful term for what I am advocating here.

of various traditions must initially postpone discussion of the ontological foundations of these respective traditions, what I have called their "cosmic dimension," when working out practical procedures in common. Anything more would require actual correspondence with some transcendent reality rather than the more minimal requirement of immanent, practical coherence.[41] Indeed, requiring any such theoretical unanimity at present could only come through violent coercion, something most people should have learned by now from the political experience of this bloody century alone.

Nevertheless, just as adherents of self-consciously religious traditions must now postpone discussion of their ontological/theistic/cosmic concerns when dealing with the moral issues that arise in secular space, so must adherents of traditions thought to be nonreligious postpone discussion of their non-ontological/atheistic/acosmic concerns here too. In effect, this means eschewing the triumphalism of both religious and secularist fanatics. For many liberals, this will mean that they can no longer insist that these cosmic concerns, which turn out to be the concerns of most natural law advocates, most of whom are religious, be denied *ab initio* as the price of admission to the democratic conversation. They will have to admit that these concerns *could* be valid. They will have to admit that these concerns are not insane illusions. And they will have to admit that these concerns are *probably* better satisfied by historical religions of revelation rather than by modern ideologies that construct for themselves historical metanarratives. And that would be the case whether or not any liberal cares to recognize such concerns in his or her own life, and whether or not he or she attempts to satisfy them through these religions accordingly. Moreover, they will have to be aware of the fact that all too often, when these concerns are repressed, various modern ideologies, which despise both revelation and reason, rush in to violently fill the aching vacuum.[42]

In terms of political discussion, liberal adherents of human rights in the modern world will have to admit the *possibility* at

---

[41] See Novak, *Jewish Social Ethics*, 77ff.

[42] See T. S. Eliot, *The Idea of a Christian Society*, 2nd edn (London, 1982), 82.

least that these cosmic concerns of those who are usually thought to be conservatives, the most immediate being the concern with natural law, *could* intend an external reality and not just be hypothetical. Liberalism will, then, have to admit the *possibility* that human rights *might* lead into natural law. And since natural law thinking today is almost always being done by adherents of religions of revelation, that will include admission of the possibility of the religious background of natural law as well. But none of these requirements, I think, should be regarded by liberals as excessive, let alone outrageous, inasmuch as none of them is a requirement for conversion of any kind. For this reason, natural law discourse should never be used as a ruse for proselytizing of any kind by its religious adherents. Indeed, adherents of natural law will also have to admit the possibility that their ontological assumptions *could* be false.

For natural law theorists, any consensus that can be achieved with liberal human rights theorists helps dispel the fear that natural law is nothing but a projection out of a particular religious tradition, a form of apologetics as it were, and that it is not really universal at all. For, as an old Jewish proverb has it, when on the right road, one is bound to meet other travelers. Thus consensuses, which for many liberals are only procedural agreements, become for natural law theorists indications of actual truth. I shall have more to say about this comparative dimension of the constitution of natural law in chapter 5.

Natural law in this context can be seen as what Kant called a "border concept" (*Grenzbegriff*).[43] On the surface, it functions like the idea of natural rights, that is, it proposes rules, procedures, and even principles for the governance of civil society. But unlike the idea of human rights, it does not claim to be self-constituting. By its real assertion of *nature*, it indicates that it is rooted in an order that transcends any immanent society. Here is where it parts company with liberalism and

---

[43] See Immanuel Kant, *Critique of Pure Reason*, trans. N. Kemp Smith (New York, 1929) B295, 311–1312; also Ludwig Wittgenstein, *Tractatus Logico-Philosophicus*, trans. D. F. Pears and B. F. McGuiness (London, 1961), 5.61.

reconnects itself to the religions of revelation from whence it emerged, in our case, to Judaism.

The usual constitution of natural law in western philosophy has been metaphysical. That is, the cosmic order in which natural law is rooted has been presented as something which itself is rationally evident. I think, though, that for a variety of reasons, both philosophical and theological, metaphysics is not the way to constitute natural law. Metaphysics is after all only one type of ontology, one approach to being. A theology of revelation is another.[44] It seems to me that the ontological constitution of natural law is better done out of a religious tradition itself, specifically out of a theological constitution of the doctrine of creation. We shall explore that route in chapters 5 and 6. In the next three chapters, we shall explore how natural law thinking can root itself in Jewish tradition, particularly the tradition of Jewish law.

[44] By "metaphysics" I mean the type of ontology beginning with Plato, and most systematically formulated by his student Aristotle, that moves up in a rational trajectory from the study of universal nature (including human nature) to what has come to be known as "natural" (as distinct from "revealed") theology (see Aristotle, *Metaphysics*, 1074b35; *Nicomachean Ethics*, 1177a10–15). For the essential differences between natural and revealed theology as they pertain to natural law, see below, pp. 129ff. and 135ff.

CHAPTER 2

Scriptural foundations

And the Lord God commanded humans saying: From all
the trees you may surely eat; but from the tree of the
knowledge you may not eat for on the day you eat from it,
you shall surely die. (Genesis 2:16–17)

THE ORIGINAL QUESTION OF NATURAL LAW

From antiquity to the present, Jewish theologians have argued
whether Judaism has a concept of natural law or not. This
debate is fundamental because it is concerned with the question
of law. Judaism is much more than law. It is more than simple
"legalism" – contrary to the views of Spinoza, Kant, and many
others – but it is not less than law.[1] Judaism without law is simply
unthinkable. But the primary law of Judaism is the revealed law
of God (*torah min ha-shamayim*). Those theologians who recognize
no place for the concept of natural law in Judaism think that the
doctrine of the revealed law of God could not be properly
maintained if the concept of natural law actually had a place
there. Other theologians, who strongly endorse the concept of
natural law in Judaism, think that without this concept (by
whatever name it happens to be called at different times in
Jewish history), Judaism would have no place for human reason.
The absence of this concept would make human reason super-
fluous, and the Torah would become unintelligible in the world.
Already in Scripture, though, revelation and reason often

---

[1] See Baruch Spinoza, *Tractatus Theologico-Politicus* ch. 3; Immanuel Kant, *Religion within
the Limits of Reason Alone*, trans. T. M. Greene and H. H. Hudson (New York, 1960),
116ff. Cf. A. J. Heschel, *God in Search of Man* (New York, 1955), 320ff.

appear together and are often bound one with the other. However, is reason dependent on revelation, or is revelation dependent on reason? That is what seems to be basically at issue between these two groups of theologians.

So, one must ask the following questions: (1) Is it possible to say that without the Torah humankind would have no intelligence, especially no moral insight? (2) Is it possible to say that human intelligence *for* revelation can only come *from* revelation? (3) But is it possible to say that the Torah is more a task *of* the Jews than it is a gift *to* the Jews? (4) And is it possible to say that revelation is only the highest form of human reason? Usually, those theologians who are in favor of natural law in Judaism would answer "no" to the first two questions, and those theologians who are opposed to natural law in Judaism would answer "no" to the last two questions. Now I happen to be in favor of natural law in Judaism as this whole book and its very title surely indicate. Nevertheless, I would answer "no" to all four of the questions above. That is, (1) we cannot cogently assert that humans without the Torah have no moral insight; (2) humans bring an intelligence to revelation before they receive governance from revelation; (3) revelation gives to the Jews more than we could ever devise on our own; (4) revelation is God's unique speech that can only be partially apprehended, never comprehended.[2] As such, I see a middle road theologically between a reduction of reason to revelation, which seems to characterize the opponents of natural law, and a reduction of revelation to reason, which seems to characterize the proponents of natural law in Judaism, especially in modern times, as we shall see in the next chapter. I think that a proper phenomenological constitution of Judaism will bear this out. In fact, I think that such a constitution is a prime task of contemporary Jewish theology in order to overcome these two extremes. This challenge is by no means easy, but it is necessary, nonetheless. Without it, Judaism is left to be either a rationalism or a fideism; but both are positions that obscure rather than uncover the larger truth.

[2] See Job 11:7–9.

One sees the necessity of this challenge in a famous proposition of Maimonides: "Therefore I say that the Law, although it is not natural, enters into what is natural."[3] The exposition of the full meaning of this proposition will, hopefully, comprise a good answer to the whole question of the relation between Torah and human intelligence. The specific questions are: How can human intelligence understand the Torah *in the world?* What is the true relation of the Torah and the world? How can they both function so that one is not reduced to the other?[4]

A famous principle of rabbinic theology, one that has assumed several different meanings in the course of the development of Judaism, is: "The Torah speaks according to human language."[5] Another equally famous principle of rabbinic theology is: "The Torah is no longer in heaven."[6] Putting the two principles together, one can say that the Torah itself is not human speech but God's speech in the sense that its first speaker is God. Indeed, the most undisputed rabbinic doctrine of all, so much so that its dogmatic status is paramount, is: "Anyone who says that the Torah is not from God, that person has no portion in the world-to-come."[7] By that qualification, the Rabbis seem to be saying that even though someone who denies the revealed law of the Torah might have to be considered part of the Jewish people here and now, such a person will not remain part of the Jewish people when they and the Torah become permanently and totally unified in the future world (*l'atid la-vo*).[8] Before that time, though, lies the present human task of the Jews – with their reason – which is to approach the Torah in this world, however imperfectly. Although God is the Torah's first speaker, humans are its

---

[3] *Guide of the Perplexed*, 2.40, trans. S. Pines (Chicago, 1963), 382. For the probable meaning of this passage for Maimonides himself, one that differs from the appropriation of it here, see D. Novak, *The Image of the Non-Jew in Judaism* (New York and Toronto, 1983), 290ff.; also, below, pp. 113ff.

[4] See D. Novak, *The Election of Israel* (Cambridge, 1995), 10ff.

[5] See B. Berakhot 31b and parallels. For its more theological use, see Maimonides, *Guide*, 1.26. For a good discussion of its original talmudic meaning, see J. M. Harris, *How Do We Know This?* (Albany, N.Y., 1995), 33ff.; also, below, p. 146, n. 69.

[6] B. Baba Metsia 59b re Deut. 29:12.   [7] M. Sanhedrin 10.1.

[8] See B. Berakhot 17a re Exod. 24:11; B. Sanhedrin 111b re Is. 28:5.

intended recipients, whose task it is to receive this gift in an authentically human way.

That task is only possible when the Torah lends itself to rational understanding in the world inhabited by its human recipients. Because of this, humankind must have its own intelligent speech in order for God's revealed speech to be intelligible to them. Thus intelligent human speech, which is human reason, is the presupposition of revelation itself. It is what makes the revelation of God's word possible in the world. For Maimonides, this is so because both the Torah and the world are creations of the same divine wisdom.[9] That is why the science (*madda*) of the Torah and the *scientia* of the world can employ the same methods. Both are the result of a creative word (*dibbur*).[10]

The remaining chapters of this book will attempt to explicate this thesis from rabbinic literature and the tradition that has been developing out of it ever since, even into contemporary times. But that tradition sees itself as rooted in Scripture. I make no apologies for reading Scripture as a traditional (that is, rabbinic) Jew. That means I believe that Scripture as a whole has a unified meaning, and that all inner contradictions are ultimately matters of perception not reality, even though more often than not one cannot adequately overcome perceived contradictions.[11] However, that does not mean that I may not perceive the ostensive meaning (*peshat*) of a number of scriptural passages to be different from some or even all received rabbinic interpretations of them.[12] That is why I have separated this discussion of Scripture from the discussion in the next chapter that deals with the teachings of the Rabbis themselves. In the issue at hand, I attempt to deal with certain scriptural texts that at least suggest a recognition of natural law in the very beginnings of Judaism, which are scriptural, of course. In this task, I shall try to draw upon the comments of modern as well as classical biblical scholars, whenever appropriate.

---

[9] See *Guide*, 1.65.   [10] See below, pp. 116ff.

[11] See Y. Peah 1.1/15b re Deut. 32:47.

[12] See Rashbam, *Commentary on the Torah*: Gen. 37:1; also, David Weiss Halivni, *Peshat and Derash* (New York, 1991), 81ff.

CAIN AND ABEL

Everyone knows that the doctrine of original sin is one that has played a crucial role in the development of Christian theology. That original sin is located by Christians in the first human couple's disobeying the commandment of God not to eat of the fruit of the tree of the knowledge of good and evil.[13] Although the doctrine has played a somewhat lesser role in the development of Jewish theology, it is there, nonetheless.[14] Yet a frequently uttered modern liberal Jewish notion is that Judaism has no doctrine of original sin, that Christianity teaches that humans are evil by nature whereas Judaism teaches that they are good by nature.[15] This is, of course, a concession to modern philosophy, especially but not exclusively to be traced back to Kant, that human morality is autonomously self-sufficient inasmuch as human will is essentially good.[16] The fact is, however, that Scripture teaches "the inclination (*yetser*) of the human heart is bad from his very youth" (Genesis 8:21), and that fact should belie any modern Jewish apologetics to the contrary.[17] Indeed, it can be asserted that both Judaism and Christianity are convinced that humans are doomed if basically left to their own devices; that grace is a necessity for the human condition. The difference between them, one that is even more crucial than the imaginary one just mentioned, is whether one is connected to the grace of God by the Torah or by Christ.[18]

Although a number of Jewish thinkers, like virtually all Christian thinkers, have located the original human fall from divine grace in the eating of the forbidden fruit in the Garden of Eden, it is well worth noting that the several scriptural terms

[13] See Rom. 5:12–14.
[14] See B. Shabbat 55a-b; Yevamot 103b; Y. Berakhot 4.2/7d; B. Baba Batra 17a; Nahmanides, *Torat Ha'Adam* in *Kitvei Ramban* II, ed. C. B. Chavel (Jerusalem, 1963), 12ff., and "Disputation," *ibid.*, I:31; also, Will Herberg, *Judaism and Modern Man* (New York, 1951), 73ff.
[15] Even the usually faithful interpreter of the rabbinic tradition, Solomon Schechter, succumbed to this modern, liberal, apologetic tendency. See his *Some Aspects of Rabbinic Theology* (New York, 1909), 262f.
[16] See *Groundwork of the Metaphysic of Morals*, trans. H. J. Paton (New York, 1964) ch. 1.
[17] See B. Kiddushin 30b.
[18] See W. D. Davies, *Paul and Rabbinic Judaism*, 2nd edn (London, 1955), 147ff.

for sin are rather conspicuously absent in that well-known narrative.[19] This could mean that what God was doing in the first commandment to humans was to present a conditional offer rather than a categorical imperative: If you want to experience good and bad – that is, to be part of the world – then you must accept your own mortality in the bargain.[20] (Of course, no orthodox Christian exegete could possibly interpret the text this way in good faith.) This might very well be the human choice to become a moral being in general before any specific moral choices present themselves thereafter. If there is any human sin here, in the sense of violating what might be called a categorical imperative, it is not the act of eating from the designated tree. Instead, it is the subsequent human attempt to see this act as making humans God's equals, thus making God no longer God. It is the sin of idolatry.[21] By being reminded of their mortality, which stands as an essential difference from God's immortality, humans are disabused – or should be disabused – of that evil assumption.

At the level of the God–human relationship, this sinfulness is manifested by denial and irresponsibility.[22] Nevertheless, how it is applied in the interhuman relationship is not evident until the incident of Cain's murder of his brother Abel. And here we see the introduction of the term "sin" and its concept as well as the introduction of a natural law type issue, natural law issues being most immediately seen in the realm of the interhuman.

The introduction of the term "sin" (*het*) comes after God's rejection of Cain and his offering in favor of Abel and his offering. No reason is given for God's preference, although the rabbinic and medieval commentators do offer a number of possibilities, as is to be expected of them.[23] Yet it is plausible to conclude from the scriptural text itself that Cain has done something wrong since God then tells him, "Is it not so that if you do well (*teitiv*), you will be uplifted, but if you do not do

---

[19] Cf. *Sifre*: Devarim, no. 339.
[20] See Nahmanides, *Commentary on the Torah*: Gen. 2:17.
[21] Gen. 3:4–5. See *Beresheet Rabbah* 19.4.   [22] Gen. 3:9–12.
[23] Gen. 4:3–5. See Louis Ginzberg, *Legends of the Jews* I, trans. S. Szold (Philadelphia, 1909), 107f.

well, sin (*hat'at*) crouches at the door, and unto to you is its desire, but you shall master it" (Genesis 4:7). Nevertheless, the only point that emerges is that Cain is responsible for his own actions. It is a matter of free choice, never one of inevitable fate. But since we do not know what he actually did that was wrong enough to earn God's rejection of his sacrifice, the point is made more for projective than for retrojective meaning. It leads us directly into Cain's succumbing to sin by murdering his brother. Why he murdered his brother is again not revealed in the text itself, but has obviously lent itself to considerable speculation.[24] However, here we do know what wrong he has done. The act is clearly one for which God holds him guilty irrespective of why he actually did it. For it is the nature of the object or victim of the act that is morally determinative, not whatever subjective rationalization the perpetrator of the act might come up with. At this point, two important things emerge in the text: (1), Cain's attempt to exonerate himself from guilt; (2), what is revealed about the reason his act is criminal.

When God asks Cain after the murder of Abel, "Where is Abel your brother?," Cain famously answers, "I do not know. Am I my brother's keeper (*shomer*)?" (Genesis 4:9). Obviously, God's question is not one calling for information about Abel's physical whereabouts. Already from the question "Where are you?" (Genesis 3:9) that had been addressed to Cain's father Adam in the Garden of Eden, it is clear that nothing can be hidden from God. This type of question is intended to require the person being so addressed by God to justify himself or herself then and there. If that is the case, then the first part of Cain's answer is certainly not one of ignorance of the visible circumstances. Abel's bleeding corpse is lying right there in front of him and God. Anyone could easily see what has just happened. Cain seems to be claiming ignorance of the law itself. He seems to be saying: "I did not – could not – know that what I did was a crime." After all, there is no record of his having been told anything like, "You shall not murder"

---

[24] See *ibid.*, 108f.

(Exodus 20:13).[25] Indeed, that is the force of this passage, which
is one of the most misinterpreted passages in Scripture. "Am I
my brother's keeper?" is usually seen as a denial of human
responsibility for one another, of the human interdependence
so often emphasized in Scripture. In other words, since Cain's
answer is taken to be a denial of this basic human responsibility,
the implied answer to him is: "Yes, you are your brother's
keeper, and you did not fulfill your duty by murdering him as
you just did!"

However, this interpretation misses the fact that the word
"keeper" (*shomer*) in Scripture denotes someone who has been
explicitly designated by someone else to look after his or her
property, and who is responsible for any damage to that
property during the time of this fiduciary relationship.[26] One
cannot be held to such a fiduciary role by implication.[27] Now if
that is so, Cain's retort is correct in and of itself, namely, there
is no record theretofore that God has explicitly commanded
him not to commit murder, let alone to actually protect his
brother from danger to his life from anyone or anything else. In
the literal sense of the term, he is surely not his brother's
keeper.

So why is he guilty anyway? The only cogent answer is that it
is already assumed that he knows murder is a crime.[28] And
how if not by his own reason? And what is that reason? Is it not
the fact that he and Abel are brothers, that is, minimally, they
are equal enough by virtue of ultimately common ancestry so

25 The rabbinic attempt was to locate the prohibition of murder in the passage, "And
the Lord God commanded the man" (Gen. 2:16). The words that seem to designate
the man as the subject of the commandment (*al ha'adam* – "to the man") are taken to
designate man as the object of the commandment (*al ha'adam* – lit. "concerning the
man" – B. Sanhedrin 56b). Even were one to accept this interpretation as the most
plausible meaning of the text from Scripture, it still has natural law implications,
namely, from the recognition of the uniqueness of human existence one learns its
inviolability.
26 See Exod. 22:6–12; Josh. 10:18; Is. 62:6–7; also, D. Novak, *Halakhah in a Theological
Dimension* (Chico, Calif., 1985), 156, n. 39.
27 See Is. 6:8–10 and Rashi thereon; also, M. Baba Metsia 3.1ff.; B. Baba Kama 79a
and B. Baba Metsia 99a.
28 Even the prescription of capital punishment for murder (Gen. 9:5–6) presupposes a
prohibition of murder already in place. To employ a talmudic question: If the
punishment has been heard, so where is the prohibition to be found? (See, e.g.,
B. Sanhedrin 54b.)

that neither of them has the right to harm the other for his own individual advantage.[29] God's retort, "The blood of your brother is crying to me from the ground" (Genesis 4:10), might very well mean that Abel's death calls for the just punishment of his murderer in the same way that his very life called for restraint on the part of his pursuer. Thus the minimal human obligation one to the other is not brotherly love, which presupposes more positive commonality than existed between the two rival brothers at the time, but, rather, "Do no harm to one another."[30] Accordingly, the original sin of humankind, namely, that which is repeated by everyone at one time or another, is twofold: the temptation to see oneself as God's equal, and as the absolute superior of one's fellow humans.[31] Idolatry thus breeds violence. The first temptation in the Garden of Eden gets played out in the first crime in the world into which all humans have been thrown out from the primordial paradise of childhood innocence and safety. This seems to be the most basic presupposition of authentic human community, which must be in place logically before any interhuman dependence, any covenant, can be instituted and maintained.

When Cain protests to God that his punishment of being "a wanderer (*na ve-nad*) in the world" is "more than I can bear" (Genesis 4:12–13), since he will be as vulnerable to destruction as was his now dead brother, God promises protection. Cain then starts his own family, and "builds a city" (Genesis 4:17), naming it after his son Enoch, which probably signifies his intention that the city exist into perpetuity.[32] To that end he is dedicated, hence the name of his son Enoch (*Hanokh*), which means "the dedicated one." The city itself would seem to be Cain's protection, both from those who would murder him and from his own homicidal temptations that seriously wounded a

---

[29] See M. Sanhedrin 4.5.

[30] Hence the most minimal moral mandate is: "What is hateful to yourself, do not do to your fellow human" (B. Shabbat 31a). For the distinction between this and the more positive and more inclusive, "You shall love your neighbor as yourself" (Lev. 19:18), see D. Novak, *Jewish Social Ethics* (New York, 1992), 182, n. 30; *The Election of Israel*, 96ff.

[31] See B. Pesahim 25b and parallels; also, J. Barton, "Natural Law and Poetic Justice in the Old Testament," *Journal of Theological Studies* 30 (1979), 3.

[32] See Neh. 12:26–29.

life worthy of human participation. What could be inferred from all this is that without socialization, humans are left unprotected from being both the victims and the perpetrators of violent death by natural forces as well as by their own hands. A justly ordered society is a requirement of human nature if human beings are to survive, let alone flourish.[33]

THE GENERATION OF THE FLOOD

The evil introduced into the world by Cain's murder of Abel was not eradicated by the establishment of the city. In fact, Scripture sees the beginning of the downfall of humankind in this political situation: "When the sons of political potentates saw how desirable (*tovot*) the daughters of common people (*benot ha'adam*) were, they took from them any wife they happened to like for themselves" (Genesis 6:2). I have translated *elohim* as "political potentates" rather than the easier translation "sons of God" because I do not think the text here is talking about sexual congress between male angels and human females.[34] Instead, it seems to be using *elohim* in a more mundane sense, for which there is some precedent in Scripture.[35] *Adam*, which literally means "human," is here contrasted with *elohim* in the sense of the ordinary masses being ruled by the extraordinary few. Following this line of interpretation, the sin here would be what in effect is some kind of politically sanctioned rape, for the women do not seem to have been consulted about their being "taken."[36] The immediate announcement of God's decree of human mortality does not seem to have stopped this political pretension. More drastic punitive action was thus called for.

The exact character of the sin of the Generation of the Flood seems to have involved the elements of illicit sexuality and violence. "And the earth was corrupted (*va-tishahet*) before God, and the earth was filled with violence (*hamas*)" (Genesis 6:11). The sexual element is further emphasized by the words, "and

---

[33] See Job 19:13–20.   [34] See Ginzberg, *Legends of the Jews*, I:124ff.
[35] See Exod. 22:7–8, 27. Cf. B. Sanhedrin 66a.
[36] See *Beresheet Rabbah* 26.5; *Yalqut Shimoni*: Beresheet, no. 43; also, B. Ketubot 3b.

all flesh (*kol basar*) corrupted its way upon the earth" (6:12). The "way of flesh," especially in the light of the passage examined in the preceding paragraph, based on the overall context and other scriptural associations, seems to refer to sexual corruption.[37] Now what is the connection between sexuality and violence? And how is this something to be known by humans rationally, even without a specifically revealed statute? For here again, humans are held guilty as Cain was held guilty for an act God expects them to already know to be a crime.

From the first crime of Cain being the archetype of all subsequent crime, we learn that it always involves violence of some type or other. Maimonides suggests that illicit sexuality leads to violence, especially violence between men fighting over women.[38] However, the matter goes deeper than that, I think. Sexuality is inherently violent; it does not just entail violence. For any act of sexual intercourse between persons itself involves the penetration of one person by another and the simultaneous devouring of that person by the other person being penetrated.[39] What saves it from being violently destructive is the positive institution of the family. Family life involves a man and a woman living together on a permanently intimate basis for the sake of having and rearing children, and remaining together even after that task for the sake of the continuity of their family identity together.[40] This is what Cain seems to have intended by his own marriage, namely, having and rearing a child, and building a city to perpetuate the identity of his family. But without that essential socialization of sexuality, it inevitably becomes the overcoming of one person by the desire of another. Physical desire per se merely intends its own satisfaction. Only when desire becomes truly personal does it intend a mutual end beyond its own internal satisfaction.[41]

Just as Cain should have known his obligation not to harm Abel by virtue of their common humanity, so his descendants

---

[37] See Exod. 28:42; Eccl. 5:5; Prov. 30:19.
[38] *Guide*, 3.49. Cf. *Beresheet Rabbah* 22.7 re Gen. 4:8.
[39] See B. Yoma 77b re Gen. 34:2 (the opinion of R. Pappa).
[40] See Novak, *Jewish Social Ethics*, 84ff.
[41] See Emmanuel Levinas, *Totality and Infinity*, trans. A. Lingis (Pittsburgh, 1969), 62.

should have known their obligation to subdue their violence, especially their sexual violence, by virtue of the communal institution of marriage. It alone enables men and women to be sexually related in mutual and creative respect precisely because their sexuality is included in and structured by something larger than the mere physical desire of separate bodies.[42] Marriage and family are the beginning of the larger human community. Any society that does not regulate sexual activity has lost its moral authority. How significant it is that when Noah and his family and the representative animals are saved in the Ark from the Flood, they enter the Ark as married couples.[43] It would seem that the experience of being in the Ark not only saved them from the physical doom that befell the rest of earthly life, but it helped them realize what it was that brought about that doom itself. And that norm is learned from the nature of the experience; the nature of the experience does not have to wait for an externally imposed norm to be morally understood. Indeed, after the Flood, Noah's drunkenness also seems to involve sexual corruption and violence, a partial regression as it were.[44]

There are further natural law implications in this narrative of the Flood and its aftermath. After emerging from the Ark, the surviving humans are told "all the seasons of the earth will not cease (*lo yishbotu*): planting time and harvest time, cold and warmth, summer and winter, day and night" (Genesis 8:22). This seems to be saying that just as the earth functions according to a law, without which it would have no sustaining order, so it is with human society itself. Indeed, human sociality presupposes a physical order surrounding it, upon which it can depend for its own continuity. But humans discover their own essential order, their own essential law, from their own social experience. Only thereafter do they discover the order of the nonhuman realm by analogy.[45]

---

[42] See *Vayiqra Rabbah* 14.5 re Ps. 51:7; also, B. Moed Qatan 5a-b.

[43] See Gen. 6:18–20.

[44] Gen. 9:23 mentions Noah's exposure of his genitals (*ervat avihem*), which might be a euphemism for actual sexual misconduct. Cf. Lev. 18:6ff.; Deut. 24:1.

[45] Thus it is worth noting here that the medieval Hebrew word used to denote a "cause" (*sibbah*) is first used in Scripture to denote an intentional act (I Kings 12:15;

Both realms are subject to God's law, but humans must freely accept that law upon themselves, unlike the physical realm onto which that order is imposed by determination. This difference between humans and all other creatures is why the shedding of innocent human blood can be avenged by other humans "because in the image of God He made humans (*adam*)" (Genesis 9:6). Human action has consequences that nonhuman behavior does not have. Only God and humans have responsibility.[46] They are never simply part of an inevitable causal chain. Humans can return or be returned to past events of their own making and be called upon to answer for them in a way that is impossible for events themselves to do in their linear trajectory. Humans like God cease from their labor (*shavat*) from time to time and look back upon it, unlike physical nature, which never ceases from it labor, which never rests, but only moves forward never looking back.[47]

ABRAHAM AND SODOM

The most unambiguous example of a natural law type position in Scripture emerges from the first unmediated covenant between persons presented there, namely, the covenant between God and Abraham. (The earlier covenant between God and Noah is essentially a covenant between God and the earth, in which Noah is included. Even Noah's response to

see I Sam. 22:22). A *sibbah* is responsible for his or her act, unlike a cause for which there is no answerability (see Plato, *Phaedo*, 98C). So, also, we use the term "law of nature" (*lex naturae* as distinct from *ius naturale* or *lex naturalis*) by analogy to moral law. For Spinoza, conversely, the analogy was in the opposite direction, namely, moral law (*ius*) imitates impersonal natural order (*lex*). See *Tractatus Theologico-Politicus*, trans. S. Shirley (Leiden and New York, 1989), ch. 4. Cf. John Finnis, *Natural Law and Natural Rights* (Oxford, 1980), 52.

[46] See Gen. 3:22 for the point of moral responsibility being what humans have in common with God, and the immortality of God being what ever divides them one from the other.

[47] Hence God judges his handiwork, the macrocosm, to be good (Gen. 1:31) and then enjoys it retrospectively from the vantage point of the Sabbath (2:2). Humans judge their handiwork (specifically, the Temple, the epitome of human effort in the world), the microcosm, similarly (see I Kings 8:56). Both God and humans assume happy responsibility for what they have done or made when it has been done well. Along the lines of the macrocosm/microcosm analogy, see Jon D. Levenson, *Creation and the Persistance of Evil* (San Francisco, 1988), 78ff.

God's commandment to save himself, his family, and representatives of the animal kingdom, is a matter of natural self-preservation, not the personal mutuality that characterizes a covenant per se.) This covenant is directly between God and Abraham and his descendants. God makes an agreement with Abraham and his people and they must remain faithful to God. "I am establishing my covenant between me and you and your descendants after you throughout the generations as an everlasting covenant: to be God for you and for your descendants after you" (Genesis 17:7). And what must this people specifically do to initially confirm the covenant? "And you shall be circumcised in the flesh of your foreskin, and it will be a sign of the covenant between me and all of you" (Genesis 17:11). So far, we see something rather unnatural in the covenant between God and Israel. It seems that Israel is not to live according to nature but, rather, to live in opposition to nature.

Nevertheless, the covenant between God and Israel presupposes the covenant God made with the earth during the time of Noah. For earlier God said to Abraham: "Be a blessing (*brakhah*) . . . and because of you shall all the families of the earth be blessed" (Genesis 12:2-3). Now how would Abraham know what that blessing is actually to be unless he had learned from the story of Noah just how God had already blessed the earth in that earlier time?[48] When it said after the Flood that "God blessed Noah and his children" (Genesis 9:1), that blessing primarily consists in God's assurance that he will deal with humankind justly, and that humans similarly deal justly with one another, "because in the image of God he made humans" (Genesis 9:6). So it would seem that Israel's blessing for the world lies in the way she is commanded, understands those commandments, and applies them. "Keep it and practice it, for it is your wisdom and understanding in the eyes of the peoples, who will hear all these statutes and say: 'surely this great nation is a wise and understanding people'" (Deuteronomy 4:6). It would seem that not only does the Torah impart wisdom and understanding to Israel, but Israel must have come

---

[48] See Novak, *The Election of Israel*, 123ff.

to the Torah with some degree of wisdom and understanding already in hand to be able to accept its teaching in practice.

All of this comes out most clearly in the dialogue between God and Abraham over the unjust situation in the cities of Sodom and Gomorrah. Like Abel's blood crying to God for the judgment of his brother who shed it, so it seems that those oppressed by the people of these two evil cities have made "a cry that is great" (Genesis 18:20), an urgent appeal for justice to be done for them.[49] God justifies taking Abraham into his confidence over his plans for them by saying, "Abraham will surely become a great and important nation, and because of you will all of the nations of the earth be blessed. For I know him, and it follows that he will command his children and household after him to keep the way of the Lord to do righteousness and justice (*tsedaqah u-mishpat*) . . ." (Genesis 18:18–19). Note that the way of the Lord initially is not what the Lord directly commands Abraham but what Abraham commands his people for the sake of the Lord. There is a prior responsibility on Abraham's part and that responsibility is one of rational morality.

Now what is the minimal condition of "righteousness and justice," which can be interpreted as "correct justice"?[50] Is it not to always distinguish between the just and the unjust, between those who have done right and those who have done wrong? This is the most minimal political condition, which is reflected in the rabbinic notion that the first collective obligation of the gentiles (and the Jews, a fortiori) is to maintain courts for the administration of justice (*dinim*), what Aristotle called "rectifying justice."[51] Without it, can any society claim the moral allegiance of its citizens? And if this minimal condition is not met by God (however mysteriously it is effected in terms of time and place), could one believe in the righteousness of God and attempt to live according to his precepts?[52] The justice of God must be the archetype for human

[49] Along these lines, see Exod. 2:23 and 22:22.   [50] See Ps. 119:164.
[51] See B. Sanhedrin 56a-b; B. Gittin 9b and Rashi, s.v. "kesherin." Re rectifying justice, see Aristotle, *Nicomachean Ethics*, 1135b25ff.
[52] See Job 35:1ff.

justice, especially for his covenanted people. Without this
cosmic justice, natural right cannot be maintained. It requires
this larger context if it is to appear as more than an unnatural
invention of finite, mortal, and fallible human beings.[53] That is
why Abraham poses as his main question to God: "Can the
judge (*shofet*) of the whole earth not himself do justice
(*mishpat*)?!" (Genesis 18:25). Just as God must deal with the
world in order to judge it cogently, so must Abraham and his
people deal with the world rationally. But here it is necessary to
say neither too much nor too little about justice and its relation
to God because here is where the direct relationship of God
with humans begins.

In their treatment of the relation of ethics and theology,
liberal religious thinkers, both Jewish and Christian, have had
much to say. Thus Hugo Grotius, whom many consider to be
the founder of modern natural rights theory, and who was
himself a Dutch Protestant, explains Abraham's query about
God's justice as asserting that justice itself even stands over
God himself.[54] That would seem to follow from what, for
Grotius, distinguishes the new natural rights theory from the
old natural law theory, which is that it is valid "even were we to

---

[53] See Novak, *Jewish Social Ethics*, 163ff.

[54] Thus he writes: "The law of nature, again, is unchangeable – even in the sense that
it cannot be changed by God. Measureless as is the power of God, nevertheless it
can be said that there are certain things over which that power does not extend; for
things of which this is said are spoken only, having no sense corresponding with
reality and being mutually contradictory. Just as even God, then, cannot cause two
times two should not make four, so He cannot cause that that which is intrinsically
evil not be evil.

"That is what Aristotle means when he says: 'Some things are thought of as bad
the moment they are named [*Nicomachean Ethics*, 1107a10] . . . Thus God Himself
suffers Himself to be judged (*de se judicari patitur*) according to this standard, as may
be seen by referring to *Genesis*, xviii.25 . . ." (*On the Law of War and Peace*, trans. F. W.
Kelsey *et al.* [Oxford, 1925], 40 = *De Jure Belli et Pacis* [Cambridge, 1953], 12–13).
Grotius is wrong theologically. God's power is inherently infinite. But the consistent
execution of justice is actually God's own limitation of that infinite power for the
sake of covenantal relationality with the world. (See D. Novak, "The Self-Contraction of the Godhead in Kabbalistic Theology" in *Neoplatonism and Jewish Thought*, ed.
L. E. Goodman [Albany, N.Y., 1992], 299ff.). Furthermore, God is only "judged"
(better, *challenged*) when he has revealed to his covenantal partner a seeming
covenantal contradiction in a possible course of action he is proposing for joint
deliberation with that partner (see Amos 3:7), as is the case here with Abraham, and
as is the case later with Moses (Exod. 32:9–14).

say there is no God" (*etiamsi daremus non esse Deum*).[55] After this (and despite Grotius' disclaimer of any atheism on his part), it is not too difficult to understand how Kant saw theology as having validity only when it is made to serve the ultimate ends of ethics.[56] Indeed, this whole line of thought can be traced back to Plato, for whom the gods are subordinate to justice as subjects are subordinate to the higher objects they can apprehend.[57] However, the pagan Plato can be more consistent than Christians like Grotius and Kant (and Jews like Hermann Cohen, who were so influenced by them) because, unlike them, he does not have to square his philosophy with the doctrine of the God who is creator of the entire world *ex nihilo*, and who is subject to nothing higher than his own will and his own truly autonomous commitments.[58]

But the teaching of Scripture (and the Rabbis thereafter) is quite clearly not what Grotius and others made it out to be, even in the dialogue between God and Abraham. God creates everything, even justice itself, and nothing in the world can stand over God as judge. "There is no wisdom, no understanding, and no counsel that can stand against the Lord" (Proverbs 21:30). Pascal was right at this point: the God of Abraham, Isaac, and Jacob is not the God of the philosophers, certainly not the God of Plato and all whom he influenced.[59]

Although justice does not stand over God, it is something higher than ordinary agreement, nevertheless. It is a principle from which one can query other persons in a mutual relationship – even God: What are you doing? That is what Abraham is doing in his dialogue with God over the verdict on Sodom and Gomorrah, a dialogue held at God's express invitation.[60] But how does this differ from judging God by virtue of human

---

[55] *On the Law of War and Peace*, prol. 11, p. 13 = *De Jure Belli et Pacis*, xlvi.

[56] See *Religion within the Limits of Reason Alone*, 95.

[57] See *Euthyphro*, 12D; *Timeaus*, 29Aff.

[58] Kant's influence on Cohen is ubiquitous in all his works – including his specifically Jewish works. See his *Religion of Reason out of the Sources of Judaism*, trans. S. Kaplan (New York, 1972), 106, 240f. Re Plato, see above, p. 18.

[59] For powerful disagreement with this notion by a contemporary Jewish philosopher, see L. E. Goodman, *God of Abraham* (New York, 1996), vii and *passim*.

[60] Gen. 18:17.

reason the way Plato judged the gods of Athens?[61] That is the heart of the theological problem of natural law.

At this point, we must now constitute a theological concept of freedom since throughout Scripture, and especially in this narrative, both God and man are free to make choices: the people of Sodom have chosen to do evil, God is deliberating about how to punish them for that evil, and Abraham has freely accepted God's invitation from God to participate in that deliberation along with him. Freedom is the personal presupposition of justice.[62] Only free beings are responsible for it. But is this connection of freedom and justice the same for God as it is for humans? To answer "yes," as liberal theology basically does, is to land ourselves in a dead-end, as we have already seen. Only when divine freedom is seen as being different from human freedom, can we then see that God is related to justice differently than humans are related to it. It is best to begin with human freedom because it is our own experience. Divine freedom requires more speculation on our part.

Human freedom, certainly as presented in Scripture, is essentially a response. It is freedom of choice (*behirah hofsheet*), not "freedom of the will" in the modern sense.[63] It is always a response to someone already there before one. Justice here comes before freedom. Humans are already contained within a world fundamentally not of our own making. Nature is the order of that world in which we find ourselves. As moral beings, we humans have the ability to be either responsible or irresponsible to the just demands of those other persons to whom we are related in our natural sociality. The consequences, both immediate and ultimate, of just responsibility are good; the consequences of unjust irresponsibility are bad. Human experience in the world is what Scripture calls eating of "the tree of the knowledge of good (*tov*) and bad (*ve-ra*)" (Genesis 2:17).[64] Human responsibility is the free choice whose

---

[61] See *Republic*, 379Cff.

[62] See Maimonides, *Mishneh Torah*: Teshuvah, ch. 5.

[63] For the difference between the two, see Hannah Arendt, *Life of the Mind* II (New York, 1978), 28f., 89; Novak, *The Election of Israel*, 138ff.

[64] Scripture teaches that God creates both what we experience as good and what we experience as bad (Is. 45:7). These polar terms are originally aesthetic and only

options are situated within the world where humans find themselves. What is within the world is what humans can choose, but they cannot choose the world itself.

Even the most radical choice of all, the choice to die, is still a choice of one location in the world in place of another. It is a relative leaving, not absolute nonbeing. Nonbeing would be an impossible escape from God's judgment. "Where can I go away from your spirit, and where can I flee from your presence? If I ascend up into heaven, you are there; if I make my bed in the world below, there you are" (Psalms 139:7–8).[65] Thus when Elijah asks God to let him die, he says to God: "Take my life" (I Kings 19:4), which surely implies that his actual desire is for a radical change of locale. Shortly thereafter the angel of the Lord tells him to "Get up! eat! because the road ahead of you is great" (I Kings 19:7).[66] That is the necessary "being-there" (*Dasein*) of the human condition.

With God, however, freedom is entirely creative. According to Scripture, only God has autonomy; only God can make laws that are not derivative from something else in the world. "Justice is God's" (Deuteronomy 1:17). (Thus Kantian autonomy is a substitution of human will for God's will.[67]) God's freedom, then, comes before justice. God is in no way necessitated to create the world or participate in it in the way that humans like all other creatures are necessarily in the world. God alone has original freedom of the will; God alone freely transcends the world. That is why later tradition read the scriptural use of the verb *bara* – "create" – as *creatio ex nihilo*, even though it could mean creation from primeval matter as some scholars, both medieval and modern, have plausibly argued.[68] Nevertheless, the cumulative implication of Scrip-

---

derivatively normative (see Maimonides, *Guide*, 1.2). The original normative terms are "innocence" (*tsedeq*) and "guilt" (*resha*), which can also be rendered "justice" and "injustice" (see Gen. 18:23–25; Exod. 9:27 and 23:7). Only we humans are capable of *resha*, and only we are accountable for it to a higher judge (see Ps. 5:5; Job 34:10–12).

[65] See D. Novak, *Law and Theology in Judaism* I (New York, 1974), 8off.

[66] Cf. Jon. 4:1ff.

[67] See *Religion within the Limits of Reason Alone*, 157 and note thereon.

[68] See Gersonides, *Wars of the Lord*, 6.1.17ff.; Levenson, *Creation and the Persistance of Evil*, 3ff.

ture, which is theologically more cogent than the previously mentioned one, is that God is not coequal with anything, even primordially.

What Abraham then asks God could be elaborately para-phrased as follows: You are the free creator of the world and everything in it. Your creation is certainly without any necessity. You could have created another kind of world altogether (as non-Euclidean geometries demonstrate), or no world at all. At this most elementary level, I as a creature am but "dust and ashes" (Genesis 18:27) and nothing more. But if you choose to be involved in the world with your human creatures, especially as their judge, then you must function as the archetype and model of justice. There is certainly more to that involvement than mere justice. There are innovative aspects of this new covenant you are making with me and my descendants, for which there are no prior grounds.[69] But there are prior condi-tions, first and foremost being that the covenant must include a morally intelligible form of polity, both in terms of the internal relationships of the members of the covenanted community one with the other, and their relationships with others outside their community. The minimum of that involvement in justice is that judicial decisions be made fairly (what we now call "due process of law").[70] You are the archetype of justice in the world, and the model of justice for the people with whom you are making this covenant. Justice is a result of your divine freedom. This freedom, unlike human freedom, is unconditional and wholly original. With us humans, however, it is different; for us, justice is a natural necessity. We humans can, of course, choose to act unjustly, but we pay dearly for such a choice, as will be the case with the guilty citizens of Sodom and Gomorrah.[71]

Natural law like the covenant is a gift from God. But the giver is always greater than the gift. In the covenant, Israel confronts the giver of the gift. In nature, though, the giver of

---

[69] See Jer. 31:30–33.

[70] And that elementary fairness sometimes requires that interhuman judgments be made on more general principles of equity rather than on specific statutes, whose application in rare cases might be contrary to elementary fairness as the first condition of judicial rulings. See I Kings 3:16ff.; B. Baba Metsia 83a re Prov. 2:20.

[71] See Ps. 53:2–6.

the gift is always hidden behind it. Justice is part of this divine gift, something about which Israel has some previous understanding. In the world in which Israel has already been living, justice is the maximum that anyone can rightfully expect. But in the covenant, justice is only the minimum. The covenant transcends nature, but as something more not less than it.

Covenantal freedom and natural or political freedom are similar in principle. God has the freedom either to make or not to make a covenant with anyone, which is like his freedom to create nature or not. When he chooses Israel, he owes them nothing, just as when he creates the world, he owes it nothing. All obligations on God's part are subsequently self-imposed.[72] But with Israel as with humans in the world it is otherwise. She only has the freedom to be responsive or unresponsive, responsible or irresponsible. The covenant and sociality are both necessities for their human participants. Thus when Israel turns away from God rather than towards him, she pays dearly. God invokes the natural created order to "testify" against Israel when this happens, which would also be the case when natural justice is violated as in the case of Sodom and Gomorrah. "I have called heaven and earth today: life and death have I placed before you, the blessing and the curse: choose life that you may live, you and your children" (Deuteronomy 30:19). That "life" is the Torah itself, which is "a tree of life" (Proverbs 3:18) in scriptural teaching. The Torah of the world is learned through human nature; the Torah of the covenant is learned directly from God.[73]

ABRAHAM AND ABIMELECH

Abraham's concern with natural justice, evidenced in his dialogue with God over the fate of Sodom and Gomorrah, is a theoretical discussion. There Abraham has nothing to do himself. Shortly thereafter, that concern becomes a matter of practical interaction, however.

[72] See Exod. 32:13–14.
[73] That "Torah of the world" is called "the Torah of man" (*torat ha'adam*). See II Sam. 7:19 and Rashi, *Commentary on the Prophets* thereon (first comment). Cf. I Chron. 17:17.

Abraham and his clan travel into Philistine territory. As he
did when he encountered Pharaoh during an earlier trip to
Egypt, Abraham passes his wife Sarah off as his sister in order
that he not be killed if she be taken into the harem of the local
king Abimelech. When Abimelech does what Abraham had
feared he would do, God tells the king in a dream that Sarah is
really a married woman and that keeping her would be a crime
entailing a death sentence.[74] Abimelech protests his ignorance
of the circumstances; after all, didn't Abraham lie to him about
who Sarah is? God then tells him in the same dream, "and now
return the man's wife (*eshet ha'ish*) for he is a prophet and will
pray on your behalf that you live" (Genesis 20:7). When
Abimelech immediately confronts Abraham about this deception, he asks him, "Just what did you discern that you did this
thing?" (20:10). Abraham answers, "Surely there is no fear of
God (*yir'at elohim*) in this place" (20:11).

Abraham's answer to Abimelech is appropriate considering
the fact that Abimelech accused him of "acts that are not to be
done" (*ma'asim asher lo ye'asu* – 20:9). Abimelech's criterion is
universal, namely, Abraham's deception is an act that should
not be done *anywhere*. It is not the violation of a local ordinance
of which he may or may not have been aware. The force of
God's telling Abimelech that Abraham is a prophet might very
well be that Abraham's specific prophetic power does enable
him to discern Abimelech's true ignorance of Sarah's status.[75]
Nevertheless, the issue is not one involving ignorance of
particular circumstances, but it is one involving the general
moral standards of the community itself. "Fear of God" means
the elementary decency that requires human beings to restrain
their desires out of fear/respect for the rights of other humans,
in this case the right to inviolable marriage, because of the way
God has created humans and their dignity. Restraint is called
for in the name of a law higher than that of human making
when desire leads to unjustified violence of any kind. To violate
the "fear of God" is to violate the order that God has enabled
humans to know through their very nature. Abraham is thus

[74] Cf. Gen. 12:10–20.   [75] See Rashi, *Commentary on the Torah*: Gen. 20:7.

allowed to lie in a situation where telling the truth would lead to a much greater evil being done. But in a community where there is political endorsement of this elementary decency, persons do not have to lie in the interest of self-preservation.

Fear of God, then, is correlative with what is not to be done. This can be seen in the scriptural account of how the Egyptian midwives saved the Hebrew infant boys from the lethal decree of Pharaoh. It is said that they did so because "they feared God" (Exodus 1:17). The commentators are divided as to whether the two chief midwives, Shifrah and Puah, were Hebrews or Egyptians.[76] However, it seems to me that they were probably Egyptians. Even though they are called "Hebrew midwives" (*ha-meyalldot ha'ivriyot*), that could very well mean "midwives of the Hebrews," namely, those in charge of Hebrew births. Why would Pharaoh entrust a program of extermination to the leadership of two women who would have ties of kinship with the victims and who would thus be much more likely to sympathize with their plight? Didn't Pharaoh enslave the Hebrews because he assumed that in the event of an invasion the Hebrews would "augment our enemies" (Exodus 1:10), which many assume were their fellow Semites (that is, "Hebrews") the Hittites? Also, the racial slur that the two midwives invented to defer Pharaoh's criticism of their failure to implement his genocidal policy, namely, "the Hebrew women are not like the Egyptian women; they are such animals (*hayot hennah*) that they give birth even before the midwife comes to them" (1:19), is much more plausible when coming out of Egyptian mouths than Hebrew ones. And, finally, Pharaoh, who is the destroyer of Hebrew homes and families, destroys Egyptian homes and families, including his own.[77] The midwives, on the other hand, by upholding the fear of God, have "houses made for them" (Exodus 1:21) by God. The term "houses" (*battim*)

[76] For the view that they were really Jochebed and Miriam (or Elisheva) respectively, see B. Sotah 11b re Exod. 1:15. For the view that they were really Egyptians, see Isaac Abrabanel, *Commentary on the Torah* thereon, and R. Samuel David Luzzatto (Shadal), *Commentary on the Torah* thereon. See also N. M. Sarna, *Exploring Exodus* (New York, 1986), 25.

[77] Exod. 12:29–30.

connotes permanence and stability.[78] It would seem, then, that their houses are Egyptian houses. The Hebrews are not going to be in Egypt much longer anyway. They will be building their houses elsewhere.

THE RAPE OF DINAH

The distinction between local ordinances and universal norms comes out in two stories in the life of Jacob.

When Jacob, fleeing his vengeful brother Esau, arrives at the home of his soon-to-be father-in-law Laban, he works for seven years in order to be allowed to marry Laban's younger daughter Rachel, with whom he instantly fell in love. After the wedding, however, Laban gives Jacob his older daughter Leah, whom Jacob does not love, in place of Rachel for the actual consummation of the marriage. When Jacob protests this deceit, Laban retorts, "To give the younger one before the older one in marriage is something not done in our place (*lo ye'aseh ken bi-meqomenu*)" (Genesis 29:26). That is, what you want is contrary to our local ordinance.[79]

Marriage has many peculiar practices that vary from place to place. So when a man is preparing to marry, he should investigate what these peculiar practices are before the actual wedding. These practices are well known to all the local inhabitants of the particular place. They have often been around there from time immemorial.[80] They are hardly a secret. These practices are either matters of written law or of oral tradition within the community. Apparently, in the grip of his passion for Rachel, Jacob did not make proper investigation of these matters. For that he had to pay a social price, which was seven more years of work in order to marry Rachel. Surely, though, no one could say that Jacob had violated any universal moral norm (but, perhaps, only the pragmatic norm of "look before you leap").

But in the story of Jacob's daughter Dinah and her violation

---

[78] See, e.g., Lev. 14:34, 25:32; Deut. 24:5; Josh. 2:18–19; II Sam. 7:1ff.; Jer. 35:7–10.
[79] See *Midrash ha-Gadol*: Beresheet re Gen. 29:26, ed. Margulies, 518.
[80] See, e.g., B. Ketubot 12a.

in the city of Shechem by the prince of that city, the moral significance of what happened is entirely different. When the matter became known to Dinah's brothers, Scripture states, "for a vile thing (*nevalah*) has been done to Israel, Jacob's daughter being raped; that is something not to be done (*ve'khen lo ye'aseh*)" (Genesis 34:7). Here we see two issues: (1), what has been done to Israel; (2), what is not to be done. Are these two issues the same or are they different? Is it "not to be done" because of "what has been done to Israel," or is it something more than that? The most plausible answer is that we have two different issues here. What is not to be done is what is not to be done *at all* – anywhere to anyone. What happened is not just the concern of Israel; it is a universal human concern irrespective of who the victim happens to be or who the perpetrator happens to be. One must see this in contrast with the justification for Laban's withholding Rachel from Jacob at first. There "what is not to be done" is qualified by "in our place." But here the same normative use of the form "to be done" is used, but without the qualification of the earlier text.

The traditional Jewish sources agree that the guilt for Dinah's rape is not only that of the prince Shechem; the citizens of Shechem are implicated in his guilt as well. But why are they guilty for what he did? It was not a gang rape after all. Maimonides answers that it was "because they saw that Shechem had robbed, they knew about it but they did not judge him."[81] (Whether the sons of Jacob had the authority to judge the people of Shechem or not is a matter of exegetical dispute, however.[82]) In other words, the act of the prince was not a random, individual violation of the law of Shechem. It seems that the communal guilt in this matter is that such an act, which universal moral reason considers evil and not to be done, could be done with impunity in Shechem. Thus the crime of the people of Shechem is not only that they did not come to the aid of the victim, Dinah, but that they saw no crime here at all. As such, "what happened to Israel" is an example of a larger moral crime. Who the victim is is itself

[81] *Mishneh Torah*: Melakhim, 9.14.
[82] See Nahmanides, *Commentary on the Torah*: Gen. 34:13.

immaterial. And what Shechem did should not be done to
anyone by anyone. The tragedy is certainly most keenly felt by
those closest to the victim, especially those having ties of
kinship with her, but the injustice is a crime against humanity.[83]
And the punishment for the crime (when humanly possible) is
different from particular vengeance. It is human retribution per
se. All of this, unlike local marriage practices, is something
about which no one can join Cain in saying "I did not know"
(Genesis 4:9) it was wrong.

JOSEPH AND POTIPHAR'S WIFE

The difference between local ordinance and universal moral
norm comes out again in the story of Joseph and the wife of his
Egyptian master Potiphar.

Joseph is sold into slavery by his own brothers and is taken
down to Egypt, where he is purchased as a slave by one of
Pharaoh's chief officials. We are told in this narrative that his
master "left everything he had in Joseph's hands . . . except the
bread that he ate" (Genesis 39:6). Now some commentators
have interpreted "the bread that he ate" to be a euphemism for
sexual intercourse with his wife, no doubt since her attempted
seduction of the handsome young slave immediately follows in
the story.[84] However, I think it is more plausible to assume that
this term be taken literally inasmuch as we learn later, from
another incident in the life of Joseph, that "Egyptians are not
able to eat bread with Hebrew because it is taboo (to'evah) for
Egypt" (Genesis 43:32). Like most of the Jewish dietary restrictions, this Egyptian dietary restriction is shrouded in mystery
and, clearly, only applies to Egyptians. Even Joseph, despite his
high rank in Egypt subsequently, is still not enough of an
Egyptian himself to be able to eat bread with the Egyptians,
even in his own home. No reason is given for the taboo, and no
one seems to question its validity in that place.[85]

But this is to be contrasted with Joseph's reasons for refusing

83 See above, pp. 6f.
84 See *Beresheet Rabbah* 86.6 and M. M. Kasher, *Torah Shlemah*: Vayeshev, 1487, n. 39.
85 See Luzzatto (Shadal), *Commentary on the Torah*: Gen. 43:32.

to accept the sexual favors of Potiphar's wife. He gives essentially three reasons. First, my master "has not denied me anything in the house except you, being that you are his wife" (Genesis 39:9). Second, "and how can I do this great evil?!" Third, "I will have sinned against God."

The first reason is that having intercourse with Potiphar's wife would be a breach of trust. Joseph has been justly treated by his master and the terms of their relationship are clear. Joseph accepts what is his and what is not his. It is very much a social contract. But what if Potiphar did not really care what happened as long as the lovers were discreet? There is such an implication in the story because Potiphar is called "a eunuch" (*seris* – 39:1).[86] Now it is true that "eunuch" is sometimes a general term for someone who personally serves a king (many of whom were eunuchs, especially those who were in contact with the female members of a royal household) even if he were not literally emasculated.[87] Nevertheless, there is the suggestion that if Potiphar was not actually incapable of intercourse with his wife, he was, nevertheless, rarely home and thus inattentive to her womanly needs. Furthermore, his reaction to the charge made by his wife against Joseph is rather mild, merely having him transferred to what seems to have been a minimum security prison, one for very special, high-ranking offenders, most of whom did not expect to be there too long. Considering the usual horror at adultery, one would have expected him to have Joseph killed for what his wife accused him of. Surely, he had the power to do so. And why does he seem to have no suspicions about his wife at all?

That is why, it seems, Joseph is not content to give this first reason concerning breach of trust as his only reason for refusing the seductive offer of Potiphar's wife. Adultery is

---

[86] See B. Sotah 13b, where it is speculated that Potiphar was castrated by the angel Gabriel in order to prevent him from homosexual rape of Joseph, for which purpose he had purchased him in the first place. Both factors, either castration or homosexuality, are plausible suggestions for his seeming disinterest in his wife, evidenced by his usual absence from their home, and her desperation in the way she pursued Joseph sexually. On the other hand, though, he could have simply been too preoccupied with his high office to care very much about domestic matters.

[87] See F. Brown, S. R. Driver, and C. A. Briggs, *A Hebrew and English Lexicon of the Old Testament* (Oxford, 1952), 710, s.v. "seris."

wrong even if not only the wife is willing and is not being in effect raped by another man, but even if the husband seems to be physically or emotionally disinterested in his wife's sexual needs and activities, that is, where the marriage is only a social facade.[88] Adultery is wrong because it violates the institution of marriage itself, an institution whose need for fidelity is recognized by most, but not all, of its participants. In other words, even if Potiphar's wife, or Potiphar himself, did not care about sexual fidelity one to the other, their entry into the marital covenant requires that they, and everyone who has personal contact with them, recognize the sanctity of this basic human institution, which is violated when infidelity is tolerated by anyone related to it. One may not privately contract what is contrary to publicly valid morality.[89] What used to be called an "open marriage" is a moral oxymoron.

Finally, Joseph asserts that succumbing to the passionate invitation of Potiphar's wife would be a sin against God. Surely, the temptation to become her lover was great, both in terms of the sexual pleasure it would afford him and the emotional satisfaction of cuckolding a man who had such power over him. But this would be a great evil, not only because it involves a fundamental contradiction of the necessary social institution of marriage, but because it violates the law of God by which the universe is run. Natural law is the law of God. Indeed, it is first manifest in the relationship of man and woman, from which all subsequent human relationships are built. But when not seen as the part of God's law that is universally intelligible to all humankind, it loses its necessary ontological foundation. As Antigone realized in her struggle with Creon, without the divine grounding and enforcement of a law, even of a law that is universally accepted as reasonable, opposition to it by human forces greater than one's own power can always be taken to be a natural confirmation of the moral validity of that greater human power.[90] By connecting natural law and divine law, one thereby acknowledges a more powerful source of law than the

---

[88] Along these lines, see B. Gittin 17a and Rashi, s.v. "mi-shum."
[89] See B. Kiddushin 19b and parallels.
[90] See Sophocles, *Antigone*, 450–457. Although, for Antigone, the gods themselves do

will of any human potentate, who after all is still finite, mortal, and fallible. And one acknowledges that mortal human powers are no match for the immortal God, either when the law is made or when the final reckoning for it comes. "I am the first and I am the last, and besides me there is no god (*elohim*)" (Isaiah 44:6). Without this ontological grounding and judgment, adherence to moral law can generate the despair of political impotence.[91] Idealism is never enough when there are real and powerful challenges to the natural law of God. That is the final and best point in Joseph's retort to the temptation posed both physically and socially, by the no doubt attractive wife, of his powerful master.

MOSES AND JETHRO

After Israel left Egypt, but before she received the Torah at Mount Sinai, Scripture states, "Jethro, the Midianite priest, the father-in-law of Moses, heard about all that God had done for Moses and Israel his people, for the Lord brought Israel out from Egypt" (Exodus 18:1). In the Talmud it is asked just what Jethro heard that made him come and convert (*nitgayyer*). Rabbi Joshua says that he heard about the victory over the Amalekites; but Rabbi Eliezer of Modiin says that he heard about the giving of the Torah at Mount Sinai.[92] This debate, like all serious debates in Judaism, is both exegetical and theological. What we need to do now is to see just how this is a debate over an essentially scriptural issue, even before it became a rabbinic issue.

As for Jethro's conversion, although that is often assumed in rabbinic texts, there is much in Scripture that seems to indicate that this was not the case. First, after accepting Jethro's advice, "Moses sent his father-in-law off, and he went by himself to his own land" (Exodus 18:27). Second, there is the passage where Moses begs Jethro to remain with the people of Israel in the desert on the journey to the Promised Land, but Jethro

not create justice, but only enforce justice that is prior to themselves ontologically. See above, p. 18.
[91] See Novak, *Jewish Social Ethics*, 163ff.   [92] Zevahim 116a.

answers, "No, I shall not go along, but I shall go to my own land and to my birthplace" (Numbers 10:30).[93] Third, when King Saul is about to rout the Amalekites, he warns Jethro's people to get out of the way "because of the kindness you showed Israel when they went up from Egypt" (I Samuel 15:6). It would seem that this advice to a gentile people is because Jethro, one of *their* leaders, came to assist Moses after the Exodus. There is no record of anyone else from that people having shown such kindness to Israel. Finally, it seems that full conversion as a religious event is something that did not come about until the period after the Babylonian Exile.[94] So, it is more plausible in terms of the text of Scripture alone to see Jethro as a sojourner among the people of Israel, and a temporary one at that.

However, the debate between Rabbi Joshua and Rabbi Eliezer of Modiin does concern a matter of scriptural exegesis per se, and that is one about the sequence of scriptural narrative. Rabbi Joshua assumes that in the case at hand, the sequence of events follows in chronological order.[95] That being so, Jethro could not have heard about the giving of the Torah because that event has not yet happened and is not yet recorded in the text. But Rabbi Eliezer of Modiin assumes that this is one of those cases where Scripture does not follow chronological order. In any good narrative, certain events are mentioned out of chronological order for the sake of emphasizing a conceptual point. For any good narrative is as much didactic as it is descriptive, often more so.[96]

---

[93] See *Sifre*: Bemidbar, no. 78, ed. Horovitz, 75, where Jethro's reason is "because *gerim* have no portion in the land." But if he had become what is later called a "full convert" (*ger tsedeq*), i.e., in the religious sense of the term rather than in the sense of being a politically disadvantaged resident-alien (*ger toshav*), then how could he possibly return to his pagan homeland? Cf. II Kings 5:17–19; Ezek. 47:22–23. This question is dealt with by the *Mekhilta*: Yitro (ed. Horovitz-Rabin, 199–200) commenting on Exod. 18:27. It asserts that Jethro went back to his homeland in order to "bring them under the wings of the Shekhinah," i.e., to fully convert them to Judaism (see Ruth 2:12). In other words, he came back to Israel for religious reasons.

[94] See D. Novak, *The Image of the Non-Jew in Judaism* (New York and Toronto, 1983), 14ff.

[95] He seems to be employing the principle of "juxtaposition" (*semukhim*). See B. Berakhot 10a re Ps. 111:8.

[96] He seems to be employing the principle "there is no strict chronological sequence (*ein muqdam u-me'uhar*) in the Torah." See B. Pesahim 6b.

The theological ground of Rabbi Eliezer's interpretation seems to be that a non-Jew cannot convert to Judaism without the full Torah already functioning in place. Without the full Torah in the hands of the people of Israel, is the conversion of a non-Jew to Judaism possible? Isn't a convert required to accept all the commandments of the Torah?[97] How could he possibly do so when they have not yet been revealed? Furthermore, just what sort of a positive law did Israel have before the giving of the Torah? One must bear in mind that when Jethro came to Moses, he gave him advice about how to make legal decisions. Those decisions are to be based on the "laws of God and his rulings" (Exodus 18:16) that Moses made known to the people. But what are they? After all, any juridical decision which is not tyrannical surely presupposes a law already in place (*nulla poena sine lege*).[98] Law must already exist before any judge can make a cogent ruling in a case before the court. And how could one convert in good conscience to a lawless community?

Clearly, though, Rabbi Joshua's exegesis is easier to argue for on exegetical grounds. But is it merely an exegetical point about a narrative sequence? Is it not, rather, dealing with the whole question of just what law Israel was living by before Sinai? That is a theological and a philosophical point, the theological point being about the content of revelation, and the philosophical point being about the content of reason.

First, even though both Rabbi Joshua and Rabbi Eliezer of Modiin are answering a question about Jethro's "conversion," only Rabbi Eliezer's view seems to be wedded to the later institution of full conversion (*gerut*), which was ultimately structured in rabbinic times. Rabbi Joshua's view only need assume that Jethro became some sort of resident-alien, what the Rabbis called a *ger toshav*, which is an institution that the Rabbis themselves recognized was one operating in biblical times, and for which there is solid scriptural evidence.[99] If that is the case, then what was the pre-Sinaitic law by which Israel was living, which could also be a feature of the community to

---

[97] See T. Demai 2.4.   [98] See Y. Yoma 1.5/39b; B. Sanhedrin 56b.
[99] See Arakhin 29a.

which Jethro was clearly attracted, however temporarily? Couldn't one say that they were living by some law that their human reason told them is God's basic law for humans in community? That law is what we now call "natural law."[100]

This answer also involves the covenant between God and Israel, which is the main interest of Scripture. For God's covenant is not primarily made with individual persons but with a people, a people that is already constituted as a community. That is quite different from an association of like-minded individuals who come together after each is convinced of a political idea. The covenant is such an association too, even in biblical times, but that association presupposes an earlier form of community that is improved but not replaced by it. But what is it that makes a community a true communion of persons and not a tyrannical regime of one group or another? From several sources, both Hebraic and Hellenic, one can answer that such a true community is one where strangers are respected as human persons. That is a community that simultaneously recognizes natural law and honors it. The stranger is, in effect, the representative of humankind per se.[101]

An authentic human community, one that is more than a simple collection of humans, is one that can make two fundamental assertions. First, we ourselves have not made all of our laws. Second, all of our laws are not valid for ourselves alone, but some very essential laws are valid for all humans in general. The first assertion speaks about nature that stands immutably in the face of all legal development. The second assertion speaks about universality, that which is not confined to the

---

100 Thus the Talmud (B. Baba Kama 100a) locates the principle of not acting according to the strict letter of the positive law in certain cases involving interhuman relations but, rather, according to more general teleological criteria (*lifnim me-shurat ha-din*), in Jethro's words to Moses to instruct the people in "what they shall do" (Exod. 18:20), words uttered before the giving of the Torah at Sinai. Moreover, in this interpretation of the scriptural passage, the words we now vocalize in the Masoretic text as "they shall do" (*asher ya'asun*) could very well have been vocalized in this talmudic text as "what [i.e., the acts themselves] are to be done" (*asher ye'asun*). For the philosophical view that "is to be done" rather than "you shall do" is the basic form of natural law propositions, see Germain Grisez, "The First Principle of Practical Reason," *Natural Law Forum* 10 (1965), 168ff.

101 See Cohen, *Religion of Reason out of the Sources of Judaism*, 116ff.; also, F. Horst, *Gottes Recht* (Munich, 1961), 244f.

singular community at hand. Only an authentic community –
and not what Plato called a "band of thieves" – only such a
community is a worthy recipient of the full revelation of God's
law in the world.[102]

In Scripture, a key sign of the true covenantal community is
the willingness and preparation of its native members to treat
strangers as sojourners in their midst. The condition for that
acceptance is that those same strangers are willing to live by
those basic laws that will also be their protection in that
community when practiced by the natives towards them. "You
shall have one justice (*mishpat ehad*), both for the sojourner and
the native born shall it be" (Leviticus 24:22).[103] Jethro is the
paradigm of such a stranger. The sign of the inauthentic
community is hatred of strangers and abuse of them. That is
what characterized Sodom as the very embodiment of what an
authentic human community is not. Thus the men of Sodom
demand of Lot, Abraham's nephew who has chosen to live in
their midst, "Where are the men who came to you tonight?
Bring them out to us so that we may know them!" (Genesis
19:5). The word "know" (*yado'a*) is, no doubt, a euphemism for
some kind of direct personal contact, whether or not it is the
"carnal knowledge" later tradition assumed it to be.[104] And
from this context it is clear that that direct personal contact is
violent. And when Lot protests, the men of Sodom answer,
"This one has come to dwell (*la-gur*) and now he is exercising
judgment!" (19:9). How different that is from Jethro's reception
by Moses and the people of Israel, indeed paralleling Jethro's
own reception of Moses when he was a fugitive from
Pharaoh.[105]

In Jethro's case, could he have come to a community that
had no acceptance of anything like the human rights of
strangers? Thus the law that is not made by humans and the
human rights of strangers belong together. For in the world that
God has made, are not all humans strangers? Is it not so that

---

[102] See *Republic*, 351D; also, Prov. 1:10–14; R. Judah Halevi, *Kuzari*, 2.48.
[103] See B. Avodah Zarah 64b.
[104] See *Beresheet Rabbah* 50.5, ed. Theodor-Albeck, 522 and note thereon.
[105] See Exod. 2:20.

basically one stranger must welcome another stranger as a
fellow sojourner, everyone's alienation being a difference of
degree rather than one of kind? "I am a sojourner (*ger*) on
earth" (Psalms 119:19). Even Israel in her own land is reminded
by God that "the land is mine, for you are sojourners and
tenants (*ve-toshavim*) with me" (Leviticus 25:23). That is why
Israel is commanded "to love the sojourner as yourself, for you
were sojourners in the land of Egypt" (Leviticus 19:34). In
other words, Israel is not to treat strangers in her midst like
enemy aliens – the way she was treated in Egypt, especially
since the story of Joseph indicates that the Israelites were
willing to live in Egypt as lawful residents.[106] And, indeed, that
alienation in the world belonging to God is taken to be the
human condition itself. "For we are sojourners before you and
tenants like all our ancestors, like a shadow are our days on
earth, and there is no abiding place (*v'ein miqveh*)" (I Chronicles
29:15). Israel's acceptance of Jethro, even her willingness to
listen to his moral guidance, is the exact opposite of the way
Lot was treated in Sodom and the way Israel herself was
treated in Egypt. Both Sodom and Egypt were in violation of
the natural law of God, even though it took miraculous
intervention to make that point sufficiently well known.

The cases from Scripture examined above are all examples of
incidences that took place before the giving of the Torah at
Mount Sinai, which marks the sealing of the covenant between
God and Israel. What they indicate, especially as pertains to
the realm of interpersonal human relations, which is the very
subject matter of natural law theorists today, is that the
normative content of the Sinai covenant need not be regarded
as originally instituted at the event of the Sinai revelation. Even
much of that content which is cultic, historical research has
been showing to have analogues and precedents in other
cultures. And that commonality is even more evident in the
ethical teaching of Scripture, which, being more universal in
essence, will have more easily discovered cognates elsewhere.

[106] See Gen. 47:4ff.

Instead, the uniqueness of the covenant lies in its overall *Gestalt*, which constitutes a full and abiding relationship between God and a people on earth. That relationship has future significance for humankind as a whole. In the end of days, "My house shall be called a house of prayer for all peoples" (Isaiah 56:7), even though as long as it stood it was only "the house built to the name of the Lord God of Israel" (I Kings 8:17). What the cases cited above have shown, I hope, is that in Scripture itself the covenant has a universal precondition as well as a universal consequence, that it has an ontology as well as an eschatology. When that is recognized, one can see that an idea of natural law is not one that was grafted onto the tree of Judaism from basically Hellenic sources. Instead, by the time the ancient and medieval Jewish theologians were ready to learn important ideas and methods from the philosophers of Athens, they already had their basic ideas from Jerusalem firmly in hand. In the next chapters, we shall see how these scriptural ideas found their development in the teachings of the Rabbis.

CHAPTER 3

Jewish ethics and natural law

For it is no empty thing for you, but it is your life.
(Deuteronomy 32:47)

JEWISH ETHICS

One of the ongoing debates among Jewish thinkers today is whether there is a doctrine (*torah*) of natural law in Judaism. The debate is being largely conducted among traditionalist Jewish thinkers, who need be concerned with the ubiquitous presence of law in Judaism. For anyone who reflects on the meaning of law itself must think about the question of natural law, whether to finally affirm it or deny it. Therefore, the question is being asked: Is the idea of natural law something authentic in Judaism, or is it a foreign import improperly grafted onto it, however ingenious that grafting might be?[1] The way to approach this question might well be to see "ethics" as the mediating term between "law," which nobody could possibly deny is indigenous to Judaism, and "natural law," which is the subject of the current debate. In other words, our introduction to the question of natural law in Judaism might very well come from the question of just what is "Jewish ethics." Whereas in the first chapter we determined just where on the horizon of democratic society there is an opening for a religiously based natural law voice to be heard, here we must see how the "world," which is the locus of natural law, finds an

---

[1] See *Jewish Law Annual* 6 (1987), pt. 1; *Jewish Law Annual* 7 (1988), pt. 1. Both of these volumes are devoted to the question of "the philosophy of Jewish law," the question of natural law being the predominant subtopic therein.

opening on the horizon of rabbinic Judaism, the Judaism that is the heritage of all traditional Jews even today.

If "ethics" be defined prima facie as a system of rules governing interhuman relations, then "Jewish" ethics is identical with Jewish law. It is *Halakhah*. More precisely, Jewish ethics is part of a system of rules that also governs relations between humans and God. Ethics, which pertains to the interhuman realm (*bein adam le-havero*), is as integral a part of Halakhah as are the Sabbath rules or the dietary rules or the rules of prayer, which pertain to the divine–human realm (*bein adam le-maqom*).[2] Because the ethical content of Judaism at this level is so obvious, some contemporary Jewish scholars of the most traditionalist type, people who usually eschew discussions of Judaism outside the context of their traditional communities of discourse and practice, have quickly and gladly entered discussions of normative ethics today. For these discussions, at least at the prima facie level, only seem to call for the comparative presentation of rules rather than the more philosophic agreement on common principles that are more general than the scope of any one tradition. The reason for this is the more case-oriented approach of normative ethics today, where the lead seems to be coming from the burgeoning field of bio-medical ethics.[3] Cases call for the immediate application of rules, unlike more theoretical discourse, which calls for the justification of principles.[4]

Nevertheless, rules themselves are insufficient for their very application in anything but the most simple and routine cases.

---

[2] For this basic distinction, see M. Yoma 8.9.

[3] Thus a prominent Orthodox Jewish ethicist, J. David Bleich, at the beginning of his thorough treatment of the issue of abortion, quotes approvingly the statement of the halakhist R. Abraham Isaiah Karelitz (*Hazon Ish*, d. 1953), namely, "Ethical imperatives are . . . at one with the directives of Halakhah; it is Halakhah which determines that which is permitted and that which is forbidden in the realm of ethics" (*Jewish Bioethics*, ed. F. Rosner and J. D. Bleich [New York, 1979], 135). When it comes to actual norms themselves, this is, of course, a quite accurate statement. It was undoubtedly made to counter liberal Jewish claims that Jewish ethical norms can be formulated outside of the content of Halakhah, even contrary to it. Nevertheless, it does not deal with the fact that ethical principles have been influential in the formulation of these very halakhic norms and the choices made in interpreting those already formulated.

[4] See D. Novak, *Jewish Social Ethics* (New York, 1992), 3ff.

More often than not rules cannot be cogently applied unless we have some understanding of what these rules intend, that is, *the reasons for which they have been devised in the first place.*[5] Since rules in the Jewish tradition are "commandments" (*mitsvot*), either commandments from God or commandments from human authorities, the principles that lie behind these rules have been termed "the reasons of the commandments" (*ta'amei ha-mitsvot*).[6] Although these reasons are "reasons *of* the commandments," they themselves are not commandments any more than a moral rule or law and an ethical principle are identical. The function of the former is to govern; the function of the latter is to explain and guide the former. Indeed, one could say, following the thirteenth-century Spanish Jewish theologian Nahmanides, that without the guidance of ethical principles in the observance of the commandments, "one could be a wretch within the law's domain (*naval bi'rshut ha-torah*)."[7]

REASONS AND INTENTIONS

In the history of Jewish thought, there have been debates about the question of the reasons of the commandments. It is often assumed that the two extremes in these debates are, on the one hand, those who hold that every commandment has a reason, and on the other hand, those who hold that none of the commandments has any reason at all. However, the latter position is an inaccurate caricature. No one could cogently argue that none of the commandments has any reason at all.

First of all, the commandments from God are in general obeyed *because* God has so commanded. That itself is a reason, not just a rule. The will of the creator is to be obeyed. It is to be obeyed because to disobey it is to deny the truth of creation,

[5] See e.g., B. Sotah 8a re Num. 5:15; B. Kiddushin 65b re Deut. 19:16; also I. Heinemann, *Taamei ha-Mitsvot be-Sifrut Yisrael* 1 (Jerusalem, 1949), 29; *Encyclopedia Talmudit*, XX:568ff., s.v. "ta'ama de-qra."

[6] See B. Sanhedrin 21a; Maimonides, *Sefer ha-Mitsvot*: introduction, sec. 5; also E. E. Urbach, *Hazal* (Jerusalem, 1971), 328; *Halakhah* (Jerusalem, 1984), 106.

[7] *Commentary on the Torah*: Lev. 19:2. Here Nahmanides agrees with Maimonides in not designating a general commandment intending the Torah in toto as one of the 613 scriptural norms. See Maimonides, *Sefer ha-Mitsvot*: introduction, sec. 4 and Nahmanides' note thereon. Along these lines, see also R. Joseph Albo, *Iqqarim*, introduction.

which is that in all areas of existence, including our moral life, "He has made us not we ourselves" (Psalms 100:3).[8]

Although there have been those in the history of Judaism who have seen all the commandments being obeyed only because they are the decrees of God, those of a more rationalist frame of mind have also thought that the commandments are to be obeyed because to obey them is to attain what the wisely beneficent creator has intended as good for us. The supreme pinnacle of this good is God's own presence in the covenant, which is called "spousal love" (*ahavat kelulotayikh* – Jeremiah 2:2). To disobey them, then, is to incur what is the opposite of good, that which is bad. That good or that bad are not only supernatural rewards or punishments but, also, intrinsic benefits or harms.[9] Indeed, whereas one is not to perform a commandment for the sake of its supernatural reward, one can certainly perform a commandment because of its own intrinsic end.[10] Of course, one is always to perform a commandment because of its source inasmuch as that source is always understood to be God. And one is to do that even when one is unclear or uncertain about whether the commandment has any intrinsic end at all, or if it does, exactly what that end actually is.[11]

These two reasons involve two theological principles, which themselves cannot be halakhic rules. Furthermore, they are reasons which require that we understand enough of *who* God

---

[8] This follows the reading of the *ketiv.* The reading of the *qrē* is "He made us and we are his," substituting *lo* for *l'o*. Theologically, it seems that the written text expresses a principle prior to that of the read text, namely, we need to be aware of the truth that we are not self-made, not fundamentally autonomous (whether in Kant's, Nietzsche's, or Sartre's sense), before we are ready for the good relationship expressed in the prepositional phrase "we are his."

[9] See B. Kiddushin 39b and Tos., s.v. "matnitin." There Rabbenu Tam argues that the Mishnah (Kiddushin 1.10), which refers to the good that comes from doing a *mitsvah*, primarily means good in this world. That good can be seen as being entailed by the very doing of the *mitsvah* itself. Thus there is a fundamental difference between doing a *mitsvah* for the sake of an extrinsic (supernatural) reward and doing it for its own sake, which can mean both because of its being God's command and because of its own intrinsic good.

[10] See M. Avot 1.3; Maimonides, *Commentary on the Mishnah*: Peah 1.1; *Mishneh Torah*: Teshuvah, 10.1–2.

[11] See *Mishneh Torah*: Teshuvah, 3.4; also, D. Novak, *The Election of Israel* (Cambridge, 1995), 246ff.

is that we are able to answer the question: *Why* is God to be obeyed?[12] That is an ontological question, which is independent of and presupposed by the epistemological question: *How* do we know it is God who has so commanded?

These two reasons are differentiated by their respective intentions. In fact, intention (*kavvanah*) is the subjective side of a commandment and reason (*ta'am*) is the objective side: one intends a reason and a reason elicits one's intention. The first reason is that God is the *source* of the commandment; the second is that God is the *end* of the commandment. As source of the commandment, God is its creator; God stands behind the commandment, as it were. As end or *telos*, though, God is the presence before the doer of the commandment, towards whom he or she acts; God stands ahead of the commandment, as it were. An end or *telos* is to be clearly distinguished from a result or consequence now absent that an act produces in the future.[13] The supernatural rewards promised for the observance of the commandments are the pinnacle of such future production.[14] In the Babylonian Talmud a "reason" (*ta'ama*) designates either a source or an intrinsic end of a commandment.[15] Therefore, what kind of reason determines what kind of intention there is to be, and vice versa.

In the commandments governing the relationship between humans and God, God is the direct source of the commandment. That is why for most of them, which are positive precepts, a blessing acknowledging God as the source of the precept is to be said prior to its performance.[16] In commandments like the recitation of the *shema* ("Hear O' Israel, the Lord is our God, the Lord alone" – Deuteronomy 6:5), which is a

---

[12] See D. Novak, *Law and Theology in Judaism* II (New York, 1976), 1ff.; *The Election of Israel*, 118f., 166ff.

[13] See D. Novak, *Suicide and Morality* (New York, 1975), 91ff.

[14] See Hullin 142a.

[15] See, e.g., B. Baba Metsia (*ta'ama* = source); B. Berakhot 23a (*ta'ama* = reason).

[16] See Maimonides, *Mishneh Torah*: Berakhot, 11.2. God is even designated as the direct source of commandments originally mandated by the Rabbis (see B. Shabbat 23a), although there is one rabbinic opinion that in the case of such commandments, one should acknowledge God as the One who commands us concerning "the commandment of the elders" (*mitsvat zeqinim* – see Y. Sukkah 2.4/53d), namely, that the mediating role of the Rabbis be acknowledged in the act itself.

Jew's personal acceptance of the kingship of God, or in the commandment to pray, God is also the direct end of the commandment by definition. Hence absence of such intention invalidates the act by depriving it of its necessary meaning.[17] Regarding other commandments in this divine–human realm, where some other object is involved (like eating *matsah* on Passover), God is the ultimate end of the act, but God is not its immediate end and thus the commandment requires much less theological intention.[18]

In commandments governing interhuman relationships, God is most often the indirect source of the commandments themselves inasmuch as most of these commandments would qualify as natural law, thus mediated by our rational reflection on created human nature.[19] And in all of them, the human objects of these acts are their immediate ends and God is their ultimate end.[20] Indeed, in several of these commandments, how one intends the human object of the act can validate or invalidate the sacred character of the act itself. In other words, such commandments require the intention of the good of the human object of them, which in many cases can be affective, namely, how the personal object is made to feel.[21] Furthermore, to confuse the direct human object with the ultimate divine object could very well lead to poor performance of the specifics of the commandment. For example, in the commandment to love one's neighbor as oneself, the neighbor needs the full and immediate attention of the one acting on his or her behalf.[22]

[17] See *Mishneh Torah*: Qeriat Shema, 2.1 re B. Berakhot 13b; *ibid*.: Tefillah, 1.1 re Exod. 23:25; *Sifre*: Devarim, no. 41; and B. Taanit 2a re Deut. 11:13. Cf. B. Berakhot 17b and Tos., s.v. "Rav Shisha"; Maharam me-Rothenburg, *Teshuvot, Pesaqim u-Minhagim*, ed. Kahana, sec. 2, no. 57; R. Jacob ben Asher, *Tur*; and R. Joseph Karo, *Shulhan Arukh*: Orah Hayyim, 70.3.

[18] See B. Rosh Hashanah 28a–b. Cf. Y. Pesahim 10.3/37c–d; B. Pesahim 115a, Tos., s.v. "matqif."

[19] See Maimonides, *Mishneh Torah*: Berakhot, 11.2, and R. Joseph Karo, *Kesef Mishneh* thereon; Nahmanides, *Commentary on the Torah*: Gen. 6:2 and 13; R. Obadiah Bertinoro, *Commentary on the Mishnah*: Avot 1.1; R. Israel Lifschitz, *Tiferet Yisrael* on M. Baba Batra 10.8: Yakhin, n. 84.

[20] See below, pp. 172ff.

[21] See, e.g., B. Kiddushin 31a–b, Rashi, s.v. "u-mevi'o" and Tos., s.v. "ve-tordo" re Y. Peah 1.1/15c; Arakhin 16b re Lev. 19:17; Y. Peah 8.8/21b re Ps. 41:2 and parallels.

[22] See B. Kiddushin 41a and Niddah 17a re Lev. 19:18; also, Novak, *Jewish Social Ethics*, 96f.

Excessive piety in the performance of such a commandment is uncalled for.

The authoritative halakhic conclusion is that all of the commandments minimally require intention of their divine source (whether immediate or ultimate) in order to qualify as *mitsvot*.[23] For those authorities who do not require intention of the divine source as a legal requirement, there is only the legal requirement that the person performing the commandment be aware of the prescribed specifics of the act itself.[24]

Aside from the commandments to accept the kingship of God upon oneself twice daily (*qeri'at shema*) and regular prayer thrice daily (*shemoneh esre*), all other commandments, whether pertaining to the divine–human relationship or to interhuman relationships, only require intention of the divine source in order to be legally valid acts.[25] But for those theologians who do stress the teleology of the commandments, even if such intention is not a legal requirement, one should optimally strive to intend the ultimate divine end of all the commandments as much as possible.[26]

Finally, the teleology of the law is best seen in the constitution of commandments from rabbinic authorities, at least since the demise of the Sanhedrin, for they have always been publicly justified by specific reasons qua purposes as well as by the general reason qua source justifying human legislation in a

[23] See *Halakhot Gedolot*: Rosh Hashanah, ed. Hildesheimer, 311; Alfasi, *Rosh Hashanah*, ch. 3, ed. Vilna, 7b; Maimonides, *Mishneh Torah*: Melakhim, 8.10–11; R. Vidal of Tolosa, *Maggid Mishneh* on Maimonides, *Mishneh Torah*: Shofar, 2.4 (cf. *Maggid Mishneh* on *Mishneh Torah*: Hamets u-Matsah, 6.3); R. Eliezer ben Joel ha-Levi, *Sefer Raavyah*: Rosh Hashanah, ed. Aptowitzer, 214 re Y. Rosh Hashanah 3.7/59a; Nahmanides, "Derashah le-Rosh Hashanah" in *Kitvei Ramban* I, ed. Chavel (Jerusalem, 1963), 241; R. Asher ben Yehiel: *Rosh*: Rosh Hashanah, 3.11; R. Jacob ben Asher, *Tur*, and R. Joseph Karo, *Shulhan Arukh*: Orah Hayyim, 60.4; R. Zvi Hirsch Chajes, *Mavo ha-Talmud*, ch. 16 in *Kol Kitvei Maharats Chajes* I (Jerusalem, 1958), 315; R. Israel Meir ha-Kohen, *Mishnah Berurah* on *Shulhan Arukh*: Orah Hayyim, 60.4, n. 11; R. David Weiss Halivni, *Meqorot u-Mesorot*: Yoma-Hagigah (Jerusalem, 1975), 404f.

[24] See B. Rosh Hashanah 28a and Rashi, s.v. "she-kaf'uhu parsiyim"; R. Nissim Gerondi (Ran) on Alfasi, *Rosh Hashanah*, ch. 3, ed. Vilna, 7b, s.v. "garsinan be-gemara" and "le-fi-khakh"; *Shulhan Arukh*: Orah Hayyim, 475.4.

[25] See R. David ibn Abi Zimra, *Teshuvot ha-Radbaz*, no. 2247; R. Joseph B. Soloveitchik, "Ish ha-Halakhah," *Talpioth* 3–4 (1944), 689.

[26] See M. Avot 2.12; Nahmanides, Notes on Maimonides, *Sefer ha-Mitsvot*, pos. no. 5; R. Joseph Albo, *Iqqarim*, 3.27.

system based on God's governance.[27] The fact is that the vast amount of law pertaining to interhuman relationships is governed much more by specific rabbinic statute rather than by directly revealed scriptural norms.[28] This is, of course, the area of human action with which natural law is concerned. Why the opponents of natural law in Judaism overlook this obvious fact is puzzling. We shall return to the question of rabbinic commandments and their reasons later; now let us confine our attention to the commandments Jewish tradition considered to be scriptural.[29]

REASONS OF THE COMMANDMENTS

The debates concerning scriptural commandments have been over three questions. (1) Do all the commandments, or do only some of them, or do none of them have specific reasons?[30] (2) Even if all of them do have specific reasons, are these reasons actually knowable by human intelligence?[31] (3) If there are reasons of the commandments, is there more than one reason for any commandment, and if so, are multiple reasons mutually

---

[27] For the requirement that specific reasons be given for rabbinic decrees, see B. Gittin 14a; B. Avodah Zarah 35a; also B. Sanhedrin 31b (cf. B. Baba Batra 173b); Maimonides, *Mishneh Torah*: Mamrim, 1.4–5; David Weiss Halivni, *Midrash, Mishnah, and Gemara* (Cambridge, Mass., 1986), 5ff.

[28] See Nahmanides, *Commentary on the Torah*: Deut. 6:18.

[29] For the essential debate regarding the criteria for designating a commandment scriptural (*d'oraita*) or not, see Maimonides, *Sefer ha-Mitsvot*: introduction, sec. 2, and Nahmanides' extensive comment thereon.

[30] The range of rabbinic opinion on the question of *ta'amei ha-mitsvot* during the talmudic period seems to be as follows: (1) none of the commandments has a specific reason and, therefore, none should be sought inasmuch as such a search is both futile and dangerous (e.g. B. Berakhot 33b; *Beresheet Rabbah* 44.1; *Bemidbar Rabbah* 19.1); (2) at least some of the commandments do have reasons, but it is dangerous to search for them (e.g. B. Sanhedrin 21b re Deut. 17:16–17); (3) at least some of the commandments do have reasons and it is beneficial to search for them (e.g. B. Eruvin 21b re Eccl. 12:12 and Rashi and Maharsha, *Hiddushei Aggadot*, s.v. "kol ha-hogeh"; *ibid.* 54b re Exod. 21:1 and Rashi thereon and his *Commentary on the Torah*: Exod. 21:1; B. Shabbat 31a and Maharsha, *Hiddushei Aggadot*, s.v. "hevanta" and Maimonides, *Mishneh Torah*: Talmud Torah, 1.12). The exponent of the last opinion is the fourth-century Babylonian *amora*, Rava, who could well be seen as the major talmudic proponent of rationalism. See below, pp. 98ff.

[31] See R. Saadiah Gaon, *Emunot ve-Deot*, introduction, ch. 6; cf. Nahmanides, *Commentary on the Torah*: Lev. 19:19.

exclusive or not?[32] But let it be noted that as the rabbinic tradition developed, especially after its encounter with philosophy beginning in the ninth century, fewer and fewer rabbinic theologians were willing to argue for the position that none of the commandments has a specific reason. Instead, the debates were more and more over whether some of the commandments or all of them have specific reasons, and just what these reasons are.[33]

Concerning the specific reasons of the commandments, there are two basic types. (1) There are reasons that seem to be based on specific history. (2) There are reasons that seem to be based on universal nature. In rabbinic parlance and conceptuality, "nature" is termed the "orders of creation" (*sidrei bere'sheet*), which is distinguished from the realm of singular historical experience (*nes*).[34] The difference between the two types of reasons is that reasons based on specific history are never universal. That is, they only pertain to the history of a particular community, one among other communities where each has its own history. Conversely, reasons based on nature are inevitably universal. That is, they pertain to humankind per se. In both realms of Halakhah, that is, both in what pertains to the interhuman relationship as well as in what pertains to the divine–human relationship, there are examples of each type of reason, the historical and the natural, at work.

Concerning the interhuman realm, the Torah justifies the institution of capital punishment for murderers with the following natural reason: "Whosoever sheds human blood by humans (*ba'adam*) shall his own blood be shed, because (*ki*) in

---

[32] See Nahmanides, *Commentary on the Torah*: Lev. 1:9.

[33] Thus the two greatest medieval Jewish theologians, Maimonides and Nahmanides, representing pro-philosophical and anti-philosophical theology respectively, both agreed in general that all of the commandments have reasons. But they differed as to just what these specific reasons are. Re their general agreement, see e.g. Maimonides, *Guide of the Perplexed*, 3.26; Nahmanides, *Commentary on the Torah*: Lev. 26:15. Re their specific differences, see e.g. Maimonides, *Guide*, 3.46; Nahmanides, *Commentary*: Lev. 1:9. See also D. Novak, *The Theology of Nahmanides Systematically Presented* (Atlanta, 1992), 2ff., 100ff.

[34] See B. Shabbat 53b. Cf. B. Pesahim 8b and 64b; B. Kiddushin 39b re I Sam. 16:2.

the image of God He made humans (*ha'adam*)" (Genesis 9:6).[35] The reason here is that being in the image of God is what human nature is essentially and that violations of it be punished commensurately.[36] On the other hand, the Torah justifies the prohibition of permanent slavery for any Israelite, as opposed to temporary indentured servitude, with the following singularly historical reason: "If he is not redeemed by any of these means [by a family member], then he shall be released in the Jubilee year, he and his children with him. For (*ki*) the children of Israel are slaves to Me, My slaves are they, those whom I have taken out of the land of Egypt; I am the Lord your God" (Leviticus 25:54–55).[37]

Concerning the divine-human realm, the Torah justifies the keeping of the Sabbath with the following natural reason: "The seventh day is a Sabbath to the Lord your God, you shall not labor: neither you nor your son nor your daughter nor your male slave nor your female slave nor your beast nor the sojourner in your gates. For (*ki*) in six days did the Lord make heaven and earth and the sea and everything therein; therefore (*al ken*) the Lord blessed the Sabbath day and hallowed it" (Exodus 20:10–11). And even though the Halakhah does not regard the cessation of work on the Sabbath as something for which non-Jews are obligated when among themselves (contrary to the prohibition of murder, for example), it is, nonetheless, something that non-Jews who live together with Jews do partake of. For Jews may not require or even request their non-Jewish employees or neighbors to work for them on the Sabbath.[38]

---

[35] See *Midrash Leqah Tov*: Yitro, ed. Buber, 69b; Hizquni, *Commentary on the Torah*: Gen. 9:6; *Zohar*: Yitro, 2:90a.

[36] See L. E. Goodman, *On Justice* (New Haven, 1991), 66.

[37] See T. Baba Kamma 7.5; B. Kiddushin 22b.

[38] For the prohibition of non-Jewish observance of the Sabbath identical to Jewish observance of it, see B. Sanhedrin 58b re Gen. 8:22 (cf. Rashi thereon, s.v. "amar Ravina"); Maimonides, *Mishneh Torah*: Melakhim, 10.9). For the prohibition of Jewish use of gentile labor on the Sabbath, see B. Shabbat 150a. Furthermore, some halakhic authorities have justified gentile observance of the Sabbath when it is based on religious commitment (see R. Israel Meir ha-Kohen, *Biur Halakhah* on *Shulhan Arukh*: Orah Hayyim, 304.3). For the universal theological significance of the Sabbath, see Maimonides, *Guide*, 2.31.

The semi-universal status of the Sabbath might be due to the fact that two reasons are given for it. The first is the reason from creation given in the Exodus version of the Ten Commandments. The second reason, though, is the one in the Deuteronomic version of the Ten Commandments, namely, "in order (*le-ma'an*) that your male slave and your female slave rest like you. And you shall remember that you were a slave in the land of Egypt and the Lord your God brought you out from there" (Deuteronomy 5:14–15). This latter reason is clearly covenantal, hence historical not natural.

On the other hand, the Torah justifies the observance of Passover with only one reason, which is historical: "You shall observe the [Festival of] Unleavened Bread, because (*ki*) on this very day I brought your ranks out of the land of Egypt" (Exodus 12:17).[39]

It would seem, then, that the proper place for Jewish ethics within the world of traditional Jewish discourse is specifically within the discourse of "reasons of the commandments" (*ta'amei ha-mitsvot*), more specifically within the discourse of reasons of the commandments "pertaining to interhuman relationships" (*bein adam le-havero*), and most specifically within the discourse that justifies these interhuman rules with natural rather than historical reasons. This task of location is important lest the whole subject of "Jewish ethics" appear to be an artificial intrusion of a discipline called "ethics" into the realm of Judaism and Jewish discourse, a foreign discipline with concerns which are inappropriate for Jews, concerns that could only distort the Jewish tradition itself. Ethics, as we have now defined it, is the reflective formulation of general principles of interhuman relations rather than the specific rules that apply to them, that is, what today is called *normative* ethics. It might be called the *theory* of Jewish *praxis*.[40] And ethics so understood is our lead into the question of natural law. There can be no idea of natural law in Judaism unless there be an authentic Jewish ethics, part of which is not exclusively for Jews.

---

[39] For the restriction of full Passover observance to Jews, see Exod. 12:43–49; B. Pesahim 3b.
[40] See Hermann Cohen, *Jüdische Schriften* III, ed. B. Strauss (Berlin, 1924), 302.

RATIONAL COMMANDMENTS

In the ninth century, the Babylonian Jewish theologian Saadiah Gaon introduced into Jewish discourse the conceptual distinction between "revealed commandments" (*mitsvot shim'iyot*) and "rational commandments" (*mitsvot sikhliyot*).[41] The distinction is helpful because it is a more philosophically precise way of looking at what divides reason and revelation, and it is a distinction that was also being utilized by contemporary Islamic and Christian theologians. The Judaic value of his distinction is that it is an authentic development of earlier rabbinic sources. Thus an early rabbinic source distinguishes between the scriptural terms *mishpatim* ("ordinances") and *huqqim* ("statutes") as follows:

"And My ordinances you shall practice" (Leviticus 18:4): These are matters written in the Torah which even if they had not been written there, reason would have required that they be written (*ba-din hayah le-kotvan*). Some examples: laws prohibiting robbery, laws prohibiting incest, adultery, homosexuality and bestiality, laws prohibiting idolatry and blasphemy, and laws prohibiting shedding human blood. Even if they had not been written [in the Torah], reason (*din*) would have required that they be written.[42]

It should be noted that this seminal text is so insistent on the rational character of some of the Torah's commandments that it repeats the point for emphasis, no doubt. This does not mean that all of the Torah's commandments are taken to be rational. For the text continues with the point that there are other commandments, designated in the scriptural verse under comment as "and My statutes you shall keep," which "the evil inclination and the idolatrous nations of the world argue against, such as the prohibition of eating pork." The text then concludes: "About them Scripture here teaches 'I am the Lord,' namely, I am He who has so ruled (*haqaqti*), thus you

---

[41] See *Emunot ve-Deot*, 3.3; also J. Faur, *Iyunim be-Mishneh Torah le-ha-Rambam* (Jerusalem, 1978), 115ff.

[42] *Sifra*: Aharei-Mot, ed. Weiss, 86a. See B. Yoma 67b. In rabbinic Hebrew, *din* denotes both law and logic, indeed, that aspect of law which is most akin to logic, i.e., most rationally evident. See e.g. B. Sanhedrin 87a re Deut. 17:8.

may not argue against them."[43] Seen in connection with the
first half of the text, the rabbinic prohibition of arguing against
these nonrational statutes seems to imply that there are no
specific arguments for them either, aside from the general
reason that God's will is to be obeyed because God is the
creator of the universe. Not only are there no specific arguments based on nature/reason for them, there are not even any
such arguments based on history/experience for them either.
Indeed, the reasons based on history/experience would only
apply to the third category of scriptural norms, the "testi-
monies" (*edot*), such as the observance of Passover.[44]

The examples given in this text for what Saadiah later called
"rational commandments" are not all in the realm of what we
would call "ethics" today (for example, the prohibitions of
idolatry and blasphemy). Even in this area, there is more to
Judaism than just ethics, as we shall see later. Nevertheless, the
other examples given (for example, the prohibitions of
bloodshed and robbery) are definitely in the realm of what we
would call "ethics." Furthermore, these ethical examples cover
virtually all of the "Noahide Commandments." There is a
persistent view among Jewish thinkers that this is the Jewish
version of natural law, although it has been just as persistently
disputed by those holding the opposite view.[45] (We shall return
to this question in chapter 6.)

The question now is just how the commandments/rules and
the reasons/principles are related. Here we must distinguish
between scriptural/divine law and rabbinic/human law.

In the case of scriptural/divine law, the rule is always prior
to the principle. That is, the principle is inferred from the rule
a posteriori. The principle functions more as an explanation
(*ratio cognoscendi*) than a sufficient reason or ground. As such, the
principle can be used to interpret the rule and even apply it.

---

[43] See *Midrash Leqah Tov*: Aharei-Mot, ed. Buber, 50b, and Huqqat, 119b. Cf. *Bemidbar Rabbah* 19.1.
[44] For the distinction between the three types of Torah commandments, see Nahmanides, *Commentary on the Torah*: Deut. 6:20.
[45] See D. Novak, *The Image of the Non-Jew in Judaism* (New York and Toronto, 1983), s.v.
"natural law"; also *Jewish Social Ethics*, esp. chs. 1–3.

But the principle can never be the basis for the dismissal of the old rule and its replacement by a new rule, even if a new rule seems to be a better means to the end that the inferred principle enunciates. This latter possibility of the replacement of a scriptural rule by a seemingly better, more rational one is seen by the Talmud as being precisely the error of King Solomon, the wisest of humans, who thought he was even wiser than the divine author of the Torah.

Rabbi Isaac said: Why were the reasons of the Torah (*ta'amei torah*) not [usually] revealed? It is because in the case of two scriptural laws (*miqra'ot*) whose reasons were revealed, the greatest one in the world [King Solomon] stumbled on account of them. It is written in Scripture, "He [the king] shall not have many wives [that his heart not be turned away from God]" (Deuteronomy 17:17)." But Solomon said, "I will have many and I will not turn away" . . . But it is written about him in Scripture, "And it came to be in Solomon's old age that his wives did turn his heart" (I Kings 11:4).[46]

Despite the fact that the Talmud warns about confusing a subsequent explanation with a prior reason, the Mishnah, in whose context this observation takes place, contains a discussion of just how the discernment of the meaning or explanation of this commandment does indeed influence how it is to be interpreted and applied.[47] Nevertheless, it can only interpret it; it cannot either ground it or uproot it by invoking any essential reason either for it or against it.[48]

However, in the case of rabbinic/human law, the principle is prior to the rule in the sense that we do know in advance the reason *for which* the rule was originally devised (*ratio essendi*). It is very much the ground of the rule. The rule is thus derived from the principle as a means is derived from the end it intends. For unlike divine law, where "My thoughts are not your thoughts" (Isaiah 55:8), in the case of human law, it is not only assumed that the intention of the human lawgiver can be fully grasped by other human minds, it is required that this intention be

[46] B. Sanhedrin 21b.   [47] M. Sanhedrin 2.4.
[48] Along these lines see Philo, *De Migratione Abrahami*, 89–93; H. A. Wolfson, *Philo* I (Cambridge, Mass., 1947), 127ff.

publicly stated sooner or later.[49] There is no rabbinic law without its evident intent/reason at hand sooner or later.[50]

Because of this, every rabbinic law made by an earlier rabbinic body can be, in principle anyway, repealed by a later rabbinic body. This can be done because the earlier law is now judged to be an ineffective means to the end it intends, or because the earlier end is no longed judged to be a public need. However, largely because of a general legal conservatism that is inherently deferential to precedent, the Rabbis made explicit repeal almost impossible *de jure* on procedural grounds. Nevertheless, because of the specifically human origins of rabbinic law (it only being generally sanctioned by divine law), it became quite easy to circumvent older rabbinic rules when it was judged that their continued application was not fulfilling their original intent, thus being contrary to the common good *de facto*.[51]

LAW AND ETHICS

In the realm of interhuman relations, at times we can see the radical reinterpretation of both scriptural norms and rabbinic norms by the use of general ethical criteria. Here the difference between scriptural norms and rabbinic norms has been more one of degree than one of kind. In this area, whether the norm be scriptural or rabbinic, the role of ethics has come closest to being actually one of governance and not just guidance. It would seem that the explanation of this greater flexibility in the area of interhuman relations is because natural law is seen as being operative here before the event of the historical revelation of the Torah at Mount Sinai. Here both the nature of the human subject as well as the human object of the law are

---

[49] See B. Avodah Zarah 35a.
[50] See B. Gittin 14a and Tos., s.v. "ke-hilkhata."
[51] For the basis of rabbinic conservatism re the formal repeal of rabbinic law, see M. Eduyot 1.5 (cf. R. Abraham ben David of Posquières, *Ravad* thereon; Maimonides, *Mishneh Torah*: Mamrim, 2.7 and R. Joseph Karo, *Kesef Mishneh* thereon). For flexibility in the radical reinterpretation of rabbinic norms in the realm of the interhuman, especially concerning economics, see e.g., Rabbenu Asher, *Teshuvot ha-Rosh*, 2.8. For the general scriptural warrant for rabbi-made law, see B. Shabbat 23a re Deut. 17:11 and 32:7.

sufficiently known to us already from reason's reflection on the created human condition *per se*.

In the area of divine–human relations, however, the character of the divine member of the relationship is unknown to us before the event of the historical revelation of the Torah at Mount Sinai. All we can learn from creation is that the creator God transcends any of the limitations of the world he creates. That is essentially a negative inference. The positive relationship of God with Israel, on the other hand, is one that God not Israel established at Mount Sinai. Its meaning, therefore, is only known a posteriori, and partially at that. Its grounds are ultimately mysterious; hence any reasons surmised about it are only partial conjectures after the fact. That is why Sinai establishes the divine–human relationship *de novo* whereas it only confirms the basic interhuman relationships, whose structures are already known a priori. This can be seen in two examples, the first involving the ethically influenced reinterpretation of a scriptural norm, the second involving the ethically influenced reinterpretation of a rabbinic norm.

We can see the ethical reinterpretation of a scriptural norm in the following example. Regarding the damages inflicted by one animal on another, the Torah states:

When the ox of one man injures (*yiggof*) the ox of his neighbor (*et shor re'ehu*) and it dies, the living ox shall be sold and its price shall be divided between the parties and they shall divide the dead animal as well. On the other hand, if it is known that it is a goring ox and had been doing so habitually and its owner had not watched it, he shall pay the equivalent value of the ox (*shor tahat shor*). Nevertheless, the dead animal shall be his. (Exodus 21:35–36)

Based on the words, "the ox of his neighbor," the Mishnah rules as follows: "When the ox of a Jew gores the ox of a gentile, there is no liability (*patur*); but when the ox of a gentile gores the ox of a Jew, whether it is not a habitually goring ox (*tam*) or whether it is one (*mu'ad*), there is full liability for damages (*nezeq shalem*)."[52] Needless to say, this implies a double standard that most people would regard as violating the ethical principle of equal responsibility entailing equal liability and

[52] M. Baba Kama 4.3. See *Mekhilta*: Mishpatim, ed. Horovitz-Rabin, 290.

equal liability presupposing equal responsibility. In fact, the ethical problem here is so blatant that the Talmud records the following incident pertaining to it:

Our Rabbis taught: The Roman government had already sent two officials to the sages of Israel ordering them to "teach us your Torah." They read it once, twice, three times. At the time of their departure they said to them [the sages of Israel]: "We have carefully examined your entire Torah and it is true (*v'emet hu*) except for this matter, "When the ox of a Jew gores the ox of a gentile . . . when the ox of a gentile gores the ox of a Jew, etc."[53]

In both the Babylonian and Palestinian Talmuds and in subsequent halakhic literature, there are various attempts to explain this law in such a way as to avoid the embarrassment it causes, especially when this law is learned even by sympathetic outsiders.[54] However, all of these attempts suffer from the same ethical flaws as the original law itself. The law itself needs to be changed somehow. But how can one change the undisputed rabbinic interpretation of a scriptural norm? The matter itself long remained at this rationally unsettled level until it was solved by the fourteenth-century Provençal commentator, Rabbi Menahem ha-Meiri. In his notes on the Babyonian Talmud he writes:

This only (*davqa*) applies to those nations not bound (*sh'einam megudarim*) by the ways of the revealed religions (*datot*) and humanly discerned morality (*nimusim*) . . . but anytime their law obligates them for the seven Noahide laws, their case before us is like our case before us. We do not favor ourselves in the case. Thus it goes without saying that such applies to the nations bound by the ways of the revealed religions and humanly discerned morality (*nimusim*).[55]

---

53 B. Baba Kama 38a. Cf. Y. Baba Kama 4.3/4b; *Sifre*: Devarim, no. 344. *Emet* here seems to be the Hebrew equivalent of *quod aequum ac bonum est* in Latin and *kaloskagathos* in Greek.

54 See Novak, *The Image of the Non-Jew in Judaism*, 60ff. For the latest scholarly treatment of this text and its cognates, one both erudite and conceptually perspicacious, see Steven D. Fraade, "Navigating the Anomalous: Non-Jews at the Intersection of Early Rabbinic Law and Narrative" in *The Other in Jewish Thought and History*, ed. L. J. Silberstein and R. L. Cohn (New York and London, 1995), 145ff.

55 *Bet ha-Behirah*: Baba Kama, ed. Schlesinger, 122. For the use of *nimusim* as human law, see Maimonides, *Guide*, 2.40.

What Meiri has done is to turn the earlier rule into a null class *de facto*.[56] That is, it remains in force *de jure*, but there was no contemporary political order, as far as he is concerned, in which it actually applied. For if the gentiles in whose society Jews are living are so unjust as not to legally recognize basic standards of responsibility for themselves and their property as well as fairness in the due process of law, then it is impossible to even imagine that Jews would turn to gentile courts for justice if their rights are not equally protected. As Maimonides noted, the Talmudic principle of "the law of the kingdom is law" (*dina de-malkhuta dina*), which allows Jews to turn to non-Jewish courts for the adjudication of secular disputes, does not apply everywhere. It is confined to those societies which have a basically just system of law.[57]

The converse, however, is equally true. That is, it is impossible to even imagine that gentiles living under Jewish rule (which until the establishment of the State of Israel had been only an academic question for more than two thousand years) would turn to Jewish courts for justice if their rights are not protected as equally as those of the Jews.[58] Furthermore, for Jewish courts to do anything less than practice evident justice is to violate the prohibition of "profaning the name of God" (*hillul ha-shem*). In rabbinic texts dealing with Jewish–gentile relations, that is a prohibition against interpreting Jewish law in a way that would strike any rational person as immoral.[59] In this case, that would be the immorality of a double standard applied to different persons both of whom are obligated by the same legal system. To do anything less would involve some sort of deceit, and that violates the later rabbinic teaching which warns that any sort of deceit (*geneivat da'at*) is prohibited, whether a Jew or a gentile is so deceived.[60]

We see the ethical reinterpretation of a rabbinic norm in the following Talmudic passage:

[56] Cf. B. Sanhedrin 71a; M. Makkot 1.10; M. Zavim 2.2.
[57] *Mishneh Torah*: Gezelah ve'Avedah, 5.18 re B. Baba Batra 54b and parallels.
[58] See B. Kiddushin 15b–16a and Tos., s.v. "b'akum."
[59] See B. Baba Kama 113a–b.
[60] Hullin 94a; Maimonides, *Mishneh Torah*: Deot, 2.6.

Rava inquired [of the members of the Academy]: If there is a conflict between one's duty to hear the reading of the book of Esther on Purim (*miqra megillah*) and one's duty to bury the dead for whom there is no one else to do so (*met mitsvah*), which duty takes precedence? Does the duty to hear the reading of the book of Esther take precedence because of the importance of publicizing the miracle (*pirsumei nisa*)? Or perhaps the duty to bury the dead for whom there is no one else to do so takes precedence because of the principle of respect for human dignity (*kevod ha-beriyot*)? After his query it became quickly evident that the duty to the dead takes precedence because an earlier authority had already ruled that respect for human dignity is so great that it even overrides (*she-doheh*) a negative commandment of the Torah.[61]

The implications of this passage must be explicated in order for us to see how it demonstrates the ethical reinterpretation of a rabbinic norm.[62]

In the *locus classicus* of the principle that respect for human dignity is so great that it even overrides a negative commandment of the Torah, the question is raised as to how a consideration of human dignity can override respect for divine dignity. There the verse is quoted, "There is no wisdom, there is no understanding, and there is no counsel that can be set up against the Lord" (Proverbs 21:30).[63] Two answers are supplied. (1) Even in the case of a conflict between human dignity and a scriptural law, human dignity takes precedence if the violation

[61] B. Megillah 3b.
[62] In the earliest treatment of the obligation to an abandoned corpse (*met mitsvah*), even the High Priest and the Nazarite, who normally are not even to have contact with their dead parents, are considered obligated to bury such a corpse when there is no one else to do so (*Sifra*: Emor, ed. Weiss, 93c re Lev. 21:1; M. Nazir 7.1; Y. Nazir 7.1/55d; *Semahot* 4.29). It seems to have been originally formulated with wartime deaths in mind, so that they would not have the indignity of being buried in a mass grave (see T. Eruvin 2.1; Y. Eruvin 1.10/19d; B. Eruvin 17a–b; R. Saul Lieberman, *Tosefta Kifshuta*: Moed [New York, 1962], 324, n. 31). Because of this, their burial gives them instant property rights over their graves, which are not to be moved except in cases of the disruption of public space, and even in such cases appropriate reinternment is required (B. Baba Kama 80b–81b; Y. Baba Batra 5.1/16a; B. Eruvin 17b; Maimonides, *Mishneh Torah*: Nizqei Mammon, 5.3 and Tum'at Met, 8.7). Later, this norm was extended to include anyone whose relatives were likely to abandon him or her in death (see B. Yevamot 89b). This is seen as being the result of applying an overall reason (*panim ve-ta'am*) for purposes of radical reinterpretation of even a scriptural norm (see B. Nazir 43b and Tos., s.v. "ve-hai").
[63] B. Berakhot 19b–20a.

of the scriptural law is one of inactivity (*shev v'al ta'aseh*) or omission rather than one of commission or performance of a positive act.[64] Thus one is required to bury a dead person for whom there is no one else to do so even if that prevents one from performing the positive scriptural commandment to circumcise one's son on the eighth day. (2) In the case of a conflict between respect for human dignity and a rabbinic law, one must violate the law even if that involves the performance of a positive act. Here there is no qualification of the principle because here there is a conflict between natural law and human law rather than one between natural law and revealed law. For in the case of such a conflict, whether involving conflicting activity or inactivity, we can assume *ab initio* that the Rabbis' primary concern was respect for human dignity. The reading of the book of Esther is a rabbinic commandment. Hence the rabbinic decision whether or not something else could ever take precedence over it is an example of this arrangement of rabbinic priorities.[65] It is to be overridden when it conflicts with the elementary dignity of the human person created in the image of God.[66]

---

[64] See B. Yevamot 90a–b; also R. Ezekiel Landau, *Teshuvot Noda bi-Yehudah*: Orah Hayyim 1, no. 35.

[65] See Maimonides, *Mishneh Torah*: Megillah, 1.1.

[66] The notion that it is obligatory to bury every corpse is best known in the West from Sophocles' play *Antigone* (24), where Antigone laments how it is contrary to cosmic justice that her brother, Polynices, has not been buried by order of the king, Creon, because of Polynices' rebellion against Creon's authority. In Jewish law, too, even criminals are considered deserving of the elementary human dignity of decent burial (see M. Sanhedrin 6.5; T. Sanhedrin 9.7; B. Sanhedrin 45b re Deut. 21:23). Although the dispensation of the High Priest, the Nazirite, and even ordinary priests from the prohibition of defiling themselves by contact with a dead body in the case of a *met mitsvah* would only apply to Jewish corpses (see Y. Nazir 7.1/55d; Maimonides, *Mishneh Torah*: Evel, 3.8), the obligation to see to it that all bodies are properly buried comes under the mandate to pursue "the ways of peace" (*mipnei darkhei shalom*), which means peace in the cosmic sense and not just the avoidance of political conflict (see T. Gittin 3.14; B. Gittin 61a; Y. Gittin 5.9/47c; Maimonides, *Mishneh Torah*: Melakhim, 10.12 and note of Radbaz thereon, and Evel, 14.12; R. Saul Lieberman, *Tosefta Kifshuta*: Nashim [New York, 1973]; Y. Y. Greenwald, *Kol Bo al Avelut* [New York, 1965], 163; cf. M. Avodah Zarah 2.1; B. Avodah Zarah 26a; Nahmanides, *Commentary on the Torah*: Num. 21:21–22). That means that Jews are to bury gentile corpses even when there are no Jewish corpses to be buried along with them (see R. Solomon ibn Adret, *Hiddushei ha-Rashba* and R. Yom Tov ben Abraham Ishbili, *Hiddushei ha-Ritva* on B. Gittin 61a; R. Joseph ibn Habib, *Nimuqei Yosef* on Alfasi, *Gittin*, ch. 5, ed. Vilna, 28a).

Since so much of rabbinic activity consists of adjudication of interhuman disputes, Maimonides warns the rabbinic judge of the ethical import of his activity: "In all of these matters let his deeds be for the sake of God and let not the respect for human dignity be light in his eyes. For it is something that overrides any negative rabbinic commandment."[67] He goes on to insist that the dignity of every Jew should be respected all the more so because they uphold the Torah of truth. Nevertheless, the respect due to fellow Jews is not one that ignores the basic respect due to every human person created in the image of God.

THE MODERN EQUATION OF JUDAISM AND ETHICS

All of the examples cited above, which show how operative ethical principles have been in the interpretation and reinterpretation of Jewish law, could be the basis for the inference that the *essence* of Judaism is ethics, that is, the universal ethics which can well be designated natural law. And, indeed, since the Emancipation and the Enlightenment, Jewish thinkers as different as Moritz Lazarus, Hermann Cohen, Ahad Ha'Am, Leo Baeck, and Emmanuel Levinas have made this claim in one way or another. This, it seems, is due to two factors, one historical, the other philosophical.

Historically, it has been the result of the economic and political emancipation of European Jewry that began in earnest in the eighteenth century. Jews had to fight against the commonly held view that their tradition did not have a universally applicable ethics, or even the potential for the development of one. It was assumed that Jewish ethics was only designed for the self-interest of the Jews, usually at the expense of whatever

---

[67] *Mishneh Torah*: Sanhedrin, 24.10. Clearly, the humans (*beriyot*) for whose dignity we are to be concerned are all humankind (see e.g. *Avot de-Rabbi Nathan* A, ch. 12, ed. Schechter, 26b re M. Avot 1.12). Elementary justice for all humankind is considered to be a norm from creation (see Y. Ketubot 5.5/30a re Job 31:15; Y. Baba Kama 8.4/ 6c; B. Kiddushin 33a; Niddah 47a; Maimonides, *Mishneh Torah*: Avadim, 9.5 and Evel, 10.12 re Ps. 145:9 and *Guide*, 1.38, 1.54, and 3.54). It is considered to be an essential Jewish character trait (see B. Betsah 32b re Deut. 13:18; B. Yevamot 89a). For a fuller elaboration of Maimonides' statement here, see below, p. 112.

gentiles they might encounter in the world. So, if Jews could not make the opposite case for themselves and their ethical tradition, there was no reason to assume that Judaism itself could function outside the ghetto in a sphere of secular equality. Thus the identification of Judaism itself with a universalistic ethics must be seen as part of the effort, which began with Moses Mendelsssohn in Germany in the middle of the eighteenth century, to argue that Judaism was not hopelessly parochial. Since Judaism can be shown to affirm universal truths and norms, Jews could become citizens of the new secularly constituted nation-states without having to leave their historical religion altogether, as was the case with Spinoza, a case that continued to haunt much of modern Jewish thought.

Philosophically, after the Enlightenment, Judaism as a minority religion had the same problem as did Christianity, the majority religion. Religion, any religion, had to convince secular culture of its social worth. For because of Kant's dominant influence, ethics was considered to be the highest level of human knowledge. It had successfully replaced both revealed theology and metaphysics as the throne before which all cultural institutions had to justify their very existence.[68] Although, in theory, Judaism and Christianity were faced with the same problem, some modern Jewish thinkers began to assert that Judaism actually had an important edge over Christianity in this process of cultural justification. This is because interhuman relations seem to play a more central role in the Jewish tradition than they do in the Christian tradition. Accordingly, ethics seems to play more of a role in the Jewish tradition precisely because, as all of these thinkers emphasized, Judaism's concerns are more "this-worldly" than those of Christianity. In this view, Christianity is a "romantic religion," to cite the title of a famous essay Leo Baeck wrote in the 1920s, whereas Judaism, Baeck argued, is the "classical religion."[69] That means Judaism is closer to Kant's true

---

[68] See Kenneth Seeskin, *Jewish Philosophy in a Secular Age* (Albany, N.Y., 1990), 158.
[69] "Romantic Religion," trans. W. Kaufmann in *Judaism and Christianity*, ed. W. Kaufmann (Philadelphia, 1958), 189ff.

ethical teaching, even though Kant himself surely had a blind spot about it.[70]

The centrality of ethics to modern Jewish thought is best seen by looking at a basic similarity in the thought of the three real philosophers among those who might be called modern *liberal* Jewish thinkers: Cohen, Buber, and Levinas. Even though the thought of Buber and that of Levinas are usually seen in contrast to Cohen's Kantian rationalism, all three of them, nonetheless, are very much beholden to Enlightenment notions of universality. One could argue that for all of them, God's only function is to provide some sort of undergirding for ethics, and that is their view of God's function in Judaism as well. And for all of them, both the singularity of revelation and the singularity of the Jewish people as the community elected to receive that revelation in the covenant, sooner or later become subsumed into universal nature.

In Hermann Cohen's case, the best place to look for his reduction of the realm of the divine–human to the realm of the interhuman is in his treatment of the question of divine love. In his posthumously published work on Jewish theology, Cohen asks: "Does God first love man, or does man first love the unique God?" His answer to this question is: "Only now, after (*nachdem*) man has learned to love man as fellowman (*Mitmensch*), is his thought turned to God, and only now (*jetzt erst*) does he understand that God loves man."[71]

What Cohen has done, of course, is to reverse the order of the covenant. For in the classical Jewish covenant with God, it is God's love which originally manifests itself to every human member of the covenant and which thus enables every member of the covenant to love every other member as his or her duty. That love is experienced by the human members of the covenant by their practice of the commandments that celebrate that love and the events that mark its most acute presence. God's love of Israel is original and Israel's love of God is thus

---

[70] See *Religion within the Limits of Reason Alone*, trans. T. M. Greene and H. H. Hudson (New York, 1960), 116ff.
[71] *Religion of Reason out of the Sources of Judaism*, trans. S. Kaplan (New York, 1972), 146f. = *Religion der Vernunft aus den Quellen des Judenthums* (Darmstadt, 1966), 169, 171.

reciprocal. Neither love is mediated through anything else, even the most intimate interhuman relationships. That is why these celebratory commandments (*edot*) are all within the realm of the divine–human relationship (*bein adam le-maqom*), even when the practice of these commandments entails the partici-pation of more than one human member of the covenant. To those outside the covenant, the duty is to practice justice towards them, but not to love them. Love presupposes cove-nantal intimacy.[72]

But, for Cohen, conversely, love is constituted in the inter-human sphere, and in its most universal context. Thus there is no direct love relationship either from man to God or from God to man that is not mediated by and constituted for interhuman love. Theologically, the error here is that revelation is essentially reduced to the supreme awareness of an order already present in creation. Functioning as He does as the theoretical foundation (*Ursprung*) of ethics, God is never the source of a direct commandment or its direct object, for Cohen.[73] Accordingly, there can be no phenomenology of the religious life *per se* in this philosophical theology of Judaism.

In Martin Buber's case, the human person does not consti-tute himself or herself autonomously, that is, alone. Buber's emphasis of the essential I–Thou character of all true inter-human relationality stresses over and over again that it is within the encountered relationship of two persons that essen-tial humanness is constituted.

From this one can see Buber's famous opposition to any role for Jewish law in the religious life. It is usually understood that this is due to the fact that any law would provide an a priori communal limit on what is supposed to be spontaneous, that is, it would reduce a true, direct personal interrelationship (*Bezie-hung*) to a relation within an abstract encompassing whole (*Verhältnis*).[74] While that is true, it is only part of the significance of Buber's seeming antinomianism. For by law (*Gesetz*), Buber

[72] See Novak, *The Election of Israel*, 105f.
[73] See *Logik der reinen Erkenntnis*, 3rd edn (Berlin, 1922), 79; *Ethik des reinen Willens*, 4th edn (Berlin, 1923), 455.
[74] See *I and Thou*, trans. W. Kaufmann (New York, 1970), 79ff.

seems to mean what is often called "ritual" law. In classical
Jewish teaching, these are the commandments wherein humans
and God are most closely and directly related. Buber holds that
the observance of these commandments actually inhibits the
true relationship with God.[75]

But where does that relationship lie? The answer to this
question can be formulated if we realize that Buber could
never be as dismissive of moral law as he is of ritual law.
Whereas Buber could, for example, dismiss observance of the
Sabbath from the relationship with God, he could not very well
do so for the prohibition of murder. For what possible I–Thou
relationship would even be possible if each person in it were
not assured that the other was committed to this prohibition?
Therefore, it seems that for Buber, if there is a direct relationship with God, it is outside the commandments in which the
direct relationship of Jews with God lies. Thus the only area of
Jewish tradition one is to be consistently concerned with would
be Jewish ethics. Moreover, there is always the possibility that
Buber did not actually recognize a direct relationship with
God, but that the recognition of God as the "Eternal Thou" is
only the ontological grounding of the possible "thouness" of
which every human being is capable.[76] Here, too, the only area
of Jewish tradition that can really be retrieved by Buber is the
area of ethics, especially its most universal aspects.

As for Emmanuel Levinas, how God is related to ethics is the
most obscure of all. On the one hand, Levinas calls for
"atheism." By this he means that ethics cannot be the way to
the God of "onto-theology," that is, the God who is constituted
by metaphysics.[77] On the other hand, though, Levinas does
speak of the "trace" of God in the realm of ethics.[78] What
Levinas is concerned with as a philosopher is the elimination of

[75] See *ibid.*, 16off.; also Martin Buber and Franz Rosenzweig, "Revelation and Law"
(*die Bauleute*), trans. W. Wolf, in *On Jewish Learning*, ed. N. N. Glatzer (New York,
1955), 109ff.
[76] See *I and Thou*, 123ff.
[77] See *Totality and Infinity*, trans. A. Lingis (Pittsburgh, 1969), 77–78.
[78] See *Otherwise Than Being or Beyond Essence*, trans. A. Lingis (The Hague, 1981), 158;
also R. A. Cohen "God in Levinas," *Journal of Jewish Thought and Philosophy* 1 (1992),
197ff.

any type of ontology that grounds the ethical relationship of humans in some larger reality, what he calls a "totality." Such a grounding inevitably subsumes the otherness (*l'autrui*) of the other person (*l'autre*) in some sort of enclosed system and thereby destroys the very phenomenality that true ethics presupposes. Thus his "atheism" is neither the assertion that there is no God, nor the assertion, siding with Nietzsche, that "God is dead." Instead, he seems to be saying that one can only allude to God from the standpoint of ethics.[79] God seems to function in his etho-centric thought as a kind of centrifugal force, which protects the otherness of the other person from being collapsed into the ultimate solipsism of a theorizing, totalizing self. Levinas explicitly says that "The direct encounter with God, *this* is a Christian concept. As Jews, we are always a threesome: I and you and the Third who is in our midst. And only as a Third does He reveal himself."[80]

Levinas does explicitly try to part company with the whole trend of modern thought, which, following Kant, sees ethics being grounded in the autonomy of the moral agent. In fact, he calls his ethics "heteronomous," that is, the ethics (*nomos*) that is elicited by the radical otherness of the other person (*heteros*).[81] Nevertheless, the range of activity between humans themselves is itself autonomous. Here too, then, the only aspect of the Jewish tradition that Levinas can authentically retrieve for his philosophy is its universal ethics. In fact, in a dialogue with a Roman Catholic bishop, Levinas states, "The authentically

[79] Note: "[L]a présence de Dieu à travers la relation avec l'homme . . . L'éthique n'est pas le collaire de la vision de Dieu, elle est cette vision même. L'éthique est une optique. De sorte que tout ce que je sais de Dieu et tout ce que je peux entendre de Sa parole et Lui dire raisonnablement, doit trouver une expression éthique." ("Une religion d'adultes," *Difficile Liberté* [Paris, 1976], 32–33.)

[80] "Ideology and Idealism," trans. S. Ames and A. Lesley, in *The Levinas Reader*, ed. S. Hand (Oxford, 1989), 247. Levinas' point here is consistent with the modern, liberal Jewish critique of Christianity as being morally inferior to Judaism. This comes out in his famous radio address of 29 April 1955, "Aimer la Thora plus que Dieu," which in effect was a polemic against the anti-Jewish Jew, the philosopher Simone Weil. For the text of this address and a sympathetic yet critical response to it from a Catholic theologian, see Frans Jozef van Beeck, S. J., *Loving the Torah More Than God?* (Chicago, 1989). A translation of Levinas' text is on 36–40.

[81] See "Philosophy and the Idea of Infinity" (1957) in *Collected Philosophical Papers*, ed. and trans. A. Lingis (Dordrecht, 1987), 47–48.

human is the being-Jewish in all men."[82] By that he means that "Israel" is a synonym for humanity *per se*.

The question faced by these modern liberal Jewish thinkers was how to actually locate this assertion of the centrality of ethics in Judaism within the classical sources. Furthermore, it was preferable that such classical sources be rabbinic inasmuch as the anti-semitic nineteenth-century Protestant theologians delighted in showing that the ethical thrust of the most "highly developed" parts of the "Old Testament" had been subverted by the "legalism" of the Talmud.

It has long been proposed that a *locus classicus* of this reduction of Judaism to ethics can be found in the passage in the Mishnah that states: "Rabbi Eleazar ben Azariah interpreted the verse, 'from all your sins before the Lord you shall be cleansed' (Leviticus 16:30), as follows: transgressions between humans and God are atoned for by the Day of Atonement (*yom ha-kippurim*); transgressions between humans themselves are not atoned for by the Day of Atonement until one appeases his fellow human."[83] At this point, it might be best to look at how Hermann Cohen interpreted this passage, for he was, to my mind, the greatest philosopher of the three thinkers we have just examined, and he was certainly the one whose thought was indispensable for the development of the thought of all Jewish philosophers after him.

To Cohen, this rabbinic passage suggests that the rectification of interhuman relations, which is surely a major ethical concern, is one that does not directly refer to God, but that it itself is foundational. It cannot be inferred from this passage that God plays no role in the ethical life. But it can be inferred that God's role, that is, the role of providing ultimate atonement, is secondary to the actual ethical task of interhuman reconciliation.[84] In other words, this passage seems to be an

[82] *In the Time of the Nations*, trans. M. B. Smith (Bloomington, Ind., 1994), 164. Also see *The Levinas Reader*, ed. S. Hand (Oxford, 1989), 264, 293; R. A. Cohen, *Elevations* (Chicago, 1994), 128.

[83] M. Yoma 8.9.

[84] "It is to be noted that the rabbinic shaping of the Day of Atonement did not fail to make reconciliation of man with God dependent (*anhängig*) upon the reconciliation between man and man." (*Religion of Reason*, 220 = *Religion der Vernunft*, 257)

anticipation of the Kantian notion that ethics is constituted by autonomous human beings by themselves rationally. Theology is thus itself rooted in ethics, not vice versa.

It is only after autonomous ethics has been constituted by practical reason that it sees a need to postulate the existence of a God, according to Kant and his followers – many of whom were Jews. The function of this God is to make ethics really and fully efficacious in the world, something that at present it certainly cannot be through merely human action. Ethics here and now is incomplete, not because of the insufficiency of its intent but, rather, because finite human beings do not have the power to themselves finally effect its totally good consequences.[85]

The problem with this ethical theology, however, is that the constitution of such a subsequent role for God makes God less than "that which nothing greater can be thought," which certainly designates the God who revealed himself in Scripture.[86] A God whose postulated role is to mediate between the ideal (or "noumenal") and the real (or "phenomenal") is no more absolute than Plato's *demiurge*, who effects a *cosmos* by relating the eternal forms above to material chaos below.[87] Hermann Cohen was keenly aware of this problem and strove mightily (although, to my mind, unsuccessfully) to overcome it by constituting a more radical God for ethics.[88]

A POST-MODERN RETRIEVAL OF ETHICS WITHIN THE COVENANT

Nevertheless, the traditional interpretation of this rabbinic text does not draw the "ethically autonomous" conclusion of many modern Jewish readers. In the more traditional reading of the text, it is not that the realm of the divine–human relationship is being reduced to the realm of the interhuman relationship.

---

[85] See *Critique of Practical Reason*, 1.2.2.5.

[86] For the accuracy of this phrase of Anselm of Canterbury for any biblically based theology, see D. Novak, "Are Philosophical Proofs of the Existence of God Theologically Meaningful?" in *God in the Teachings of Conservative Judaism*, ed. S. Siegel and E. B. Gertel (New York, 1985), 188ff.

[87] See *Timaeus*, 29Aff.   [88] See *Religion of Reason*, ch. 1.

Instead, it is quite the reverse, that is, the interhuman realm is being included in the divine–human realm. The source of the law is God, whoever its more proximate source or more proximate end might be. But when God is the object of the law, the relation to the source of the law is more direct. When humans are the object of the law, the relation to the source of the law is less direct.[89] That is why Maimonides concluded that blessings (*berakhot*) are only mandated for commandments that pertain directly *to* God.[90] It is not that the interhuman commandments are not part of divine law. It is just that they do not involve the more direct relation with God as do the divine–human commandments.[91] Nevertheless, the ultimate end of any commandment is "for the sake of God," irrespective of who its more immediate object is.[92]

The commandments, whatever their immediate object, are essential expressions of the covenantal reality established by God with us by revelation. Therefore, even if we are able to discern the specific reasons for each and every one of the individual commandments, that would in no way detract from the overall revealed *Gestalt* of the commandments as *Torah*. That *Gestalt* is that each of the commandments bespeaks God's own personal involvement in the life of the elected community in the world.[93] God's involvement could only be revealed by God himself.[94] Thus Jewish ethics, to be authentically Jewish, whatever rationally evident meaning it might have, must be essentially covenantal.

If natural law is an apt designation of the universal ethics one finds in the Jewish tradition, it is now appropriate to see

[89] See B. Yoma 87b re I Sam. 2:25.
[90] See *Mishneh Torah*: Berakhot, 11.2 and R. Joseph Karo, *Kesef Mishneh* thereon. Cf. R. Solomon ibn Adret, *Teshuvot ha-Rashba* 1, no. 18.
[91] See *Commentary on the Mishnah*: Avot, introduction (*Shemonah Peraqim*), ch. 6; *Mishneh Torah*: Melakhim, 8.11. From these two texts a number of scholars have inferred that Maimonides was opposed to the idea of natural law. However, I have argued that he is only denying the ultimate sufficiency of natural law ethics without a suitable theology to undergird it. He is not denying its immediate moral necessity. See *The Image of the Non-Jew in Judaism*, ch. 10.
[92] See above, n. 26.
[93] See Y. Rosh Hashanah 1.3/57b; *Vayigra Rabbah* 35.5; also D. Novak, *Halakhah in a Theological Dimension* (Chico, Calif., 1985), 116ff.
[94] See B. Berakhot 7a re Exod. 33:23; B. Rosh Hashanah 17b re Exod. 34:6.

how the tradition constitutes that universal, natural law, ethics within the covenant itself. That will require an understanding of how the tradition connects creation and its nature with revelation – which is the subject of the next two chapters.

In the next chapter, we shall examine how Maimonides places the law in a teleological context, both ethically and ontologically. In chapter 5, though, I shall critically examine that teleology as well as that of Maimonides' predecessor, Saadiah, on the grounds of covenantal theology. Nevertheless, there is so much to be learned from Maimonides' teleology, whether or not one accepts his foundations for it, that it is certainly important to examine it after our initial introduction to teleology in Judaism.

CHAPTER 4

Maimonides' teleology of the law

Observe it and practice it, for it is your wisdom and
discernment in the eyes of the peoples.   (Deuteronomy 4:6)

LEGAL DISPUTATION

It is best to begin looking at Maimonides' natural law theory by
considering the way he categorizes the law itself. For Maimonides devised the most coherent conceptuality for dealing
with Jewish law, both as a whole and in all its parts. If natural
law be taken as the most evidently rational aspect of Jewish law,
then Maimonides' rational ordering of the law itself is the best
introduction to his treatment of what we would now call
natural law (even though Maimonides himself did not use that
specific term). We shall see that Maimonides attempts as much
as he can to provide for Jewish laws reasons that are universally
valid and universally intelligible, but without the sacrifice of
revelation we saw in some of the modern Jewish thinkers
examined in the previous chapter.

Normative Judaism has been aptly designated as affirming
the doctrine of the *dual* Torah.[1] This means that one part of
God's law is revealed directly in written form (*torah she-bikhtav*)
and the other part is presented through the dicta of human
authorities (*torah she-b'al peh*). Although the Oral Tradition does
supplement the Written Torah's silence on certain matters,
much of it interprets the Written Torah where that Torah is not
silent but vague.[2] It is here that disputes about the meaning of

---

[1] See Jacob Neusner, *Meaning and Method in Ancient Judaism* (Chico, Calif., 1979), 59ff.
[2] See, e.g., M. Hagigah 1.8.

the law arise. Since the community requires law, and since law brings a certain general uniformity to communal practice, there must be a method for the resolution of legal disputes.[3] Already in the early rabbinic sources, two main approaches to the resolution of legal disputes are found.

The first approach looks to the recovery of lost tradition. The tradition is assumed to have all the answers to legal questions, but it is not fully accessible because of the inadequate apprenticeship of students to their teachers and masters, who are the true repositories of that whole tradition. Thus it is noted, "When the arrogant (*zehuhei lev*) increased, disputes (*mahloqot*) increased in Israel and the Torah became two Torahs. When the disciples of Shammai and Hillel increased, who had not sufficiently apprenticed themselves (*she-lo shimshu kol tsorkhan*), disputes increased in Israel and the Torah became two Torahs."[4] So it seems disputes about the law are largely due to the moral fault of the students of the law. Owing to insufficient diligence as disciples of the Sages (*talmidei hakhamim*), they inevitably lost much of the Oral Tradition that their teachers could have indeed imparted to them were it not for their slothful inattention. This inattention is seen as what weakened their connection with the tradition. It would seem, then, that the rectification of this situation and the resolution of most, if not all, disputes depends on a renewed revelation of this tradition. Thus the archtraditionalist, Rabbi Eliezer ben Hyrkanus, who said that he never taught anything he did not receive as a tradition from his teachers, also invoked heavenly voices to support his position in a halakhic dispute; indeed, he did so to end the dispute (and, probably, all other disputes as well) permanently.[5]

The second approach can be seen in the very retort to Rabbi Eliezer's invocation of heavenly voices to prove his point made

---

[3] For generality as an essential characteristic of law itself, see B. Yevamot 42b; Hullin 9a; Maimonides, *Guide of the Perplexed*, 3.34.

[4] T. Sotah 14.9, ed. Lieberman, 237 from Ms. Erfurt. See R. Saul Lieberman, *Tosefta Kifshuta*: Nashim (New York, 1973), 755.

[5] Re his traditionalism, see B. Sukkah 28a; T. Sotah 15.3, ed. Lieberman from Ms. Erfurt; B. Sotah 47b (with note of Rashi, s.v. "nignaz"); re his invocation of a *bat qol*, see B. Baba Metsia 59b.

by his colleague Rabbi Joshua ben Hananiah. He stated the principle "the Torah is not in heaven," which is a principle frequently invoked thereafter. It asserts that the law is to be determined by means other than renewed revelation.[6]

Maimonides is clearly an advocate of this second approach. Disputes arise, not because of the moral fault of inattention to one's teachers and masters, but rather because they are matters of genuine intellectual disagreement. So, it is more and better reason that is required as the necessary correlate of revelation, not more revelation or even retrieved revelation.[7] The disputes arose because the later generations of scholars were simply not as intellectually gifted as their predecessors. This was a lack for which one cannot be morally faulted. Furthermore, Maimonides points out that the disputes did not arise in matters of pure tradition, namely, in those few matters about which none of the Sages ever disagreed. Their disputes were confined to the vast majority of legal matters for which there was no such pure tradition. This was the area of the law where new interpretations had to be formulated by intellectual means (*iyyun*). The question, then, is by which intellectual means is this to take place. What are the best intellectual methods for resolving such disputes and, hence, arriving at the truth of the law and extending it into new areas? What is required is the restoration of an intellectual atmosphere where there are far fewer disputes about the truth of the law because there has been a restoration of the true science of the law, one adequate to the law's own truth.[8]

In a later treatment of this fundamental problem, Maimonides points out that "when the Great Court [the Sanhedrin] existed, there were no disputes in Israel."[9] For when a dispute about the law arose, the Great Court either referred to

---

[6] See B. Eruvin 6b-7a re Deut. 30:12 and Tos., s.v. "k'an." For rabbinic views that the lost tradition can be retrieved by ratiocination, see Temurah 16a; B. Baba Kama 5a, and Tos., s.v. "le-hilkhoteihem."

[7] *Commentary on the Mishnah*, introduction, Heb. trans. Y. Kafih (Jerusalem, 1964), I:11–112. See D. Hartman, *Maimonides* (Philadelphia, 1976), 111ff.

[8] See *Guide*, introduction and 3.54 for the appeal to the true science of the Torah.

[9] *Mishneh Torah*: Mamrim, 1.4 re T. Hagigah 2.9, and T. Sanhedrin 7.1 (also, B. Sanhedrin 88b). See B. Hagigah 16a, Tos., s.v. "Yose ben Yoezer."

an already extant tradition (*mi-pi qabbalah*), or it reached its own decision and, in effect, made a new law. However, this only indicates that disputes among the legal authorities themselves were not disclosed to the public. The lack of disputes simply means that full political sovereignty enabled the final decision of the court to have unanimous authority. It does not, however, tell us how these disputes were argued behind closed doors when the Sanhedrin deliberated in camera.[10] It does not tell us how one side in a dispute argued its point of view and how it convinced the majority to accept it, thereby rejecting the opposing points of view. Nevertheless, in the text immediately following, Maimonides indicates that since the dissolution of the Great Court, disputes have increased and that each side must now "give a reason (*ta'am*)" for it own point of view.[11] But what are these "reasons"? How are they argued so as to be convincing to the wise? The answer to this question depends upon a closer look at Maimonides' view of the structure of the law.

THE RATIONAL STRUCTURE OF THE LAW

Following a late rabbinic teaching that became quite influential on his predecessors, Maimonides confines perpetually binding divine law to the 613 commandments assumed to be found in the Pentateuch.[12] But the problem with this assumption is that if one were to count every prescriptive statement in the Pentateuch, many more than 613 prescriptions would be found. So, what constitutes a divine commandment (*mitsvah*)? This is Maimonides' main task in the lengthy introduction to his enumeration of the 613 commandments, *Sefer ha-Mitsvot*, which itself is the introduction to his comprehensive work on Jewish law, *Mishneh Torah*, which he himself

---

[10] Re the secrecy of the Sanhedrin's deliberations, see B. Baba Kama 92b and B. Sanhedrin 31a.

[11] Mishneh Torah: Mamrim, 1.4.

[12] The talmudic source is B. Makkot 23b–24a. Maimonides' most immediate precedent for his enumeration and ordering of the divine commandments is *Halakhot Gedolot*, although he frequently disagrees with this work's selection of commandments. See, e.g., *Sefer Ha-Mitsvot*, pos. no. 1.

called "our great work."[13] This is a fundamental question for Maimonides as a theorist of the law.

When one looks at the fourteen criteria (*shorashim*) Maimonides employs in his introduction to *Sefer ha-Mitsvot*, one might arrive at the following definition of a divine commandment: *A divine commandment is a specific prescription, having a number of particular details, which is commanded for the sake of a more general reason.* Thus the more particular details (*diqduqim*) are subsumed under a specific commandment, and the specific commandment is subsumed under a general reason (*ta'am*).[14] Neither reasons connected to specific commandments nor even more general reasons for the commandments as a whole are themselves commandments. Instead, they are principles that determine the nature of the commandments and what is therefore to be the proper intention (*kavvanah*) of those who practice them. As for the particular details, even they gain more rational validity by being seen as parts of larger normative wholes than they would have if they were taken as the disjunct, almost random rules that they appear to be *prima facie*.[15]

As for the reasons of the commandments, Maimonides consistently asserts in a number of places that even though Scripture only mentions reasons in connection with a few of the commandments, we must assume that all the commandments do have them. For to assume otherwise would be an affront to the wisdom of the divine lawgiver.[16] The fact that most of these reasons are only implicit should not, however, prevent our independent discernment of what they are, although the task seems to be infinite. Finally, the exclusion of what could be termed "ad hoc directives" (*sh'ein nohagot le-dorot*)

---

[13] *Guide*, 3.29. Whether this judgment was speaking of the quantity of *Mishneh Torah* in comparison to the *Moreh Nevukhim* or its importance in comparison to it is a subject of great debate. See D. Novak, "Philosophy and the Possibility of Revelation: A Theological Response to the Challenge of Leo Strauss" in *Leo Strauss and Judaism*, ed. D. Novak (Lanham, Md., 1996), 192, n. 69.

[14] See *Sefer ha-Mitsvot*: introduction, nos. 4, 5, 7, 11.

[15] For the notion that ordering into larger classes brings with it more essential understanding of the norms so classified, see *Sifre*: Devarim, no. 306, ed. Finkelstein, 336, 338f; Y. Sheqalim 5.1/48c; B. Pesahim 105b and Rashbam, s.v. "ve-sadrana ana."

[16] See *Mishneh Torah*: Me'ilah, 8.8; *Guide*, 3.31.

seems to be because their reasons are no more general than these directives themselves, hence they are lacking according to the criterion of universal perpetuity.[17]

The reasons of the commandments are the purposes we discern for which they have been formulated in the first place. Nevertheless, no matter how well we might discern what the reasons are, we are never able to simply deduce from them all the particular details of the commandments. Thus the irreducible authority of revelation and its tradition in the law lies in the irreducibility of these very details. Even if we could answer every "why" about the law, we could never answer every "how" about it.[18] Later, Maimonides addresses this point by saying, "Those who imagine that a cause may be found for suchlike things are as far from the truth as those who imagine that the generalities of a *commandment* are not designed with a view to some real utility."[19] By emphasizing the rationality of the law, without resorting to the totalizing rationalism characteristic of some modern Jewish thinkers, Maimonides saves revelation from being reduced to reason, and he saves the law from being reduced to divine caprice. Furthermore, by seeing the reasons of the commandments (*ta'amei ha-mitsvot*) as their *purposes*, Maimonides' teleology is built upon solid rabbinic precedent.

We can see how Maimonides builds on this precedent when we look at the development of the meaning of the Hebrew word *ta'am* and the Aramaic word *ta'ama*. In late biblical Hebrew and Aramaic, it simply means a rule itself as in "Everything that is by decree (*min ta'am*) of the God of heaven is to be done diligently" (Ezra 7:23). In early rabbinic sources, it usually means either a scriptural source in general, or one determined by simple exegesis, or one derived by more complicated hermeneutics.[20] In later rabbinic sources, it comes to mean the purpose of a law, that is, why it was so formulated to begin with.[21] That purpose can be either one we (more often

---

[17] *Sefer ha-Mitsvot*: introduction, no. 3.   [18] See R. Joseph Albo, *Iqqarim*, 1.8.
[19] *Guide*, 3.26, trans. S. Pines (Chicago, 1963), 509.
[20] For the first meaning, see e.g. T. Menahot 6.19. For the second meaning, see e.g. Y. Hagigah 2.1/77c–d. For the third meaning, see Y. Hagigah 2.3/78a.
[21] See B. Sanhedrin 21a.

than not) assume was in the mind of the divine lawgiver when we examine a scriptural law (*d'oraita*), or one we know was in the mind of human lawgivers when we examine a rabbinic law (*de-rabbanan*). We know the latter because it has been publicly argued for.[22]

The emphasis of *ta'am/ta'ama* as purpose was made in fourth-century Babylonia by Rava, who is a key figure in the development of the Halakhah. Rava refers to such teleological reasoning as *torat ta'ama*, namely, "the doctrine of purpose."[23] In fact, we can readily see him in many ways as being Maimonides' closest rabbinic predecessor. For Rava, more than any of the other Sages, seemed to have stressed the rational aspect of the Torah.[24] He expanded the range of law designated as rabbinic as much as possible, and thereby narrowed the range of scriptural law as much as possible. Rava's legal theory might best be seen in a statement where he says "How foolish are ordinary people: they stand for a Torah scroll, but they do not stand for a Sage (*gavra rabba*)."[25] The occasion for this statement is Rava's insistence that the Rabbis, for good reasons, actually interpreted a scriptural law in a way that clearly does violence to the ostensive meaning of the scriptural text at hand. Indeed, it was Rava who seems to have limited the use of the term "reason" (*ta'ama*) to designate a *telos*. His approach was most effective in the area of rabbinic legislation, where there are no specific scriptural norms to be interpreted and thus specific legislation begins *de novo*.

All rabbinic legislation, as distinct from scriptural law and Mosaic traditions (*halakhot*), requires a reason.[26] For example,

---

[22] See B. Avodah Zarah 36a–b.   [23] B. Berakhot 23b.
[24] See, e.g., B. Kiddushin 32a–b re Ps. 1:2; B. Eruvin 21b and 68b; B. Taanit 8a; B. Makkot 23b.
[25] B. Makkot 22b.
[26] See B. Gittin 14a and parallels (see Tos., s.v. "ke-hilkhata"; B. Baba Batra 144a, Tos., s.v. "ke-hilkhata"). Also, unlike Mosaic traditions, one can draw inferences from one rabbinic law to another precisely because of their rational character (see Maimonides, *Mishneh Torah*: Mekhirah, 6.8; cf. Zekhiyyah u-Mattanah, 6.15). However, sometimes reasons for rabbinic laws were not initially publicized lest the process of rabbinic reasoning be made to look ineffectual if the particular law failed to gain popular acceptance (see B. Avodah Zarah 35a; also, E. E. Urbach, *Halakhah* [Jerusalem, 1984], 108).

the Rabbis were quite concerned with the actual Torah justification for writing the Scroll of Esther (*megillah*) and including it
in the canon of Scripture. After hearing about earlier discussions where specific scriptural warrants were proposed for this
canonical inclusion, the second-century Babylonian Sage
Samuel of Nehardea stated: "Had I been there, I would have
given a better argument than all of them. It says (Esther 9:27)
'they upheld it and accepted it,' namely, they upheld in heaven
what they had already accepted on earth."[27] To this statement
Rava added that "all of the other arguments are refutable (*eet
lehu pirkha*) except Samuel's which is irrefutable."[28] Now how
does the interpretation of Samuel differ from those of the other
Rabbis? The answer is that Samuel's interpretation does not
derive the warrant for this canonical inclusion *from* a verse at all.
Instead, it interprets a verse as describing a human enactment,
one which received *subsequent* divine approval. Obviously, in
order for such approval to be won, the enactment itself had to
be based on a consideration of the purposes of the Torah in
general, one of which is surely to directly relate all instances of
great deliverance to an awareness of the presence of God and to
thus affirm that nothing is accidental.[29]

MAIMONIDEAN TELEOLOGY AND THE LAW

Maimonides' connection to Rava's rationalism comes out when
we compare the following two texts.

Rava said that at the time a person is brought into the court of
heavenly justice, they say to him, 'Did you conduct your business
dealings honestly? Did you set aside time for the study of the Torah?
Did you engage in procreation? Did you look forward to salvation?
Did you reason wisely (*pilpalta be-hokhmah*)? Did you infer (*hevanta*) one
thing from another (*davar mi-tokh davar*)?'[30]

---

[27] B. Megillah 7a.
[28] See, also, B. Hagigah 10a for Rava's colorful endorsement of the most rational
interpretation offered by earlier authorities. Moreover, Rava uses the verse from Est.
9:27 to also describe the reacceptance of the Torah by the Jewish people after the
destruction of the First Temple (B. Shabbat 88a).
[29] See Maimonides, *Mishneh Torah*: Taaniyot, 1.1–13 and *Guide*, 3.36.
[30] B. Shabbat 31a.

Maimonides paraphrases Rava's words about "inferring one thing from another" as follows:

A person is obligated to divide his time for learning into three parts: one third for Scripture; one third for the Oral Tradition; and one third for understanding and discerning the end of a matter from its beginning. He should derive one thing from another, compare one thing to another, and understand by means of the methods through which the Torah is interpreted (*nidreshet*) until he knows the root of these methods; how he can derive what is forbidden and what is permitted from these things he has learned from revealed tradition (*mi-pi ha-shmu'ah*). This is what is called *gemara*.[31]

Although Maimonides speaks of "the methods through which the Torah is interpreted," which is a rabbinic term covering the various hermeneutical devices used in scriptural exegesis, it seems that he meant more than this. For he is suggesting a methodology sufficient to explain all aspects of the law, much of which is not the product of scriptural exegesis.[32] Maimonides' real concern here is to suggest a methodology adequate for the true science of the law. Along these lines he speaks of three types of ratiocination: (1) discerning the end of the matter from the beginning; (2) deriving one thing from another; (3) comparing one thing to another. I would suggest that these three types of ratiocination can be termed: (1) teleological inference; (2) deduction; (3) analogy. In other words, teleological inference is not the same as deduction. In a deduction, the premise is a whole and the conclusion a part thereof; in a teleological inference, the premise is a part of the whole which is concluded therefrom.[33]

This comes out even more sharply when we look at Maimonides' later treatment of Rava's dictum in the *Guide of the Perplexed* (where, quite significantly, he presents it as the opinion of "the Sages"). There he writes that "a man is required first to obtain knowledge of the Torah, then to obtain wisdom, then to

---

[31] *Mishneh Torah*: Talmud Torah, 1.11 based on B. Kiddushin 30a. See, also, B. Sotah 20a, Rashi, s.v. "ve-hadar," and *ibid.* 22a, Rashi, s.v. "she-morin."

[32] Maimonides may well have meant "interpreted" (*nidreshet*) to be interpretation that is wider than strictly scriptural exegesis (cf. T. Ketubot 4.9ff.; B. Baba Metsia 104a and Tos., s.v. "hayah").

[33] See Aristotle, *Posterior Analytics*, 86a4–10; *Nichomachean Ethics*, 1095a30.

know what is incumbent upon him with regard to the legal science of the Law – I mean the drawing of inferences concerning what one ought to do."[34] Thus between acquiring the data of Scripture and Tradition and properly applying it, comes "wisdom . . . being the verification of the Torah through correct speculation (*ba'iyyun ha-amiti*)."[35] Wisdom is the knowledge of ends. As he writes at the very beginning of the *Guide*, "The term wisdom (*hokhmah*) is applied in Hebrew . . . to the apprehension of true realities (*ha'amitot*), which have for their end (*takhlit khavanatam*) the apprehension of Him, may he be exalted . . . [and] it is applied to acquiring moral virtues."[36] Furthermore, this teleological inference strengthens analogy in a way deduction cannot. In explicating this point, I shall attempt to show that the legal logic of Rava enabled Maimonides to employ the philosophical logic of Aristotle with genuine Jewish integrity. This point is seen quite well when we compare two texts of Maimonides, both of which deal with the role of medical science in the process of halakhic decision making.

The first text concerns the question of how one is to determine whether or not an animal had been suffering from a fatal condition (*treifah*) before being slaughtered. Such a determination is the basis of the judgment of whether or not the meat of this animal is fit for Jewish consumption after the animal has been slaughtered (*kasher*). Maimonides writes:

One is not to add onto the number [seventy] of these fatal conditions. For there are conditions that might affect an animal . . . over and above those the Sages of earlier generations enumerated . . . and even if it be known to us from medical science (*me-derekh ha-refu'ah*) that they are terminal . . . you only have [in this matter] that which the Sages designated, as it says in Scripture, 'according to the law which they shall instruct you' (Deuteronomy 17:11).[37]

---

[34] *Guide of the Perplexed*, 3.54, p. 634. See *ibid.*, intro., 5. For the origin of the phrase "the end of a matter from its beginning," see Y. Sotah 8.10/23a re Eccl. 2:14.

[35] *Guide*, 3.54, p. 632.

[36] *Ibid.*, p. 632. See,also D. Novak, *The Image of the Non-Jew in Judaism* (New York and Toronto, 1983), 185ff.

[37] *Mishneh Torah*: Shehitah, 10.12–13. For a problematic self-contradiction on this point by Maimonides, however, see *Teshuvot ha-Rambam* II, ed. Blau (Jerusalem, 1960), no. 309 re Shehitah, 8.23; also, R. Joseph Karo, *Bet Yosef* on *Tur*: Yoreh De'ah, sec. 33 in

What we see here is that no comparisons are to be made on the basis of current medical information; nothing is to be added or subtracted irrespective of what we now actually know scientifically. Indeed, Maimonides' choice of Deuteronomy 17:11 as his scriptural warrant for this view is significant because the verse ends with the words, "you shall not depart from what they [the sages] will tell you, neither to the right or to the left." These words have two very well-known rabbinic interpretations, with which many of Maimonides' readers would certainly be familiar. The first interpretation is that this is the warrant for the authority of the Rabbis to add to the law rules that are not found in Scripture.[38] The second interpretation is that the rulings of the Sages are to be obeyed "even if it seems to you [that they are teaching] left is right or right is left."[39] In other words, at least in some areas of the law, no specific reasons are required for the understanding and application of the law. Scripture and Tradition alone suffice.

The second text from Maimonides concerns the question of human viability, that is, which wounds in a human being are considered fatal and which are not. Significantly, a human being who is fatally wounded is called a *treifah*, which is the very same term designating an animal suffering from a fatal condition, as we just saw. In the case at hand, determination of whether a murder victim was already a *treifah* would be a prime factor in judging whether his or her murderer would be subject to the death penalty or not. To be sure, the act of murder is prohibited regardless of the medical condition of the victim.[40] Nevertheless, if it is determined that the victim was indeed a *treifah*, then the murderer would not be executed.[41] This is because there is an insoluble doubt as to whether the victim died as a result of the act of the murderer or from his or her

the name of Rashba, and R. Yom Tov Lippmann Heller, *Divrei Hamudot* on R. Asher (Rosh: *Hullin*, 3.42, n. 221).

[38] B. Shabbat 23a.
[39] *Sifre*: Devarim, no. 154, ed. Finkelstein, 207.
[40] See M. Niddah 5.3; B. Shabbat 151b.
[41] B. Sanhedrin 79a and parallels; also, *ibid.*, 37b (following T. Sanhedrin 8.3); B. Makkot 7a.

previously fatal wound. In cases of doubt concerning human life (even the human life of the murderer), one is to follow the more lenient legal practice.[42] However, the resolution of the doubt concerning the condition of the victim could offer a more certain, a more scientific, criterion for what to do with the murderer. In other words, if we find that the victim's previous wounds are not fatal after all, then we no longer have any more doubt that the murderer should face the death penalty. Thus Maimonides writes:

> If one was is the very throes of death because of a humanly caused act (*goses bi-yedei adam*), for example, one who was beaten until he was on the verge of death: the one who murdered him is not to be executed by the court . . . Every person is assumed to be in good health (*be-hezqat shalem*) . . . until it is known for sure that he is suffering from a fatal wound (*treifah*) and the physicians (*ha-rof'im*) say that this wound has no cure (*ta'aleh*) in a human being, that he will die from it and from nothing else.[43]

Now in this ruling, unlike the previous one, we do follow the opinion of the physicians, and these opinions are the result of comparing one case to another. Why do we make comparisons when judging who is a human *treifah*, but not when judging what is an animal *treifah*? That comparisons are not to be made in cases of animal *treifah* is already presented in the Talmud, but there no reason is given.[44]

It would seem, though, that for Maimonides there would be an answer to this distinction between a human *treifah* and an animal one. For a human *treifah* is of concern in a murder trial. And the reason for the prohibition of murder is clearly evident. As Maimonides himself put it, "even though there are sins more serious than murder (*shefikhut damim*), none of them [like murder] entails the destruction of civilization (*yishuvo shel*

---

[42] B. Yoma 83a and parallels.

[43] *Mishneh Torah*: Rotseah, 2.7–8. See R. Joseph Karo, *Kesef Mishneh* on 2.7, who shows how this follows Rava's specification on B. Sanhedrin 78a (see Tos., s.v. "be-goses") that a humanly caused *goses* and a *treifah* have the same status, precisely because both are humanly caused (*iy'aved beiyh ma'aseh*). For Maimonides' general acceptance of medical-scientific consensus for halakhic purposes, see *Commentary on the Mishnah*: Yoma 8.4.

[44] B. Baba Batra 130b. See T. Sanhedrin 7.7; Niddah 7b; Y. Hagigah 1.8/76d and parallels.

olam)."[45] Conversely, in the case of the laws of the slaughter of animals for food, Maimonides cites them in an earlier work as the prime examples of "a traditional commandment (*mitsvah shim'it*) for which there is no reason (*ta'am*)."[46] Furthermore, even if we do have some notion of the reason of the commandment in general, as he asserts in a later work, we still have no notion of how the various specifics of this commandment are correlated with that general reason.[47]

Such, of course, is not the case with the laws dealing with murder. There the teleology, both general and specific, is clearly evident. As such, comparisons of specific points are possible and required in a way that could not be so in dealing with laws concerning the slaughter of animals for food.[48] Where a teleological continuum (an *entelechy* in precise Aristotelian terms) is present, one can draw analogies between the various specifics in a way one cannot do when the specifics are not seen as being in correlation with an overarching end.

Although we have seen that a teleological tendency is already present in talmudic sources, whose Babylonian authors especially cannot be assumed to have been influenced by the Aristotelian corpus (or by any Greek philosophical school), Maimonides was greatly influenced by Aristotle and the Aristotelians by his own admission.[49] This influence can be seen, especially, in his philosophy of law, a point missed by most philosophical students of Maimonides' work, who concentrate on his metaphysics. His Aristotelian teleology enabled him to enunciate a legal logic, developing the insights of the Rabbis, most particularly Rava.

---

[45] *Mishneh Torah*: Rotseah, 4.9. See *ibid.*: Me'ilah, 8.8.

[46] *Commentary on the Mishnah*: Berakhot 5.2, ed. Kafih, I:42. See Y. Berakhot 5.3/9c. For other laws that are considered incomparable because the reasons for their exceptional characteristics are unknown, see B. Shabbat 132a and parallels; B. Moed Qatan 7b; B. Sanhedrin 27a.

[47] See *Guide*, 3.26.

[48] For the suggestion that the greater rationality of the law pertaining to interhuman relations than that of the law pertaining to divine–human relations thus requires more ratiocination in cases of the former than in cases of the latter, see R. Israel Lifschitz, *Tiferet Yisrael* on M. Baba Batra 10.8: Yakhin, n. 84.

[49] See *Guide*, 1.71, where Maimonides says that he agrees with Aristotle "with great regard to any point he has demonstrated" (trans. Pines, 182). That covers a good deal.

Before, I purposely selected two examples where Maimonides discusses medical science not only because Maimonides himself was a distinguished physician and medical theorist, but because Aristotle uses a medical example when presenting a fundamental aspect of his teleology.

If it has a common significance (*kata ti koinon*), it must fall under one science . . . A diagnosis and a scalpel are both called medical, because one proceeds from medical science and the other is useful to it. The same is true of 'healthy'; one thing is so called because it is indicative of health, and another because it is productive of health; and the same applies to all other cases.[50]

Elsewhere, using the same medical model, Aristotle says that "what denotes and what produces health are 'commensurately' related (*to symmetros echon*) to health."[51] Teleology explains how many things are related to one another and can thus be properly compared. They are so interrelated because they are all related ultimately to one good – one end (*pros hen*).[52] Thus in the text above, without the common relation to health as an end, a diagnosis and a scalpel would have almost nothing in common. Any analogy between them without this teleological connection would be highly tenuous. Thus we can better see how Aristotelian teleology was not employed by Maimonides as something foreign to somehow or other explain Judaism or be synthesized with it but, rather, as a way to accelerate the growth of the whole Jewish tradition of "reasons of the commandments" that has deep rabbinic, and even scriptural, roots.

MAIMONIDES' USE OF LEGAL TELEOLOGY

Maimonides regarded the essence of positive rabbinic legislation (*taqqanah*) to be (1) "the proper ordering (*hasdarah*) of matters between humans"; and (2) "the improvement of the

---

[50] *Metaphysics*, 1060b36–1061a7, trans. H. Tredennick (Cambridge, Mass., 1935), 64–65.
[51] *Topica*, 107b6–10, trans. E. S. Forster (Cambridge, Mass., 1960), 318–319.
[52] See *Nicomachean Ethics*, 1096b26–32; *Posterior Analytics*, 95a1–15; also, J. Owens, *The Doctrine of Being in the Aristotelian Metaphysics*, 3rd rev. edn (Toronto, 1978), esp. 119ff.

world in religious matters."[53] In the *Guide of the Perplexed*, he
sees these same two ends, namely, "the improvement of the
body" (*tiqqun ha-guf*) and "the improvement of the soul" (*tiqqun
ha-nefesh*) as the two purposes for which the divine law of the
Torah was instituted.[54] This correlaton between divine law-
making and human law-making is consistent with the *Guide*'s
conclusion that the greatest purpose of the entire law is *imitatio
Dei*.[55] In fact, since revealed law is already completed but
human law is still in the making, teleology plays a more
constructive role in the area of human law. Moreover, the
content of revealed law, being already given by God, is
immutable. No change here is possible.[56] It can only be
partially described in teleological categories and these categories can only be partially used in its application. But with
human law, conversely, both the content and the application
admit of a totally teleological interpretation. As such, *imitatio
Dei* can be seen at least as much in the making of new human
law as in the understanding of the old revealed law. Finally,
there is no ultimate conflict between the two types of law
because human law is made for what are perceived by the
Sages to be the transcendent purposes of the revealed law. In
essence, then, both are divine law.[57]

For Maimonides, the range of rabbinic, human-made law is
wider than for any other medieval Jewish legal theorist because
he opines that this category of law not only covers what is
explicitly called a rabbinic "enactment" (*taqqanah*) or "decree"
(*gezerah*), but also covers any law the Rabbis derived by
scriptural exegesis, unless they specifically designated the law

---

[53] *Commentary on the Mishnah*: introduction, I:11–112.
[54] *Guide*, 3.27. This twofold purpose is emphasized throughout Maimonides' *œuvre*. See,
e.g., *Iggeret Teman*, trans. B. Cohen (New York, 1952), iv; *Mishneh Torah*: Gezelah, 6.11.
Nevertheless, *tiqqun ha-guf* is understood primarily in terms of the "body politic."
Mamonides explicitly rejects any suggestion that the words of the Torah have literal
curative powers. See *Mishneh Torah*: Avodah Zarah, 11.12; also I. Twersky, *Introduction
to the Code of Maimonides* (New Haven, 1980), 483.
[55] See 3.54 (end) re Jer. 9:23.
[56] See *Commentary on the Mishnah*: Sanhedrin, ed. Kafih, II:143–144 (principle 8);
Mishneh Torah: Melakhim, 12.2.
[57] See *Guide*, 2.40; also, Novak, *The Image of the Non-Jew in Judaism*, 290ff.

"a Torah matter" (*dvar torah*).[58] Thus the vast body of rabbinic
exegesis of Scripture is only taken to be an allusion to Scripture
(*asmakhta*).[59] As such, in the vast majority of cases, rabbinic
exegesis of Scripture is only an informal connection to an
actual scriptural passage, being grounded in the power of the
Rabbis to legislate for the Jewish people. That is why Maimonides (to my knowledge at least) never cites any such
scriptural allusions when codifying rabbinic law but, rather,
only cites either reasons already given by the Rabbis themselves
or reasons of his own for the legislation.

What Maimonides has done is to assign vast importance to
the role of practical reason. This can best be seen in his
treatment of the question of the preparation of rabbinic
legislation and its possible repeal. As we shall soon see, the two
processes are symmetrical inasmuch as the positive procedures
of legislation are paralleled by the negative procedures of
repeal.

Maimonides sees two prerequisites for responsible rabbinic
legislation: (1) the authorities must deliberate "according to
what seems proper in their eyes" (*ke-fi mah she-nir'eh*)"; (2) they
must discern the likelihood whether the proposed legislation
will be accepted by the majority of the lawabiding members of
the community.[60]

It would seem that the first prerequisite involves teleological
reasoning. That can be seen in the way Maimonides designates
the process of repeal (*bittul*). There he invokes the criterion of
the Mishnah that a later court may not repeal the legislation of
an earlier court "unless it is greater in wisdom and in
numbers."[61] Since the court he is speaking of is the Sanhedrin
of seventy-one members, how can any later court be larger?
Maimonides' answer to this question is straightforward: The
larger number refers to the larger number of Sages (outside the
actual seventy-one members of the Sanhedrin) who approve

---

[58] See *Sefer ha-Mitsvot*: introduction, sec. 2.
[59] Cf. note of Nahmanides thereon. See *Mishneh Torah*: Ishut, 3.20 and notes of
R. Abraham ben David of Posquières (Ravad) and R. Joseph Karo, *Kesef Mishneh*
thereon.
[60] *Mishneh Torah*: Mamrim, 2.5.   [61] *Ibid.*, 2.2 re M. Eduyot 1.5.

the later legislation to replace earlier legislation. But how does one determine who is wise, let alone whose wisdom is greater than someone else's? Here Maimonides says that the later court has discerned "another reason" (*ta'am aher*) for its proposed repeal of the earlier legislation.[62] It seems that they either disagree with the reason for the original legislation on rational/ teleological grounds, or they see new and better means to the original end.

More conservative Jewish jurists roughly contemporary with Maimonides saw two areas of rabbinic legislation to be beyond repeal. The first such area concerns those decrees that the Rabbis made in order to protect the laws of the Torah itself from violation (*kedai l'asot siyyag*). The second such area concerns those decrees that received wide popular support in Jewry when they were first legislated.[63] The first area of law seems to be so close to the immutable laws of the Torah itself as to share their very immutability. The second area of law seems to assign to initially popular precedent a veto against any future overturning of it. Maimonides, however, accepts neither of these restrictions. In effect, he seems to assume that practical reason, indeed all reason, is only as good as its contemporary arguments make it.

In the case of decrees made to protect the sanctity of scriptural laws (the best examples being rabbinic additions to the scriptural Sabbath laws), Maimonides writes that this restriction only applies when the earlier ruling "has spread (*pashat*) throughout all Israel."[64] That is, it only applies when its authority is *still* respected by the vast majority of Jews here and now. By implication, though, if this is *no longer* the case, then repeal would be justified. This point is further brought out by Maimonides' insistence that if a much later court conducted an investigation (*badaq*) and found that a formerly popular decree had now lost its popularity, that later court itself has the

---

[62] *Ibid.*, 2.1.
[63] See Rashi on B. Avodah Zarah 36a, s.v. "lo pashat," and Tos., s.v. "ve-ha-tenan" re Y. Shabbat 1.4/3c, and R. Joseph Karo, *Kesef Mishneh* on *Mishneh Torah*: Mamrim, 2.7.
[64] *Mishneh Torah*: Mamrim, 2.3.

authority (*reshut*) to repeal it.[65] It seems that he requires such formal repeal, even though the law itself has already fallen into disuse, because keeping an ineffective law on the books, so to speak, might very well weaken the effectiveness of the law itself as a whole.[66]

In fact, Maimonides goes so far as to say that even without these popular grounds for repeal, any law, even a law of the Torah, can be repealed temporarily (*le-fi sha'ah*), even by those having less authority than the earlier Sages (*qatan min ha-rish'onim*), when they determine that such a temporary measure is needed here and now "to return the masses to lawfulness" (*le-dat*).[67] That, of course, is a judgment of practical reason functioning above and beyond the specifics of the law themselves. One can thus conclude that for Maimonides, practical reason governs the lives of the Jewish people except where there is a specific law of the Torah, and even that can be temporarily repealed if that same practical reason determines that there is here and now what we might call a "teleological emergency," which calls for radical action on the part of the authorities without delay.

In the area of adjudication, which unlike legislation does not require the actual institution of the Sanhedrin, the role of practical reason is on the one hand more circumscribed, but on the other hand less so. It is less circumscribed since, unlike explicit rabbinic legislation, adjudication does not require any institution like the Sanhedrin. It is the day-to-day business of rabbinical judges (*dayyanim*), requiring nothing more than a normatively constituted Jewish community anywhere for whom these judges can function.[68] Nevertheless, it is more circumscribed since the cases brought before judges are usually quite specific, most often being subsumed under one or another of

[65] *Ibid.*, 2.7. Even when the power of formal repeal was no longer in effect due to the absence of the Sanhedrin, Maimonides still uses the criterion of contemporary acceptance to justify departure from earlier (even talmudically established) rules and procedures. See, e.g., *Mishneh Torah*: Ishut, 16.7 and note of R. Vidal of Tolosa, *Magid Mishneh*, and Malveh ve-Loveh, 11.11 and note of R. Joseph Karo, *Kesef Mishneh* thereon; also, R. Isaac bar Sheshet Parfat, *Teshuvot ha-Rivash*, no. 392.

[66] Along these lines, see B. Avodah Zarah 35a; B. Baba Batra 31b–32a.

[67] *Mishneh Torah*: Mamrim, 2.4. See B. Sanhedrin 46a.

[68] See B. Gittin 88b; Maimonides, *Mishneh Torah*: Sanhedrin, 5.8–9.

the norms that make up the whole Halakhah.[69] But even here, Maimonides is able to assign a prominent role to practical reason, and to do so with much the same conceptuality he employed in his constitution of the process of legislation.

This can best be seen by looking at how Maimonides formulates the range of the authority of rabbinical judges in civil cases.

A judge is to judge in civil matters according to the way his intelligence inclines (*she-da'ato noteh*) to ascertain the truth (*emet*). And when he is certain (*hazaq be-libbo*) about the matter, even if there is no clear proof (*r'ayah berurah*), then he should conclude (*dan*) according to what he knows . . . The matter is left to the mind of the judge according to what appears to him to be the truth.[70]

Then Maimonides asks:

If that is so, why did the Torah insist upon two witnesses? That is because anytime two witnesses actually do come before the judge, he is to judge according to their testimony, even though he does not really know whether what they testified is true or a lie (*sheqer*).[71]

Notice how Maimonides constitutes the judicial function. He has avoided two possible extremes, namely, either assuming that the presence of two witnesses is a *conditio sine qua non* of any civil proceeding and without which no judgment can be rendered at all, or assigning a role to practical reason so large that it can simply make up law as it goes along, albeit being guided by general principles.[72] Maimonides' middle path, as it were, is to state that when two witnesses are not present, then – and only then – may the judge take matters into his own judicial hands, guided solely by his own discernment of the truth. Such ascertainment, to be sure, might very well miss the mark inasmuch as it is practical reason and not the type of theoretical reason that admits of precise demonstration. But if

---

[69] Cf. B. Eruvin 63b and parallels; Maimonides, *Guide*, 3.34.

[70] *Mishneh Torah*: Sanhedrin, 24.1 based on B. Sanhedrin 6b re II Chron. 19:6.

[71] *Ibid.*

[72] In his earliest work, *Millot ha-Higayon*, sec. 14, ed. Roth (Jerusalem, 1965), 112–113, Maimonides criticized this total reliance on practical reason for human practice. Later, as we have seen, he makes more room for practical reason but, nevertheless, making it take second place to revealed law – but when and only when that law is unambiguous. Cf. Plato, *Statesman*, 294A-C; Aristotle, *Politics*, 1286a8ff.

the judge is morally and intellectually honest, then at least it is not a lie, which could be the case with witnesses who know how to lie effectively and who have not been disqualified in advance because of their being morally disreputable.[73] In other words, practical reason takes over when the superior wisdom of the Torah is specifically silent. The Torah's commandments, then, are only a negative not a positive condition, that is, they need not be present in every case; they must only not be directly and permanently contradicted.

Now, of course, all practical reason is not necessarily teleological. Here Maimonides might very well only be discussing the practical wisdom of a judge to insightfully surmise from the character of the litigants and the circumstances at hand just who is right and who is wrong. In fact, he actually follows the previously quoted text by cautioning contemporary judges not to take upon themselves such broad discretionary powers because they are not as intellectually qualified as earlier generations (a point we have seen at the very beginning of this chapter). But, nevertheless, he goes on to say that if the judge's opinion inclines in the direction of one of the litigants, then he should "reason (*ve-nosē ve-noten*) with the litigants until they agree . . . or submit to arbitration (*pesharah*), or he should remove himself from the case."[74] The first option might very well be to simply convince the litigants of the judge's own insight into the case and its participants. The last option might very well be based on the law that a judge who is partial to one litigant over another should disqualify himself from adjudication.[75] But the option to submit to arbitration is based on teleological considerations. For arbitration is presented in the Talmud as something that increases peace (*shalom*) as the common good (*bonum commune*) precisely because after arbitration, which is by defini-

---

[73] For the limitations of the very institution of legal testimony (*edut*), see *Mishneh Torah*: Yesodei ha-Torah, 8.2. For the various moral qualifications required of witnesses to be bona fide, see *ibid.*, Edut, 10.1ff. (See R. Joseph Karo, *Kesef Mishneh* thereon for the various talmudic sources.)

[74] *Mishneh Torah*: Sanhedrin, 24.2. For the background of post-talmudic attempts to limit the range of judicial discretionary powers, see I. Schepansky, *Ha-Taqqanot be-Yisrael* III (Jerusalem, 1992), 222ff.

[75] See B. Ketubot 105b re Exod. 23:8; B. Shevuot 30a re Lev. 19:15; *Mishneh Torah*: Sanhedrin, 21.1ff.

tion a compromise among the parties themselves, nobody is innocent and nobody is guilty as would be the case after a trial.[76] In effect, there is greater equality here than would be the case in a trial with its winner and its loser and, therefore, greater commonality in which the community as a whole has a direct interest. For the common good as the good of community itself, which should be the goal of all society, is enhanced by everyone not exercising their personal right to full justice for themselves alone (*bonum sibi*). The question of what is preferable, a formal legal proceeding or arbitration, is debated in the Talmud.[77] But Maimonides codifies the view that arbitration is preferable (*mitsvah*), thus opting for teleology when it can possibly replace strict legal deduction.[78]

At the end of this chapter in Maimonides' overall discussion of the procedures of Jewish courts, he writes the following about the teleology of practical reason as adjudication:

All of these matters are to be according to the way the judge judges them to be right for the occasion (*ra'ui le-kakh*) and what the time requires. And in all of them, let his deeds be for the sake of God, and let not human dignity (*kevod ha-beriyot*) ever be light in his eyes.[79]

And then at the very end of this chapter, Maimonides speaks about the additional dignity due to those of the Jewish people who "uphold the Torah of truth." That, for him, is the honor of the Torah itself (*kevod ha-torah*). He then concludes by saying, "the honor of the Torah is nothing but acting according to its laws and its ordinances." At first glance, this phrase is a bit odd since it would seem to contradict the beginning of the chapter, where Maimonides has just assigned to judges a very wide range of authority for the use of their extra-legal powers of practical reason. Now he seems to say they must only judge according to the strict letter of the law and remain silent when it is silent. Yet perhaps what Maimonides is hinting at here is that the true content of the Torah is not only its literal laws but, even more, the truths it teaches, truths to which humans are to aspire in

[76] See B. Sanhedrin 6b.   [77] *Ibid.*
[78] *Mishneh Torah*: Sanhedrin, 22.4.
[79] *Ibid.*, 24.9. For similar language regarding the royal function, see *Mishneh Torah*: Melakhim, 4.10; also, D. Novak, *Jewish Social Ethics* (New York, 1992), 193ff.

their attraction to God. Thus it is only by constantly seeking these truths that a judge can truly judge here on earth, even though he can never be demonstrably certain that he has truly achieved justice in any particular case. All particular judgment is tentative, especially when it applies to only one case at a time. And this is precisely why the ends of the law must, in effect, create rulings when the specifics of the law are not at hand.

REASON: PRACTICAL AND THEORETICAL

One cannot fully understand Maimonides' approach to practical reason unless one understands how he relates it to theoretical reason. The following passage is the key to that understanding:

Accordingly, if you find a law (*shariyah*) the whole end of which and the whole purpose of the chief thereof, who determined the actions required by it, are directed toward the ordering of the city . . . and if in that Law attention is not at all directed toward speculative matters . . . you must know that that Law is a nomos and that the man who laid it down belongs . . . to those who are perfect only in their imaginative faculty.

If, on the other hand, you find a Law all of whose ordinances are due to attention being paid . . . to the body and also to the soundness of belief . . . with regard to God . . . and that desires to make men wise . . . you must know that this guidance comes from Him, may He be exalted, and that this Law is divine (*al-shariyah al-alahiyah*).[80]

That this statement not only applies to the Jews and their law, but just as much to the gentiles and their law, is brought out earlier by Maimonides in his discussion of the Noahide laws in the *Mishneh Torah*. There he writes that if a person follows the Noahide laws because he regards them as divine law, he is assured of the bliss of the eternal, transcendent realm (*olam ha-ba*). However, even if he only follows them because they are rationally evident solely on political/moral grounds (*mipnei hekhre ha-da'at*), he is then still considered one of the wise.[81]

It would seem that Maimonides recognizes three types of

---

[80] *Guide*, 2.40, pp. 383–384 = *Dalalat al-ha'irin*, ed. S. Munk (Jerusalem, 1931), 271.
[81] Melakhim, 8.11. See Novak, *The Image of the Non-Jew in Judaism*, 276ff. for the conceptual implications of the disputed text of Maimonides here.

practical reason in the following ascending order: (1) The practical reason of ordinary jurists, who simply accept the laws of their particular society as given and make deductions from them in the process of ordinary adjudication. All law, for them, is positive statute. (2) Then there is the practical reason of philosophically inclined jurists and statesmen, who attempt to base legal and political reality on rationally evident principles about human sociality by a process of ordinary ratiocination (*qiyas*).[82] (3) Finally, there is the practical reason of true metaphysicians, those who correlate practical reason and theoretical reason in one continuum.[83]

By his insistence that there is a real continuum between practical and theoretical excellence in the divine law, Maimonides comes much closer to the position of Plato than to that of Aristotle, his usual authority on other philosophical questions. In his lucid introduction to his equally felicitous translation of the *Guide*, Shlomo Pines notes in aligning Maimonides with Plato and against Aristotle, "Plato's position is different, philosophy in its highest reaches cannot be held to be a purely private occupation. Man qua metaphysical animal is obligatorily tied up with man the political animal."[84] Indeed, as Plato himself put it in probably the most famous passage in the *Republic*, "Unless . . . either the philosophers will exercise kingship in Greek cities, or those who are now kings and rulers will philosophize authentically and ably . . . there will be no end of troubles for the Greek cities . . . nor for the human race."[85] Pines goes on to convincingly argue that this Platonic notion of the metaphysical grounding of politics came to Maimonides through the admitted influence of the Muslim philosopher Alfarabi.[86]

Despite the greater importance of practical excellence for Platonists than for Aristotelians, because of its necessary con-

---

[82] Re *qiyas*, see J. R. Wegner, "Islamic and Talmudic Jurisprudence: The Four Roots of Islamic Law and Their Talmudic Counterparts," *American Journal of Legal History* 26 (1982), 44ff.

[83] For the distinction between a metaphysically inclined jurist and one not so inclined, see *Commentary on the Mishnah*: introduction, ed. Kafih, I:20–21; *Guide*, 3.31 and 54.

[84] *Guide*, translator's introduction, lxxxviii. Cf. Aristotle, *Nicomachean Ethics*, 1177a25–30.

[85] *Republic*, 473D, trans. P. Shorey (Cambridge, Mass., 1930), 1:509.

[86] *Guide*, translator's introduction, xc-xcii.

nection with theoretical excellence, its importance is still due to its participation in an *entelechy* where concern with theoretical objects is the prime *telos*, that which gives meaning to everything beneath it. To reverse this teleological hierarchy would be totally contrary to the metaphysical foundations of Platonism. And yet, Maimonides seems to have done just that in his conclusion to the *Guide*. For this reason, the conclusion to this most philosophical of all his works has been problematic to all Maimonidean commentators, especially modern commentators who have tried to see Maimonides as a consistent, even systematic, philosopher. Indeed, the problem that this conclusion raises in relation to Maimonides' earlier dependence on Plato and Aristotle, both of whom assumed, *mutatis mutandis*, that *theōria* is superior to *praxis*, has been actually welcomed by some Kantian students of Maimonides' thought. For they see Maimonides reversing the ancient preference for *theōria* over *praxis*, a point later developed by Kant.[87]

At the end of the *Guide*, Maimonides writes:

It is clear that the perfection of man that may be glorified in is one acquired by him who has achieved, in a measure corresponding to his capacity, apprehension of Him, may He be exalted, and who knows His providence extending over all His creatures as manifested in the act of bringing them into being and in their governance as it is. The way of life of such an individual, after he has achieved his apprehension, will always have in view loving-kindness (*hesed*), righteousness (*tsedaqah*) and judgment (*mishpat*), through assimilation to His actions, may He be exalted.[88]

Hermann Cohen, the great German Jewish philosopher and theologian, made much of this problematic conclusion to the *Guide*. In effect, Cohen takes Maimonides' theological conclusion to be nothing less than a true anticipation of Kant, writing, "Therein lies the key point in Maimonides' theory of divine attributes, that he reduces and confines the concept of divine attributes to the ethical attribute, and therewith the concept of God to the ethical concept of God."[89] In this

---

[87] See *Critique of Pure Reason*, B671ff.   [88] *Guide*, 3.54, p. 638.
[89] "Charakteristik der Ethik Maimunis," *Jüdische Schriften*, III, ed. B. Strauss (Berlin, 1924), 246.

interpretation of the end of the *Guide*, Cohen is subsequently followed by Zvi Diesendruck, Samuel Atlas, Steven Schwarzschild, and Kenneth Seeskin.[90] Nevertheless, most other Maimonidean scholars have followed the opinion of Julius Guttmann, who stated in regard to Maimonides' doctrine of divine attributes, "Cohen failed to do justice to its metaphysical presuppositions."[91]

Alexander Altmann better describes Maimonides' concluding view of practical reason as "the practical consequence of the intellectual love of God."[92] Nevertheless, although this seems to me to be correct, even Altmann does not show how his consequence is constituted by Maimonides himself. For Maimonides, truth must be shown, be it theoretical or practical.[93]

The solution to this problem, it seems to me, without resorting to the forced neo-Kantian interpretation mentioned above, is to see how Maimonides moved beyond the extreme intellectualism of Aristotle and first came closer to the unified position of Plato and Alfarabi, and then ultimately suggested a unified view that reaches to the very ontological foundations of Judaism.

It should be noted that Maimonides preferred Plato's theory of creation to Aristotle's theory of the immutability/eternity of the superlunar universe because "the opinion of Plato – according to which the heavens too are subject to generation and corruption, this opinion would not destroy the foundations

---

[90] Disendruck, "Die Teleologie bei Maimonides," *Hebrew Union College Annual* 4 (1928), 499ff.; Atlas, *Netivim be-Mishpat ha'Ivri* (New York, 1978), 10ff.; Schwarzschild, "Moral Radicalness and 'Middlingness' in the Ethics of Maimonides," *Studies in Medieval Culture* 11 (1977), 87ff.; Seeskin, "The Positive Contribution of Negative Theology," *Proceedings of the Academy for Jewish Philosophy*: 1986–1987, ed. N. M. Samuelson (Lanham, Md., 1987), 87ff. For a critique of this whole line of interpretation, see Novak, *The Image of the Non-Jew in Judaism*, 311, n. 64.

[91] *Philosophies of Judaism*, trans. D. W. Silverman (New York, 1964), 357. Also, see Pines, *Guide*, translator's introduction, cxxii.

[92] "Maimonides' Four Perfections," *Essays in Jewish Intellectual History* (Hanover, N.H., 1981), 73. See, also, D. H. Frank, "The End of the Guide: Maimonides on the Best Life for Man," *Judaism* 34 (1985), 485ff.

[93] See *Mishneh Torah*: Qiddush ha-Hodesh, 17.24; also, *Commentary on the Mishnah*: Shemonah Peraqim, intro. re M. Avot 4.1.

of the Law and would be followed not by the lie being given to miracles, but by their becoming admissible."[94]

Miracles as innovative acts of God are inadmissable in a strictly Aristotelian universe because there is nothing that could be said or done to change the way things are from eternity. However, if the world as we know it came into being by a creative act, then another creative act can always change it. Plato does not state what the essence of the creative act is. He simply says that God "brought order out of disorder."[95] Furthermore, there is always a residue of disorder (*hypodochē*) requiring, as it were, subsequent creative acts to bring order to it.[96] To be sure, Plato believed that God engaged in some kind of internal discourse in the sense that the cosmos is made "according to the word" (*kata logon*).[97] But one cannot say that the word itself was creative. For Maimonides, though, God's creative act is a word (*dibbur*) because creation and prophetic communication are in essence the same divine act. As Maimonides writes: "Similarly . . . it has been said that the world derives from the overflow (*al-faiz*) of God and that He has caused to overflow to it everything in it that is produced in time. In the same way it is said He caused His knowledge to overflow to the prophets."[98] Thus both ethics and metaphysics are grounded in divine discourse, which God conducts as both creator and revealer. The prophet, then, imitates God in both teaching and ruling.

Imitation of God as ethical action and not just metaphysical contemplation does not mean that Maimonides subordinated metaphysics to ethics. Instead, it means that a metaphysics of creation leads to an active ethics precisely because both are essentially discursive rather than merely descriptive acts. For Plato, God's word is *subsequent* to the true, unspoken, being of the universe. For Maimonides as a Jewish thinker, conversely, the true being of the universe is the *consequent* of God's word. Accordingly, the practical wisdom of the prophetic metaphysi-

---

[94] *Guide*, 2.25, p. 328.   [95] *Timaeus*, 30A.   [96] *Ibid.*, 51A.   [97] *Ibid.*, 30B.
[98] *Guide*, 2.12, p. 279 = *Dalalat al-ha'irin*, 195. For the created status of the Torah, see *ibid.*, 1.65. For rabbinic precedent, see M. Avot 6.10, *Sifre: Devarim*, no. 316, and B. Pesahim 87b re Prov. 8:22.

cian consists of two parts. (1) There is the creative introduction
of the elements – in this sense the ends (*tela*) – for which the
truly fulfilling human community continually strives. (2) There
is his practical judgment, teleologically demonstrable, whereby
he simultaneously functions as statesman and jurist, answerable
to the very norms he has introduced. On the first level, will and
wisdom are identical. They are the creative introduction of
intelligible, ordered, being.[99] On the second level, however, will
is subsequent to wisdom. Will here becomes choice, which can
only be made by the criterion of prior standards. Will *per se*,
though, establishes its own standards.[100] It alone is purely
prescriptive.

Now even for Plato, God too is subject to the eternal Forms,
only having relative leeway in the world of Becoming. And,
because these Forms are intelligible but not themselves creative
– they do not speak – the word (*logos*) is still in essence
descriptive rather than creative, functioning *ex post facto* rather
than *ab initio*. For Maimonides, on the other hand, God is
subject to nothing but his own identical will and wisdom. That
is why the earlier Jewish doctrine of *creatio ex nihilo* must be
defended against any philosophy that denies it, at least *via
negationis*.[101] There are no correlations between God and
anything else. Everything is subsequent to him.

Because creation is a communication from the creator to the
creature, the creature who possesses the power of intelligent
speech can engage in contemplation of creation.[102] And since
that contemplation is of an active, transitive, and intelligent
power, that contemplation can – indeed must – overflow into
active, transitive, intelligent human action, which is creative
political action as practical excellence. Thus it would seem that
contemplation has been brought down to the level of action
and action has been brought up to the level of contemplation.
The Torah is a contemplative work since it teaches the highest

[99] See I. Efros, *Studies in Medieval Jewish Philosophy* (New York, 1974), 164–165.
[100] For this crucial difference between the classical Judeo-Christian notion of *behirah hofsheet* or *liberum arbitrium* and the modern, post-Kantian, notion of *Willensfreiheit* or autonomy, see Hannah Arendt, *The Life of the Mind: Willing* II (New York and London, 1978), 28f.
[101] See *Guide*, 2.15.   [102] See *ibid.*: introduction, p. 6.

truths about God and how the world is related to him.[103] And the Torah is a practical work since it directs its adherents to what is good: what is to be done.[104] Truth and goodness are coherently bound up together in the Torah. The divine creator is simultaneously the divine lawgiver.

This idea is not found in Plato, Aristotle, or the Stoics. According to the brilliant research and insight of Helmut Koester, they had no idea of natural law as it came to be understood after Philo – and that "after Philo" includes Maimonides.[105] For "natural law," as distinct from the ancient notion of "law imitating nature" (*kata physin*), or the modern notion of "law of nature" (*lex naturae*), does not mean human activity somehow patterned *after* nature, or the patterns *within* nature somehow seen as "lawlike" by analogy. In both, law has no certain ontological status. Instead, *natural law* (which, to be sure, is a term Maimonides does not use, but which can be applied to his legal theory) means the most general law that God has decreed for human creatures. It is discoverable by the use of their theoretical reason when it pertains to what is descriptively true *about* their world, and by practical reason when it pertains to what is prescriptively good *for* their lives in that world. Therefore, the commandments of the Torah have both cognitive and effective functions. Both, however, are ultimately creative.

Practical excellence as *imitatio Dei* introduces into the history of ideas a new form of practical freedom. It is more than simple free choice because it itself introduces its own ends; it is not simply an application of standards already in place. But it is

---

[103] For a midrashic attempt to see *torah* and *theōria* as etymologically similar, see *Midrash Konen* in *Bet ha-Midrash* II, ed. Jellinek (Leipzig, 1855), 23.

[104] The attempt to make the Torah devoid of any theoretical truth, and thus to make it unworthy of the highest attention of a truly rational mind, had to wait for Spinoza. See his *Tractatus Theologico-Politicus*, ch. 15. For discussion of how deep that rejection of the Torah's truth value goes, see D. Novak, *The Election of Israel* (Cambridge, 1995), 22ff.

[105] "NOMOS PHYSEOS: The Concept of Natural Law in Greek Thought" in *Religions in Antiquity*, ed. J. Neusner (Leiden, 1968), 521ff. This article, which most of the scholarly literature seems to have missed, is a *tour de force* having monumental implications for natural law theory and, indeed, for the whole "Athens–Jerusalem Question," namely, the relation of theology and philosophy.

still less than what we mean by autonomy after Kant. That is because this freedom can only function in a subordinate partnership with God's creative intelligence.[106] The limitations of human mortal creatureliness – the essential finitude of the human condition – makes this metaphysical grounding the *conditio per quam* of true practical reason. Without it, the roles of God and man would be reversed, as indeed they are for Kant and all who follow him.[107] But for Maimonides, that would be basing practical wisdom on what is demonstrably false since he believed that the primacy of God is rationally evident.[108] Moreover, truth is both logically and ontologically prior to good.[109] As such, the human person participates in divine creativity first by deriving his or her wisdom from that creativity through contemplation of its effects, and then creatively applying part of it in establishing the city of God on earth. In affirming that, Maimonides gave great philosophical expression to a uniquely Jewish idea.[110] It shows him to be a thinker who was much more than a follower of Plato, Aristotle, or Alfarabi, however much he may have learned from all of them. Both his agenda and his insights were originally Jewish. We have now seen that both in his jurisprudence and in his ontology.

What we have seen here is that Maimonides provides the most impressive way of looking at Judaism teleologically, which is an essential component of natural law thinking. However,

---

[106] See D. Novak, *Jewish–Christian Dialogue* (New York, 1989), 148ff.

[107] Thus, for Kant, man is the end (*Zweck an sich selbst*) and God is the means to the achievement of the highest good. Note *Critique of Practical Reason*, 1.2.2.5, trans. L.W. Beck (Indianapolis, 1956), 130: "It is also not to be understood that the assumption of the existence of God is necessary as a ground of all obligation in general (for this rests, as has been fully shown, solely on the autonomy of reason itself). All that here belongs to duty is to the endeavor to produce (*die Bearbeitung zu Hervorbringung*) and to further the highest good in the world, the existence of which may thus be postulated though our reason cannot conceive it except by presupposing a highest intelligence." (= *Kritik der Praktischen Vernunft*, ed. K. Vorlander [Hamburg, 1929], 144.) Hermann Cohen was well aware of this problem Kant poses for a Jewish believer who is also a Kantian. He strove mightily (and I think tragically) to overcome it. See his *Ethik des reinen Willens*, 4th ed. (Berlin, 1923), 455. Cf. Novak, *The Election of Israel*, 58ff.

[108] See, e.g., *Guide*, 2.33.   [109] See *ibid.*, 1.2.

[110] For an insightful discussion of how the Jewish idea of creation influenced Muslim and Christian reworkings of the relation between speculative and practical reason, see David B. Burrell, *Knowing the Unknowable God* (Notre Dame, Ind., 1986), 73ff.

even though one can adopt many of his teleological explanations of Judaism, regarding both its theory and its practice, one can still question the acceptability of his overall teleological view by both theological and philosophical criteria. To simply accept Maimonides' theology as dogma rather than being persuaded or dissuaded by it through rational argument places Jewish "Maimonideans" in much the same awkward position many Thomists find themselves in relation to the authority of Thomas Aquinas. That is, it is the paradox of a refusal to argue with, for, and against a thinker who himself presented rational arguments for his views. Therefore, critical review of the foundations of Maimonides' theology is certainly in order. That critical review will partially occupy us in the next chapter.

CHAPTER 5

Natural law and created nature

If my covenant does not endure by day and by night, then
I will not have established the laws of heaven and earth.
(Jeremiah 33:25)

LAW AND NATURE

Any theory of natural law must sooner or later consider just
what it means by "nature." This is a difficult task inasmuch as
nature is a notoriously slippery idea. Nevertheless, without the
proper constitution of nature, a theory of natural law will
inevitably become a description of features of the human
condition too vague to have any normative meaning at all.
Thus, for example, one can generally observe that there is no
human community that has permitted murder. As an empirical
generalization, all that this states is that there seems to be no
human community that permits unlimited killing – and no
human community that prohibits all killing (minimally as we
see in justifications of killing in self-defense, either individual or
social). But that in no way tells us precisely enough who may
not be killed and who may be killed and why. It does not tell us
what are the grounds for the prohibition of murder anywhere.
So also, one can generally observe that there is no human
community that permits one to have sexual relations with
everyone else – and no human community that prohibits all
sexual activity. (In those cultures in which celibacy is permitted,
that permission has always been made to a small minority of its
members, who are still dependent on the larger procreating
community for their continuity.) As an empirical generalization,

all that this states is that there seems to be no human community that permits unlimited sexuality. But here again, in no way does that tell us precisely enough with whom one may not have sexual relations and with whom one may have them and why. It does not tell us what are the grounds for the prohibition of fornication anywhere. Therefore, natural law cannot be theorized out of sociology, anthropology, or modern historical-critical investigation, namely, out of any descriptive social science at all. Although natural law intends an objective reality, that reality is not known by means of the most wide-ranging induction.

As we saw in chapter 3, natural law is constituted out of ethical theory. It consists of the principles that moral rules presuppose and which offer guidance as to how these rules are to govern human relationships in a historical community. Natural law reasons for certain commandments, specifically those that govern most interhuman relationships, are those reasons that are assumed to have normative validity universally. Accordingly, the "nature" in natural law must be seen as an essentially normative concept, one immediately connected with the demands made upon humans in their various historical communities.

A cogent natural law theory must correlate the concept of law and the concept of nature. For law without nature becomes the expression of the will of someone powerful enough to utter it effectively, be it God or a human being – the only two persons whose commandments have been heard. Law without nature is law without a discernible reason. And nature without law becomes the experience of impersonal forces, which themselves are incapable of making any demands on rational beings. (That is why the term "laws of nature" is an anthropomorphic metaphor.) Nature without law is a pattern waiting to be appropriated by being free enough to make law or be addressed by it.[1] Indeed, human beings are the only beings we know who are addressed by law. Law presupposes addressees who are

---

[1] That is why Thomas Aquinas rightly notes that all law, including natural law, requires "promulgation" in order to qualify as law (see *Summa Theologiae*, 2/1, q. 90, a. 4). Natural law being inherent in the created order, could be promulgated by no

intelligent enough to hear it and free enough to either accept it
or reject it. Thus law presupposes addressees who hear before
they speak. Conversely, God speaks before he hears, and that is
why he makes laws but laws are not addressed to him.[2] And,
conversely, nature neither speaks nor hears; therefore, it is
neither the source of law nor its addressee.[3] God is too free to
be addressed by law; nature is not free enough to be addressed
by law.

Joseph Albo, the fifteenth-century Spanish Jewish theologian
who introduced the term – but not the concept – "natural law"

one other than God. And in order to know it as such, one would have to infer that
law *per se* is part of the divine design of the universe.

[2] It is only in the covenant that laws are addressed to God by himself, namely, God
binds himself to norms resulting from his own irrevocable promises. In this sense,
God is autonomous in the strongest sense of auto-nomy. These norms are seen to be
the content of God's covenantal relationship *with* Israel, namely, they *both* practice
them *together*. Hence the theonomy under which Israel lives in the covenant is distinct
both from human autonomy whereby humans give commands *to* themselves, and
from "divine command" heteronomy whereby God merely gives commands *to* Israel
in an external, nonreciprocal way (cf. D. Novak, *The Election of Israel* [Cambridge,
1995], 248ff.). But norms cannot be heteronomously addressed to God because such
address would presuppose an authority higher than God himself, hence God would
cease to be absolute. For the notion of divine autonomy, see Y. Rosh Hashanah 1.3/
57b re Lev. 22:9; B. Berakhot 32a re Exod. 32:13. For the notion, though, that God
submits himself to the interpretation of his autonomous law by the Sages of Israel,
see B. Baba Metsia 59b re Exod. 23:2; *Shir ha-Shirim Rabbah* 8.13 re Hab. 3:3. For
further discussion, see D. Novak, *Halakhah in a Theological Dimension* (Chico, Calif.,
1985), 116ff.; *Jewish Social Ethics* (New York, 1992), 45ff.

[3] In his critique of the idea of natural law, Hans Kelsen writes, "Nature has no will and
therefore cannot enact norms. Norms can be assumed as immanent in nature only if
the will of God is assumed to be manifested in nature. . . [That] is a metaphysical
assumption, which cannot be accepted by science in general and by legal science in
particular" (*The Pure Theory of Law*, trans. M. Knight [Berkeley, 1967], 221). However,
for Kelsen, following Logical Positivism's view of science, "nature is a system of
causally determined elements" (*ibid.*). Nevertheless, if one assumes that human beings
are free enough to be addressed by law, then nature *per se* cannot be totally
determined because human nature is a part thereof, indeed, the part which is able to
formulate a concept of the whole. And wouldn't even Kelsen have to admit that
human life is inconceivable without law; hence isn't law an essential aspect of human
nature? As such, one cannot separate law and nature or freedom and reason. Of
course, nature itself as structure does not promulgate laws, but in the case of natural/
moral law, the designation of *human* nature is the *reason* for the promulgation of the
law by one free *person* to another. If one sees human nature as part of a total cosmic
nature, then the ultimate promulgator of natural law is the creator God. However,
that is an inference abstracted from the experience of lawfulness; it is not its
presupposition as Kelsen seems to think. Coming from the wisdom of God, natural
law reasons are discernible before one affirms the divine authority who promulgated
that rational law ("the will of God" in Kelsen's words). See above, pp. 16ff.

into Jewish theology, divided law into three categories: (1), natural law (*dat tiv'it*); (2), conventional law (*dat nimusit*); (3), divine law (*dat elohit*).[4] Although he may very well have been influenced by Thomas Aquinas' distinction between *lex naturalis*, *lex humana*, and *lex divina*, the distinction is extremely helpful in understanding the role of law in Judaism, nevertheless.[5] As I shall try to show, the introduction of the term *nature*, hence *natural law*, into a Jewish theology of law is an improvement over the more vague term "rational commandments" (*mitsvot sikhliyot*) used earlier. Following Albo's lead, I think the relation of *nature* and *law* contained in the term *natural law* must be seen in the context of the interrelation of the three types of law he so insightfully outlined. That is, natural law must be understood in relation to divine law above it and human law beneath it, a point initially demonstrated in chapter 3.

LAW, NATURE, AND TELEOLOGY

In terms of the relation of law and nature, I see four basic options for the natural law theorist and, indeed, each of the four has had its proponents in the history of Judaism. Furthermore, since the question of ends is essential to any theory of law, all of these options involve *teleology*. Thus in a philosophically developed Jewish theory of natural law, the concept of the "reasons of the commandments" (*ta'amei ha-mitsvot*), which we examined in the last two chapters, now becomes a Jewish perspective on the true end or *telos* of human active existence in the world.

So, we now need to examine some different Jewish teleologies. But our examination should not be a mere taxonomy of earlier opinions. Since our quest is a normative quest for what is true and how we should respond to that truth in good action, a person so moved needs to indicate a preference for one of these teleologies over the others and argue for it. That pre-

---

[4] *Iqqarim*, 1.7.
[5] See *Summa Theologiae*, 2/1, q. 93, a. 2ff. For the question of Aquinas' influence on Albo, see D. Novak, *The Image of the Non-Jew in Judaism* (New York and Toronto, 1983), 346, n. 4.

ference should be for the one that sheds more light than the others on our situation at this point in time within the ongoing development of our own tradition. In other words, it should have maximum correspondence with the sources of the tradition, and it should provide more coherent guidance than its alternatives for judging our current needs and effectively dealing with them.[6]

All teleologies assume that there is a hierarchal order in the world, one whose recognition enables us to call the world *cosmos* not *chaos*. After this fundamental apprehension, only four options are possible, it seems to me. Three of these teleological options we shall now examine; the fourth I shall present in the next chapter.

First, it can be assumed that this order of the world is itself ultimate reality and that the highest human task is to reverently perceive it. That approach is essentially one of *theōria*, which comes from the Greek word *theōrein*, "to gaze." This view has long been called "metaphysical" because it is our ultimate concern with what is beyond (*meta*) the physical, the ordinary world in which embodied humans live and work.[7] All other

---

[6] By "correspondence" I do not mean specific correspondence at each and every point but, rather, a general correspondence to a *Tendenz* of the tradition. Along these lines, see W. V. Quine, "Two Dogmas of Empiricism," *From a Logical Point of View*, 2nd rev. ed. (New York and Evanston, 1963), 42f. To demand such specific correspondence, without significant counterexamples, would make any normative judgment of what Judaism teaches impossible since normative judgment is essentially selective. It only addresses itself to *a* question at hand, hence its task is never totalizing. It always has to leave out more of the tradition than it could possibly include in any of its judgments (see e.g. B. Baba Kama 15a and parallels). To demand such totally impossible correspondence for any Jewish judgment would make Judaism normatively inoperative. That should strike anyone who knows anything about how Judaism operates as being utterly counterfactual. If Judaism isn't *nomos*, then what could it possibly be? Too many modern "studies" of Judaism, based as they are on historicist premises (consciously or unconsciously), state many truths *about* Judaism while simultaneously precluding the truth *of* Judaism (i.e., *torah*) to be spoken. The task of modern Jewish scholarship, which is the heir of nineteenth century *Wissenschaft des Judenthums*, must now be a philosophical examination of its methodological principles in order to see whether or not they are consistent with the assumption that Judaism is alive not dead. But, there is surely no way to return to a pre-modern type of scholarship. Modernity must be critically emended. Fundamentalism is not a viable intellectual option inasmuch as the enunciation of *the* truth of the tradition cannot simply ignore truths learned elsewhere. The two require coordination.

[7] Although the word "metaphysics" comes from Aristotelian philosophy, the metaphysical impetus is more originally Platonic. See Plato, *Theatetus*, 176A–B.

human activity, confined as it is to mundane, finite tasks in the world, that is, *praxis*, must be subordinated to the higher supermundane task of *theōria*. As we shall soon see, this is what Maimonides appropriated for Judaism, largely from Plato and Aristotle.

Second, it can be assumed that the order we perceive in the world only has meaning when placed in the context of what we ourselves make *of* the world. The world's meaning lies within us not in or above the world itself. The highest human task, then, is to properly incorporate that order into the higher order of our own making. It is the assertion of the primacy of human inventiveness: the human person as *homo faber*. Kant's notion of autonomy gave human inventiveness its most impressive philosophical grounding. It is the approach of *praxis*, which comes from the Greek word *prattein*, "to make."[8] As we saw in chapter 3, this is what Hermann Cohen appropriated for Judaism, largely from Kant.

Thirdly, one can combine the theoretical and practical approaches to the world as follows. On the one hand, we recognize the priority of a maker over any material that maker can use. As such, we see our own *praxis* as giving us a priority over that which we use or can use. It is the priority of subject over object, of intelligence over intelligibility. But, on the other hand, we recognize that we ourselves are part of an order greater than anything we ourselves could possibly make. Therefore, we conclude that the world itself is the product of a mind far greater in power than our own. And since our highest principle of order is purpose, we conclude that the orderer of the order of which we are part is a purposeful intelligence.[9] To assume anything less would involve the absurdity of concluding that there is an unintelligent cause of our own intelligence, and

---

[8] See Novak, *The Election of Israel*, 128ff.

[9] The logic of the argument from design has been enunciated no more lucidly than by Etienne Gilson in *God and Philosophy* (New Haven, 1941), 140f.: "Being an absolute, such a cause is self-sufficient; if it creates not only being but order, it must be something which at least eminently contains the only principle of order known to us in experience, namely, thought. Now an absolute, self-subsisting, and knowing cause is not an It but a He. In short, the first cause is the One in whom the cause of both nature and history coincide, a philosophical God who can also be the God of a religion."

the absurdity of concluding that there is a nonpurposeful cause of our own purposefulness.[10] "Could it be that he who planted the ear himself does not hear; that he who formed the eye himself does not see?" (Psalms 94:9).

So far, though, we have only asserted that there is a purposeful order of the cosmos and that our own purposefulness somehow fits into it. But *what* is the end of that cosmic purposefulness, and *how* does our own purposefulness fit into it? That is the question addressed by the ninth-century Babylonian Jewish theologian Saadiah Gaon, who is considered the first major rabbinic thinker to incorporate the methods and findings of philosophy into traditional Jewish discourse. Nevertheless, let it be emphasized that whatever new conceptualities are worked out by such philosophically influenced Jewish thinkers, the basic subject matter in which they are interested and the basic vocabulary they must retain in dealing with it, come from the primary sources of the tradition: Scripture and Talmud (by which I include all the rabbinic texts). Saadiah's teleology was certainly influenced by his reading of the philosophers, but its original impetus and final application are both located squarely within the Jewish tradition. Accordingly, we can accept the Jewish authenticity of his teleology, whether we accept it for ourselves here and now or not.

SAADIAH'S TELEOLOGY

For Saadiah, the fundamental questions are: *For whom* is that order created? What is its end? His answer is that man is the end of this purposeful, orderly creation.[11] Saadiah well appropriated a teaching of the Mishnah: "Everyone should say that for my sake (*bishevili*) was the world created (*nivra*)."[12] What this means, at least in his theology, is that the world in general is beneficent, and this is especially and supremely so in and for the creation of humans.

Natural law, for Saadiah, is an aspect of the creation of

---

[10] See Thomas Aquinas, *Summa Theologiae*, 1, q. 19, a. 4 and a. 5.
[11] *Emunot ve-Deot*, 4, introduction.
[12] M. Sanhedrin 4.5. Cf. B. Sanhedrin 38a; Novak, *Jewish Social Ethics*, 145ff.

multiple goods by the one God.[13] Natural law is the recognition
of those goods which humans can actively pursue and which
are readily discernible by them. The imperative comes from
the very attractiveness of these goods. That is a matter of what
some have called "general revelation." Other goods that are
less readily discernible require what some have called "special
revelation."[14] Such special revelation is itself an act of divine
beneficence. It enables most people of ordinary intelligence to
actively attain many goods which they could never discern for
themselves, and it enables even people of extraordinary intelligence to actively attain some goods far sooner than would be
the case if they were simply left to their own pursuits.[15] Thus
the difference between divine law (what Saadiah called *mitsvot
shim'iyot*, "revealed commandments") and natural law is one of
degree rather than one of kind.[16] For even revelation is from
within creation itself, which is the origin of both types of law.
As for human law, it is a further specification of the law of
creation, whether divine or natural. One could say that
Saadiah's constitution of the relation of nature and law, the
relation that a theory of natural law requires, is that *nature is for
law*, that is, our lawfulness is intended by the beneficent order
revealed to us by nature in its various workings on our behalf.
Ultimately, the theoretical is for the sake of the practical.

Saadiah's teleology has had a recurring attractiveness to
many Jews. It has sufficient support in the primary scriptural
and rabbinic sources of the tradition, especially because of how
seriously it takes the scriptural doctrine of creation. And it is
not wedded to any specific scientific paradigm of the physical
world that is incommensurable with the current scientific
paradigm (a problem with Maimonides' teleology, as we shall
soon see). Yet there is a fundamental theological problem with
what might be termed its "naturalism." That problem is
connected with its reduction of revelation to creation. Because

[13] See note of L. E. Goodman on Saadiah Gaon, *The Book of Theodicy: Commentary on the Book of Job*, trans. L. E. Goodman (New Haven and London, 1988), 99ff.
[14] See John Calvin, *Institutes of the Christian Religion*, 1.2.1.
[15] *Emunot ve-De'ot*, introduction, 6.   [16] *Ibid.*, 3.3.

of that, it seems to me, Saadiah could not very well constitute the key scriptural doctrine of covenant (*berit*).

It can be maintained, I think, that in Saadiah's theology everything is for the sake of the world, especially for the sake of humans, namely, as they are already situated within the world. This even includes the human relationship with God. Humans receive everything from God by means of the world (with effort appropriate to authentic human dignity, to be sure).[17] Thus the human relationship with God is not only *in* the world, a point common to any theology of creation, but it is always *through* the world as well.

But here it seems a fundamental element from the tradition has been lost. For the doctrine of the covenant teaches that there is a relationship with God, indeed *the* relationship with God, that although *in* the world is clearly not *of* it or *through* it. That relationship, as Franz Rosenzweig best taught us earlier in this century, is not *about* the world either.[18] It does not simply supply us more truth about the world than our unaided intelligence could learn, or could very readily learn. Instead, it enables our relation *to* the world to be ontologically (even if not usually chronologically) subsequent to our direct relationship *with* God. It places the world in its true place ultimately. The subject of revelation is *God-with-us*, not *we-with-the-world-because-of-God*. So when the Psalmist says, "the nearness of God, that is what is good for me (*tov li*)" (Psalms 73:28), that means that God is nearer than anything else in the world possibly could be *for* me. And soon before that, when he says "who is there for me in heaven, and along with You (*imekha*) I desire none on earth" (73:25), that means that there is nothing that could come *between* God and me in the covenant, that everything else must wait so to speak.[19] For at this level of covenantal exultation (which being precious is rare), "all who are far away from it (*reheqekha*) are lost" (73:27). That is what it means to declare "my flesh and my heart, my steadfast heart, fail me since God is my portion (*helqi*) throughout all worldly time (*l'olam*)"

---

[17] *Ibid.*, 3, introduction.
[18] See *The Star of Redemption*, trans. W. W. Hallo (New York, 1970), 16of.
[19] See *Devarim Rabbah* 1.18 re Exod. 31:17.

(73:26).[20] In rabbinic teaching, as we saw in chapter 3, the more direct relationship with God intended by the commandments that pertain to what is "between (*bein*) humans and God" has a priority over the less direct relationship with God intended by the commandments that pertain to what is "between (*bein*) humans themselves."[21] The latter must fit into the former, not the former into the latter. A theory of natural law must fit into the context of the covenant.

This aspect of the tradition, which Saadiah could not constitute in his theology, is especially significant for modern Jews for whom modernity has emphasized the phenomenality of history as being distinct from that of nature. As Dilthey clearly saw, the way we constitute the realm of freedom and purpose (what he called *Geisteswissenschaften*) is essentially different from the way we constitute the realm of necessity and causality (what he called *Naturwissenschaften*).[22] The greatest modern Jewish theologian to my mind, Franz Rosenzweig, whatever his critique of other aspects of modernity might have been, built on modernity's insistence on the independence of history from nature. He did that because the very centrality of temporality (*Zeitlichkeit*) to Jewish revelation and its tradition has some essential commonality with that modern insistence.[23] History, not nature, is the integral realm of persons and their interrelationships.

Of course for some, that has meant the abandonment of any sense of the importance of natural law for Judaism. But that too easy abandonment has led just as easily to the normative graveyard of historical relativism. Both authentic normativity and its presupposition of freedom together presuppose an anti-

---

[20] I have translated *l'olam* as "wordly time" following Martin Buber's and Franz Rosenzweig's translation of it as *Weltzeit* throughout their own Bible translation (see Novak, *The Election of Israel*, 262f.). Rosenzweig's influence can be seen in this exegesis of Psalm 73; indeed, he selected this psalm himself to be read at his funeral and to be inscribed on his headstone. It was read at the funeral (12 December 1929) by Martin Buber (see Nahum Glatzer, *Franz Rosenzweig*, 2nd edn [New York, 1961], 175f.).

[21] *Above*, pp. 88ff.

[22] *Introduction to the Human Sciences*, trans. R. J. Betanzos (Detroit, 1988), 83ff.

[23] See Karl Löwith, "M. Heidegger and F. Rosenzweig or Temporality and Eternity," *Philosophy and Phenomenological Research* 3 (1942), 55ff.

relativistic affirmation of truth. That is something George
Orwell among others has powerfully taught us in this century, a
century whose widespread contempt for truth has often led to
the easy denial of right law and human freedom in favor of
apathy or brutality.[24] So, instead, what we need is to recon-
stitute our theory of natural law to be more consistent with a
more intense historical sense without collapsing nature into
history, however.

MAIMONIDES' TELEOLOGY

From our present philosophical perspective, Saadiah's teleology
has a strength and a weakness. Its strength is that it is general
enough not to be wedded to any specific scientific paradigm.
Thus one can be convinced by the argument from design,
which forms the basis of Saadiah's cosmology, and still operate
within any of the subsequent scientific paradigms that have
been operative since his own time. But its generality, which
keeps it out of trouble on the scientific front, is also its
weakness. For his teleology, which we might term pluralistic,
lacks the univocal universal hierarchy that the teleological
quest is itself searching for.

   This designation of the weakness of Saadiah's teleology on
the ontological front is where we might well locate Maimonides' criticism of it and his own determination to think out
a more systematically satisfying teleology. This is especially so
in Maimonides' teleological constitution of the "reasons of the
commandments" (*ta'amei ha-mitsvot*), which, as we have already
seen in the last two chapters, is the traditional matrix for the
development of a Jewish natural law theory.

   Maimonides' criticism of Saadiah's concept of "rational
commandments" has often been misinterpreted to mean that
he rejects the notion of rational commandments altogether.[25] If
that is so, then it is concluded, especially as a point within the
current debate about natural law in Judaism, that Maimonides

[25] See *Commentary on the Mishnah*: Avot, introduction (Shemonah Peraqim), ch. 6. Cf.
    Emunot ve-Deot, 9.2.

is opposed to the very idea of natural law, certainly within the Jewish tradition. That, however, as I have shown elsewhere, is an erroneous interpretation of Maimonides' critique.[26] When that critique is properly understood, it is not only not a rejection of the idea of natural law in Judaism, it is actually a considerable development of it from the legacy of Saadiah.

One could characterize Maimonides' critique of Saadiah's teleology of the commandments as being a critique of a theory that is not teleological enough. What Saadiah's teleology lacks is an overall hierarchy, namely, a teleology having one supreme end that orders everything beneath it according to each respective entity's capacity to approximate it. Thus what Saadiah's teleology and hence his natural law theory lacks for Maimonides is a properly constituted metaphysics. The authentic relationship with God, especially for humans whose intelligence is below that of the angels but above that of the beasts, is not primarily with God as the efficient cause of the universe. For the latter type of relationship would always have to be mediated by some sort of cosmic nexus. Instead, the authentic relationship with God is with God as the supreme *telos*, the intelligible and intelligent apex of the entire cosmos.[27] That apex can be reached by human intelligence, beginning in philosophy and ultimately graced by prophecy.[28] The very operation of that intelligence in its fullest and highest sense intends a vision of God not mediated by the world or anything in it, a vision of God beyond God's envelopment in any concealing mist. It is a vision for which Moses, the prophet of all prophets, must remove the veil that separates him from all other people.[29] Therefore, in the theory of natural law that emerges from this philosophical stance, *law is for nature*, that is, our lawfulness is for the sake of affirming and approximating the highest order of nature: God. *Praxis* is ultimately for the sake of *theōria*.

To know God as the End of all ends, however imperfectly in a world where one's soul is incarnate in a finite, mortal body, is

---

[26] See Novak, *The Image of the Non-Jew in Judaism*, 278ff.
[27] See *Guide of the Perplexed*, 1.69. [28] See *Mishneh Torah*: Yesodei ha-Torah, 7.5.
[29] See Exod. 34:34–35.

the summit of intellectual excellence, what Maimonides called
the "ordering of the soul" (*tiqqun ha-nefesh*).[30] Furthermore,
following Plato, he saw the ordering of the moral life, which is
the ordering of the society of an essentially political creature, as
the necessary step before the ordering of the soul.[31] This
secondary ordering he called the "ordering of the body" (*tiqqun
ha-guf*). By "body" he meant what later philosophers called the
"body politic."[32]

Yet for Aristotle, true intellectual excellence leads one away
from the life of the political body never to return.[33] But
Maimonides, being a theologian in a tradition where the law as
the structure of the polity is never to be transcended by anyone
(at least in this world), had to think in a way closer to Plato
than to Aristotle, therefore, in constituting the relation between
moral excellence and intellectual excellence as reciprocal.[34]
That is, one moves up from the life of the body to the life of the
soul, and then one brings the enlightenment of the soul back
down to properly rule the life of the body. The excellence of the
soul entails the excellence of the body. And the excellence of
the soul presupposes an ordered bodily life.[35] For Maimonides
and others thinking along these same lines, this is because the
ordering of the body is an ordering that does not allow any of
the body's appetites, or even all of them together, to claim
ultimacy. For anyone who was that attached to bodily ends
would not only not be leading a truly ordered moral life, but
such a person would also not have the proper desire for the
ends of the soul, which are the locus of true human fulfillment.

Maimonides saw all of the commandments of the Torah in
the context of this reciprocal relation of body and soul, a
relation that participates in the cosmic relation of matter and
form. In this sense, all of the commandments of the Torah are
natural law. They all contribute either to spiritual betterment
or to political betterment. That does not mean that one can
give a rational explanation for every one of the details of every

---

[30] *Guide*, 3.27.   [31] See *Republic*, 484Dff.   [32] *Guide*, 3.27.
[33] See *Nicomachean Ethics*, 1177a10ff.   [34] See above, pp. 113ff.
[35] See Leo Strauss, *Philosophy and Law*, trans. E. Adler (Albany, N.Y., 1995), 124ff.; also
D. Novak, *Suicide and Morality* (New York, 1975), 22ff.

law.[36] But that usually means not all of the details of the ritual law, especially the many details of the sacrificial system, a system which even by Maimonides' time had become totally detached from anyone's experience. Yet when it comes to the moral law, what for us is the locus of natural law, Maimonides seems to have been able to explain just about every detail quite rationally. For moral law and its details are all either part of our own experience or are quite close to it. In fact, Maimonides had the more rationally developed theory to explain the reasons of the commandments than any other Jewish thinkers. To this day, many of his rationales are invaluable when presenting Jewish views on many questions of general normative concern. As we saw in the chapter 1, intelligent participation in such generally normative discussions involves the development of a theory of natural law out of the sources of the Jewish tradition. Maimonides certainly did that with great brilliance.

Whereas Maimonides was better able to constitute a direct divine–human relationship unmediated by the world than Saadiah could, one cannot describe that constitution as truly covenantal either. For the relationship Maimonides constitutes is more than anything else a relation *to* a God who seems to closely resemble the God of Aristotle. It is a relation where only God and not man is the object of love. All concern is in one direction: from man to God.[37] Maimonides in no way ever attempts to constitute a truly responsive role for God. There is no real reciprocity here. But the covenant is surely characterized by constant transaction between God and Israel, with that activity being mutual. Even when God is actively saving Israel, Israel's participation in her salvation is not wholly passive. She is required to do something *with* God in response to what God is doing *for* her. In fact, there is a trend in rabbinic teaching, which is considerably developed in kabbalistic theology, that sees what Israel does *with* God as also being *for* God as well.[38] That is the theological problem with Maimonides' natural law

---

[36] See *Guide*, 3.49.   [37] See Novak, *The Election of Israel*, 225ff.
[38] See e.g. *Shemot Rabbah* 15.5; also D. Novak, *Halakhah in a Theological Dimension* (Chico, Calif., 1985), 120ff.

theory. Minimally, it is noncovenantal; maximally, it is counter-covenantal.

The philosophical problem with Maimonides' natural law theory is one that a number of modern philosophers have noted about all Aristotelian and neo-Aristotelian ethical theories. That problem is that teleological ethics, where real and not projected ends are intended, seems to presuppose a teleological natural science.[39] Teleology is only real, that is, prior to the human intention of the ends it proclaims, when these ends are not confined to human intelligence, but are part of a larger order than that populated by humans alone and constructed by them. Only when man is seen as acting within a cosmic teleology can the purposeful action of humans be presented as more than the projections of human will. That is what fundamentally distinguishes a *telos* from an ideal in the modern sense.[40] That is especially so for someone like Maimonides, who so heavily invested in the importance of natural science for theology. In his view, one truth encompasses both the Torah and the world.

The strength of Maimonides' more highly developed teleology as compared to that of Saadiah worked to its persuasive advantage when the reigning scientific paradigm was Aristotelian-Ptolemaic. But with the shift in scientific paradigms after Galileo and Newton, the earlier paradigm seems to be irretrievable. That is certainly so in astrophysics, where all Aristotelians have located the teleology *towards* which human intelligences aspire. It is the teleology of the heavenly bodies, which before Galileo were assumed to be separate intelligences higher than that of earth bound humans. These higher intelligences inspire human intelligences to aspire to be like them in their knowledge of the unmoved mover, the God who is End of

---

[39] See Ernst Cassirer, *The Logic of the Humanities*, trans. C. S. Howe (New Haven, 1961), 165ff.; Leo Strauss, *Natural Right and History* (Chicago, 1953), 8; Jürgen Habermas, *Communication and the Evolution of Society*, trans. T. McCarthy (Boston, 1979), 201; Alasdair MacIntyre, *After Virtue* (Notre Dame, Ind., 1981), 152.

[40] Thus Kant sees an ideal as the final cause of an idea of pure reason (*Critique of Pure Reason*, B838). It is thus a projection of the rational will (*ibid.*, 845B; *Religion within the Limits of Reason Alone*, trans. T. M. Greene and H. H. Hoyt [New York, 1960], 54). Following Kant, Hermann Cohen confines ideality to the human sciences. See *Religion of Reason out of the Sources of Judaism*, trans. S. Kaplan (New York, 1972), 353f.

all ends.[41] Biological teleology, which some forms of natural law theory still seem to regard as normative, was never normative for humans in the view of Aristotle and his authentic disciples. Any order less intelligent than our own is more often than not something to be manipulated *by* us, not something for us to respect and aspire *to*. The only order having an inherent normative pull on us is one that is more intelligent than our own.

Hence, despite the many specific things we can learn from Maimonides in connection with our search for natural law materials, I think his overall theory has insurmountable difficulties for us.

THE EPISTEMOLOGICAL QUESTION

The previous teleologies we have just examined, functioning as they do as ontological foundations of the natural law theories of their respective proponents, have suffered from theological and philosophical inadequacies. A further philosophical inadequacy from which they suffer, one that is epistemological, must be termed a "perspectival" inadequacy or the fallacy of too easy generalization. That is, as many opponents of natural law have often argued, how do we know that when we assume something to be universal, we are not in fact merely projecting certain minimal general standards of our own particular culture onto the universe? Thus, for example, it does not logically follow from the recognition that no human community can endure where there is unrestricted sexual conduct to conclude that no nonmarital sex can be allowed. For missing between the premise and the conclusion is a minor premise defining marriage. Since there is no universal unanimity on that point, but only much cultural diversity, the move from the premise to the conclusion is logically invalid.

It seems that to adopt a natural law position is to presuppose that one can sit on some sort of Olympian perch and look down and judge the practices of any and every culture beneath

---

[41] See Novak, *Jewish Social Ethics*, 141ff.

oneself by immutable criteria. It seems that one must, in effect, speak *sub specie aeternitatis*. But can one ever be so removed from one's own culture to be able to do that without prejudice? If we assume, as argued in chapter 1, that no constructed philosophical language can ever claim true priority over the historical language from which it has been abstracted so that the old language can be deduced from the new one, then there is no such Olympian perch that is not primarily rooted in the mud of the earth. Hence one can only speak *sub specie durationis*, that is, within history. This indictment of universality and its attendant teleology must be addressed for there to be a cogent natural law theory, especially when our greater sense of historical and cultural diversity has strengthened the perspectival perspective. Unfortunately, too many natural law theorists have chosen to either ignore this challenge or to dismiss it too quickly.

Yet are not such terms as "nature," "universal," and "teleological" used in one guise or another in the languages of historical cultures? Do they not have clear equivalents in the traditional discourse of Judaism, which is always our case at hand here and now in this inquiry? How then can we cogently use these terms and the concepts they name, which have shown themselves to be necessary for any natural law theory, but speaking of them from *within* that tradition rather than imposing them *onto* it?

Here I think a historical analysis of the tradition of natural law thinking itself might be helpful in our inquiry. For natural law thinking has its own history, which is not confined to any one cultural tradition, but seems to represent a cross-cultural effort. Indeed, natural law thinking became an inter-cultural pursuit. Of course, some scholars have tried to see natural law as an idea determined by Greek philosophy, which has thereafter been simply taken up by Roman jurisprudence, and then by Judeo-Christian-Islamic theology.[42] However, I think a better scholarly case can be made for a true interrelation between the three traditions just mentioned, so much so that elements from one cultural strand can illuminate elements from

---

[42] See A. P. d'Entrèves, *Natural Law* (New York, 1965), 20ff.

another. At this point, I shall try to show how elements from the strand of Roman jurisprudence can illuminate my attempt to understand how the idea of natural law operates in Jewish theology. (This is similar to the appropriation of elements from the Greek philosophical strand by Saadiah and Maimonides.)

NATURAL LAW IN ROMAN JURISPRUDENCE

To understand natural law thinking in Roman jurisprudence, one must always keep in mind the relation of three terms: (1) *ius civile* ("civil law"), which is the positive law made for Roman citizens by their designated authorities; (2) *ius gentium* ("law of nations"), which is the positive law made by the Roman authorities for certain non-Romans living under their rule; (3) *ius naturale* ("natural law"), which is the law inherent in nature and thus, even if made by someone, it is not made by any human authorities.[43]

Originally, *ius gentium* was the law made for non-Romans who had long lived under Roman rule, before the vast expansion of that rule when Rome changed from a republic to an imperial form of government. It was administered by a Roman official, the *praetor peregrinus*, who might be termed in our language the "minister of resident-alien affairs."[44] But even at this early stage, when *ius gentium* was more closely related to the cultural singularities reflected in *ius civile*, it still had to take into consideration certain more general aspects of the human condition in order to properly relate to these "others" living under its rule. For even though Rome was the source of the law, its addressees were a variety of non-Roman communities. As such, it had to seriously concern itself with the commonalities between the rulers and the ruled, as well as commonalities between the various communities themselves being ruled from without. This process of generalization can be characterized as the search for overlappings *between* oneself and others rather

---

[43] See E. Levy, "Natural Law in Roman Thought," *Gesammelte Schriften* I (Cologne, 1963), 4ff.; H. J. Jolowicz and B. Nicholas, *Historical Introduction to the Study of Roman Law*, 3rd edn (Cambridge, 1972), 102ff.

[44] See David Daube, "The Peregrine Praetor," *Journal of Roman Studies* 41 (1951), 66ff.

than the constitution of some universal whole, totally *containing* onself and others.[45] That is, I think, a major contribution to the epistemology of natural law, one that has received little if any notice heretofore.

This culturally internal need to constitute some sort of *human* commonality eventually led to a new view of *ius gentium*, which was constituted after *ius gentium* ceased to function as a real institution of Roman law. In this later view, *ius* gentium came to mean those political practices that seemed to be commonly practiced by all the nations.[46] So, whereas in the early view, *ius gentium* might be termed "Roman law *for* the (conquered) nations," in the later view, it might be termed "the law *among* the nations themselves" (*inter*-national). It is now what can be located *between* them.

Here is where *ius naturale* receives a constitution that is abstracted *out of* a historical matrix. It is not a transcendental constitution of an ideal law under which any real law is subordinate, that is, whose validity is derived therefrom.[47] This latter approach, as we saw above, creates many of the very problems that have afflicted natural law when constituted by philosophers. It is necessary, instead, to abstract a notion of nature and the law to which it is related in order to explain how the commonality inherent in *ius gentium* is real and enduring and not just contrived or accidental, that is, ephemerally mutable. Thus the move from *ius civile* to *ius naturale* has been mediated by the concept of *ius gentium*. That is an extremely important point for our inquiry because it is an attempt to constitute a universal sphere on one's own cultural horizon without attempting the impossible task of constituting a universal whole to totally contain one's cultural matrix and all others as well, a whole transcending any time or place, what Thomas Nagel has aptly called "the view from nowhere."[48] The sphere of the universal is constituted as a consequence of

---

[45] See above, pp. 19f.   [46] See Ulpian in *Digest*, 1.1.1.

[47] Thus, contra Thomas Aquinas (*Summa Theologiae*, 2/1, q. 95, a. 4), *ius gentium* is not "derived (*derivatur*) by way of a conclusion that is not very remote from its [natural law's] principles" (*Basic Writings of Thomas Aquinas* I, ed. A. Pegis [New York, 1945], 789).

[48] *The View from Nowhere* (New York, 1986).

the constitution of a comparative dimension. Ironically enough, a concept like that of *ius gentium*, which was developed in the context of Roman imperialism, provides us with a more modest philosophical handle on the question of universality than could be provided by the philosophers.

The efforts of the Roman jurisprudents, however, were quite vague when they tried to constitute *ius naturale*. That might well be so because like most contemporary jurisprudents (let alone virtually all practicing lawyers and judges) they were not that much interested in such abstract, theoretical questions. Moreover, their vagueness also might well be attributed to the influence of the thinking of the Stoics on the question of natural law. But the Stoics themselves – even that most philosophical of the Roman lawyers, Cicero – were quite vague about what they meant by such terms as "right reason" (*recta ratio*).[49] That vagueness was due, I think, to the inability of the Stoics to develop an adequate teleology and the adequate theology it seems to require. That is why natural law theorists in the Middle Ages, once they were able to retrieve Aristotle's political theory, and especially his metaphysics, quickly adopted his more illuminating categories over those of the Stoics.

The search for *ius naturale*, however vague it might have been in the Roman context, did bequeath at least one very important thing for our own inquiry into natural law. That is, it implied that when one looks for some commonality among the foreign communities with which one has to intelligently work out a *modus vivendi* to live in peace with them, one must also constitute what his or her own community has in common with them essentially. And for that commonality to be truly intelligible, it must be seen as rooted in nature, which is a sphere which *every* community must see as its precondition for emergence in the world. This happens when thinkers in that community engage in true cultural introspection, namely, reflection on the natural conditions that make the emergence of their own culture possible.

That consideration begins, as we have seen, with the consti-

---

[49] See *De Legibus*, 1.7ff.

tution of a horizon on which *others* can properly appear.[50]
Initially, when taking a *ius gentium* type perspective, that horizon
is constituted as a foreground. It is what is intended to lie
outside of us; it *confronts* us here and now. But when we move
deeper, from a *ius gentium* type perspective to a *ius naturale* type
perspective, we begin to constitute that horizon as a background. It is what is intended to lie antecedent to us, *behind* us
as it were. It is *ius naturale* type questioning that leads us to
inquire into our own origins, that is, into those intelligible
preconditions that have enabled one's own community to both
appear and endure in the world.[51] Accordingly, these origins
ever accompany the historical development of the community.
To bury them and forget them is to lose one's communal
bearings in a fundamental sense; it is to become truly disor-
iented in the world. Therefore, the question of *ius naturale*, as
we have appropriated the concept at this point of our inquiry,
involves the question of the interrelation of nature and history,
and the question of the interrelation of externality and origin
on the horizon of our own tradition.

At this point, having learned a good deal from Roman law,
we can take what we have learned back home to the realm of
Judaism. For the question of nature and history and the
question of externality and origin are more richly constituted
for all those interested in natural law by the theological
constitution of the interrelation of the events of creation and
revelation and, subsequently, by the philosophical constitution
of the ideas of nature and history.

CREATION AND REVELATION

As Franz Rosenzweig taught modern Jewish theology quite
well, any aspect of Judaism is best understood when seen within
the interrelation of three events: creation, revelation, and

---

[50] See above, pp. 9ff. My use of the term "horizon" is quite close to Husserl's use of it.
See *Ideas*, trans. W. R. Boyce Gibson (New York, 1962), 2.27.
[51] By "origin" I mean what Hermann Cohen called *Ursprung*, and what Aristotle called
archē (see *Logik der reinen Erkenntnis*, 3rd edn [Berlin, 1922], 79; *Metaphysics*, 1012b35ff.).
It is to be contrasted with *Anfang*, which is a point which is already within one's own
history.

redemption.[52] However, if an event is something which one experiences, that is, something with which one can be cotemporaneous, then the only one of these "events" that so qualifies as a literal *event* is revelation. Creation as primal origin is necessarily prior to the experience of any creature. It is an experience only God could have. And redemption as the ultimate end of history is neither the experience of humans nor even of God because it has not happened at all to anyone yet. It is only within the reach of God's action.[53] No one is or has ever been contemporaneous with it. Creation is humanly irretrievable past; redemption is humanly unattainable future.[54]

Revelation is God's presence to us, with us, and for us. Its is the ever-present giving of the Torah (*mattan torah*) to Israel.[55] As such, it must always be our fundamental standpoint in the present when looking at either the past or the future. Initially, Torah is the point from which we look for our retrievable past, that is, what we have from tradition (*masoret*).[56] And it is the point from which we look for our attainable future, that is, what we can reasonably anticipate in this world.[57] But, more profoundly, Torah is the point from which we look for our irretrievable past, which is creation, and for our unattainable future, which is redemption.[58]

Any Jewish universalism must be constituted by reference to a primordial origin or to an eschatological consummation. The idea of natural law does figure in the interrelation of revelation and redemption, namely, when the universality of

---

[52] See *The Star of Redemption*, 250. [53] See B. Berakhot 34b re Isaiah 64:3.

[54] That is why the investigation of these matters is dangerous to those who are not spiritually prepared for their profundity (see M. Hagigah 2.1 and Maimonides, *Commentary on the Mishnah* thereon).

[55] Rosenzweig better than anyone else showed how revelation must be understood as presence/present (*Gegenwart/Heutigkeit*) and not as a historical memory. See *The Star of Redemption*, 177; also *Sifre*: Devarim, no. 33 re Deut. 6:6; Novak, *The Election of Israel*, 151f.

[56] See e.g. Y. Pesahim 6.1/33a; Temurah 16a.

[57] See e.g. M. Avot 2.12 (the statement of R. Simon) and Maimonides, *Commentary on the Mishnah* thereon. Such reasonable anticipation is the basis of virtually all rabbinic legislation, which is made on the anticipation of what people are likely (*shema*) to do in the imminent future (see e.g. B. Avodah Zarah 36a–b).

[58] See B. Eruvin 13b; M. Sanhedrin 10.1.

nature and the substance of history finally become one.[59] But its main function comes out of the interrelation of revelation and creation, when nature and history are still separate and distinct. For only this interrelation is connected to our present experience.

The great mistake of what I have called etho-centric (usually liberal) modern Jewish thought has been its grounding of revelation in the world.[60] This modern world is taken to be what human reason (or consciousness for those thinkers less rationalistic) can readily bring to presence. Revelation, then, becomes the epitome of human effort itself. But that has fundamentally confused what we can learn for ourselves with what God alone can teach us. Furthermore, liberal Jewish thought has reduced revelation to redemption by constituting it as potential for human progress.[61] But that conflation has confused what we can do for ourselves with what only God can do for us. Authentic Jewish eschatology is not to be confused with Utopianism.[62] Thus by identifying revelation essentially with natural law instead of seeing natural law functioning at the juncture of revelation and creation, liberal Jewish theology has confused the necessary distinctions and interrelations between all three prime events Judaism affirms.

Because the nature from which we learn natural law is rooted in irretrievable creation, it is not simply what we ourselves can simply bring to presence. Nature is not an object right before us about which we can argue using the truth

[59] That is best expressed by the verse that, in the Jewish liturgy, has become the anticipation of redemption in the *alenu* prayer that concludes almost every service, namely, "And the Lord shall be king over all the earth; on that day he shall be unique (*ehad*) and so shall his name" (Zechariah 14:9). Thus the historical/political order will be fully ruled by God *then* as the physical/natural order is ruled by God *now* (see *Sifre: Devarim*, no. 31/end). That will be accomplished by God apocalyptically. Conversely, one can see Hegel's notion of the ultimate unity of nature (*Ansichsein*) and history (*Fürsichsein*) effected by the self-development of reason (of which human reason is our only example) as being the major expression of the modern attempt to secularize the ancient eschatological hope (see *Phenomenology of Spirit*, preface, trans. A. V. Miller [Oxford, 1977], 11). Cf. Novak, *The Election of Israel*, 152ff.

[60] See above, pp. 82ff.

[61] See Hermann Cohen, *Religion of Reason out of the Sources of Judaism*, trans. S. Kaplan (New York, 1972), 250.

[62] See e.g. B. Kiddushin 39b; Hullin 142a.

criteria of correspondence. It is something that can only be grasped abstractly from within our historical present, a present whose content is continually provided by revelation. The truth criterion here is much more one of coherence.[63] This is especially so when we speak of nature in the context of human action inasmuch as the truth of practical reason is character-ized much more by coherence than by correspondence.[64]

Nature is not the ground of history any more than revelation is derived from creation. Yet created nature is vital, and to eliminate concern with it is to lose something essential in the covenant. To eliminate a distinct concern with it is to confine God's relation to the world to God's relationship with Israel. When this is done, as indeed it was done by the kabbalists, one loses any Jewish constitution of nature and natural law because, in effect, there is no constitution of the external world. It is no accident, then, that there is nothing even resembling the idea of natural law in Kabbalah.[65]

So, if created nature is not the ground of revelation nor is it reduced to revelation, just what is its relation to revelation? I would answer that creation and its order, that is, nature, is the necessary precondition for revelation to occur. Just what does this mean?

When we speak of nature in natural law, we are primarily concerned with human nature, namely, those structures that make authentic human life possible. It is a *conditio sine qua non*. When we speak of revelation, we are primarily concerned with God's address to a historical human community, God's speaking with the community for the sake of their mutual and ongoing relationship, which is the covenant. Only secondarily and derivatively do we intend something essentially nonhuman when we say "nature;" and only secondarily and derivatively do we intend an individual Jew when we say "revelation."[66] Nonhuman nature is minimally the wider physical support for human nature, which we subsequently constitute.[67] The indi-

---

[63] See Novak, *Jewish Social Ethics*, 76ff.   [64] See Plato, *Crito*, 46B, 48A–D.
[65] See Novak, *The Image of the Non-Jew in Judaism*, 268.
[66] See e.g. B. Rosh Hashanah 18a re Deut. 4:7 and Isaiah 55:6.
[67] See Gen. 8:22–9:7 and *Beresheet Rabbah* 34.11.

vidual Jew is one who is to personally internalize what has been
given to the community and to develop its meaning for them.
Even Moses' solitariness is for the sake of Israel.[68] Therefore,
the juncture of revelation and creation is human community.
This is where revelation is to occur in the world. Indeed, since
revelation is God's speech to humans in their own language,
where else could it possibly occur except within a real human
community in history?[69] Wittgenstein was right when he
insisted there are no private languages.[70]

Accordingly, natural law or its equivalent is what a number
of more rationalistically inclined thinkers within the Jewish
tradition have seen as something that had to be in place for
Israel to be enough of a human community, with insight into
the nature of human sociality, to be able to accept the Torah
from God. Only then can their existing polity be elevated and

[68] See Exod. 32:32 and B. Rosh Hashanah 16b.
[69] This point is based on the rabbinic principle "the Torah speaks as does human
language" (*dibrah torah ke-lashon benei adam*). In its original presentation, it expresses
the view of R. Ishmael that Scripture speaks as does ordinary human language,
including repetition of words for rhetorical effect (see *Sifre*: Bemidbar, no. 112 re
Num. 15:31; Y. Shabbat 19.2/17a; also Gersonides [Ralbag], *Commentary on the Torah*:
Exodus – Pequdei [end], ed. Venice, 116a). For the classic study of the theological
roots of this view and the opposing one of R. Akibah, see the two-volume work of
my late revered teacher Abraham Joshua Heschel, *Torah min ha-Shamayim b'Ispaqlaryah shel ha-Dorot* (London, 1962), esp. I:3ff. Later, rationalist Jewish theologians like
Maimonides invoked this principle to justify Scripture's use of anthropomorphic
language to describe the acts of God. Thus the exoteric language of Scripture is for
ordinary believers, who can only think imaginatively about anything, even about
God, whereas only extraordinary believers can understand the deeper, esoteric
meaning of the text (see *Mishneh Torah*: Yesodei ha- Torah, 1.9ff.; *Guide*, 1.26, 33, 46).
But, even for Maimonides, Scripture in general speaks as does human language
because the Torah is a created entity (*Guide*, 1.65), hence *in the world*, where human
language is the only vehicle to intelligibility available. The specific difference is
between ordinary and extraordinary human language, the latter being occasionally
used in Scripture and, therefore, to be interpreted literally, unlike the former, which
is used more often and is to be interpreted figuratively (see e.g. *Mishneh Torah*:
Yesodei ha- Torah, 1.8; Teshuvah, 5.1ff.). Despite my own differences with Maimonides over where exactly to draw the line between literal and figurative meaning
in Scripture (see *The Election of Israel*, 200ff., 225ff., 262f.), I accept the general
premise underlying his whole view of language, namely, that the language of
revelation must be one already employed in the world.
[70] See *Philosophical Investigations*, 2nd edn, trans. G. E. M. Anscombe (New York, 1958),
1.242ff.; also R. Rhees, "Can There Be a Private Language?" in *Wittgenstein the
Philosophical Investigations*, ed. G. Pitcher (Garden City, N.Y., 1966), 267ff. See above,
p. 19.

become a holy people, God's portion in the world. Creation is
not only for the sake of revelation, which would mean that it is
solely for the sake of man; indeed, solely for the sake of Israel.
The author of Job dispelled the notion of the anthropocentric
character of creation in God's speech to Job out of the whirl-
wind. "Where were you when I laid the foundation of the
world?" (Job 38:4). And Amos dispelled the notion of the
Israelocentric character of history when he spoke God's word
to Israel saying, "Did I not bring Israel up out of Egypt, but
also the Philistines from Caphtor and the Arameans from
Kir?" (Amos 9:7) Created nature is more than just potential for
revelation, which would totally subsume it within a particular
revelation. Instead, created nature is the sphere of finite human
possibilities, some of which are realized in history by revelation
and its content. But, and here the comparative dimension of
natural law thinking enters the picture, one can see these finite
human possibilities being realized in other historical communities as well as in Israel.[71]

The interest in creation and its structures from the standpoint of Jewish revelation is minimally that creation makes it
possible for that revelation to occur within its sphere. Maimonides speaks of the Torah as not natural but "entering into
nature."[72] This is what enables Israel to accept God's law,
which would be unintelligible if she were not aware of law's
initial function as a natural limit on human projection. Natural
law, then, is the recognition of the normative significance of the
limits of nature. It can only operate in human community; any
use of it elsewhere is metaphorical. That is how the normative
idea of nature functions. It is not a name for the sum of all
phenomena but, rather, it is the name for that which functions
as a limit on the chaotic expansion of activity that regards all
limits as mere obstacles to be overcome because they all can be
overcome. Such frantic activity is fueled by the illusion of

[71] See D. Novak, *Jewish–Christian Dialogue* (New York, 1989), 129ff.
[72] *Guide of the Perplexed*, 2.40. I am here using Maimonides' statement in a way he
himself probably did not mean it (see Novak, *The Image of the Non-Jew in Judaism*,
290ff.); nevertheless, his phraseology as I have appropriated it here does express
with beautiful precision a fundamental doctrine found in rabbinic theology. See
above, p. 29.

invulnerable immortality by essentially fallible, finite creatures, who continually hope to be immortal and invulnerable like the God who made them.[73] Natural law emerges when humans realize that all their historical acts have limits just as human life itself has an outer limit. Only with this recognition can the world be cosmos.[74] Since leaving the Garden of Eden, our mortality and all that it entails is part of our continuing process of the de-*finition* of ourselves in the world.[75]

In the next chapter, we shall explore how the idea of natural law as created limit functions in a theory of the horizons of Judaism, especially as that pertains to human personhood and its rights.

[73] See Gen. 3:3–5 and *Beresheet Rabbah* 19.4.
[74] See Reinhold Niebuhr, *The Nature and Destiny of Man* I (New York, 1941), 251ff.
[75] See *Beresheet Rabbah* 9.5 re Gen. 1:31 and Ezek. 28:13.

CHAPTER 6

Noahide law and human personhood

This is the record of human progeny: On the day God
created man, in the likeness of God He made him, male
and female He created them.
(Genesis 5:1–2)

NOAHIDE LAW

The debates over natural law in the Jewish tradition have
inevitably become debates over the meaning of the Noahide
laws. The Noahide laws or "the seven commandments of the
children of Noah" (*sheva mitsvot benei Noah*) are those norms the
Rabbis considered to be binding on all humankind, who,
following scriptural narrative, are the descendants of Noah.
They are the survivors of the universal cataclysm of the Flood.
In the version of these laws in the Tosefta and the Talmud, they
are presented in the following order: (1) the requirement to
establish a judicial system in society (*dinim*); (2) the prohibition
of blasphemy (*birkat ha-shem*); (3) the prohibition of idolatry
(*avodah zarah*); (4) the prohibition of wanton destruction of
human life (*shefikhut damim*); (5) the prohibition of adultery,
incest, homosexuality, and bestiality (*gillui arayot*); (6) the prohibition of robbery (*gezel*); (7) the prohibition of eating a limb
torn from a living animal (*ever min ha-hai*).[1]

Those who have argued against natural law in Judaism have
characterized this doctrine of Noahide law, in one way or

---

[1] T. Avodah Zarah 8.4; B. Sanhedrin 56a. Note another version of the order of the
Noahide laws, that of R. Isaac (*ibid.*, 56b), which lists the prohibition of idolatry as
the first commandment. This order is followed by Maimonides (*Mishneh Torah*:
Melakhim, 9.1), who, undoubtedly, wanted to further emphasize the theological
foundation of all law. See above, pp. 132ff.

another, as a Jewish version of *ius gentium*.[2] What they have
meant, whether they actually use the term *ius gentium* or not, is
the original meaning of *ius gentium* that we saw in the previous
chapter, namely, law made by Romans for non-Romans over
whom they had political power, thus being a judicial policy for
the resident-aliens.[3] So, for them, Noahide law is law made (or
enforced) by Jews for non-Jews. But this interpretation of the
doctrine is implausible.

Unlike the Romans who created the real, practical institution
of *ius gentium*, the Rabbis who formulated the doctrine of
Noahide law did not have any such power over any group of
non-Jews. That is why we have no record in rabbinic texts of
any actual case being adjudicated under Noahide law.[4] (The
biblical institution of the *ger*, meaning a resident-alien, had long
since ceased to operate when the doctrine of the Noahide and
Noahide law were formulated.) Hence, the attempt of some
contemporary Jewish scholars to speak of a "Noahide Code,"
as if this were simply one more department of operative
Halakhah, is inaccurate and highly misleading.[5] Furthermore,
without there being any Jewish power over non-Jews, why
would any non-Jew choose to be ruled by Jewish law but not
have all the rights that fully Jewish status, gainable by means of
conversion (*gerut*), would afford? And in the Middle Ages, when
the category of the Noahide was helpful to Jews in their
dealings with Christians and Muslims, who were deemed to be
on a higher moral level than the ancient pagans, Noahide law
was viewed much more like the later meaning of *ius gentium* in
Roman law, namely, points in common between *ius civile* (for
which the Jewish analogue is the Torah: Scripture and Rabbinic Tradition) and the actual practices of the gentiles at hand.
It did not represent Jewish might *over* the gentiles but, rather,
Jewish recognition of right, that is, moral/legal commonality
among diverse communities in humankind.[6] As for the real

2 See Boaz Cohen, *Jewish and Roman Law* I (New York, 1966), 26f.
3 Above, pp. 139f.
4 See D. Novak, *The Image of the Non-Jew in Judaism* (New York and Toronto, 1983), 28ff.
5 See e.g. J. David Bleich, *Contemporary Halakhic Problems* I (New York, 1977), 315f.
6 See D. Novak, *Jewish–Christian Dialogue* (New York, 1989), 141ff.

power Jews do have over non-Jews in the State of Israel today, that power is structured by a totally secular system of law, one whose ties to classical Jewish law are at most highly selective.[7]

The rabbinic presentation of these laws attempts to derive them from actual scriptural statements that seem to be about humankind *per se*. Nevertheless, it has long been recognized that the use of these verses does not mean that they are regarded as the actual sources of these laws but, rather, they are used as allusions (*asmakhta*) at best.[8] In other words, the Rabbis were engaged more in speculating about the overall teaching of Scripture and its analogues in the outside world than they were engaged in strictly legal exegesis when they were developing the doctrine of Noahide law.

The speculative character of rabbinic thought on the issue of Noahide law, of course, strengthens the case of those who have argued for natural law in Judaism, and who have located natural law primarily in the doctrine of Noahide law. For if the Noahide laws have never been a vehicle of real Jewish political power over any other, non-Jewish community, and if these laws are basically imagined (that is, abstracted from generalizations) rather than strictly derived from specific authoritative texts, then what else could they be except the product of speculation? And that, as we have indeed been seeing, is how natural law thinking operates. It is an integral part of a philosophy of the law. Noahide law functions more as a system of principles than it does as an actual body of rules. This is brought out by the very generality of these seven laws; they are more like categories than like immediately prescriptive precepts.[9]

We have seen in the last chapter that there are two ways of engaging in natural law thinking. One way, which is epitomized by Saadiah and Maimonides, is to speculate teleologically, namely, to reflect on what the ends of law are and how natural law precepts are the proper means to fulfill them.[10] The

---

[7] See Menachem Elon, *Jewish Law* IV, trans. B. Auerbach and M. J. Sykes (Philadelphia and Jerusalem, 1994), 1620ff.

[8] See R. Judah Halevi, *Kuzari*, 3.73; R. Bahya ben Asher, *Commentary on the Torah*: Gen. 2:16.

[9] See Novak, *The Image of the Non-Jew in Judaism*, 46, n. 110.

[10] Above, pp. 125ff.

"nature" in *natural* law in this way of thinking is an all-
encompassing whole, each of whose parts is a good attracting
intelligent human action. The other way, which I began to
present in that chapter, is to reflect on the inherent negative
limits of the human condition and to see law as the way of
practically affirming the truth of that limitation of a finite
creature, a limitation apprehended by its intelligence. The
"nature" in *natural* law in this way of thinking is internal
structure, that is, what limits personal and communal pretensions.[11]

The actual content of the law comes from specific positive
law-making. It is the ordering of the singular substance of a
historical culture for the sake of those ends the authorities in
that culture see as good and thus truly worthy of its members,
ends about which the members of the community can be
persuaded. In Judaism, those ends are covenantal. Natural law
is a contributing factor in that law-making, but it is never the
only factor. Hence natural law does not function as the
normative whole of which positive law is the applied part
thereof. Positive law is not deduced from natural law, but is
only explained and guided by it. Its function, then, is essentially
heuristic. Accordingly, even when natural law is invoked as the
teleological justification for some positive legislation, as in cases
of the invocation of the principle of the common good, that
invocation is penultimate.[12] That is, the common good is
instrumental; it is for the sake of the real ultimate ends of *that*
community.[13] Neither negative limits nor positive means are
those ultimate ends. And the difference between them is that
the negative limits are more general than the positive means;
hence they are more abstract and so more easily recognizable
as natural law.

---

[11] Thus natural law is a limit (*peras*), but not a *telos*. Borrowing from Aristotle: every
telos is a *peras*, but not every *peras* is a *telos*. See *Metaphysics*, 1022a14.

[12] Thus invocation of the principle of *tiqqun olam*, which is the rabbinic equivalent of
bonum commune, always turns out to be for the ultimate sake of covenantal ends. See
e.g. M. Gittin 4.1ff; B. Ketubot 56b; also D. Novak, *Jewish Social Ethics* (New York,
1992), 206ff.

[13] For the difference between instrumental/penultimate ends and noninstrumental/
ultimate ends, see Aristotle, *Nicomachean Ethics*, 1094a1ff.

The relation of negative form and positive content might be illumined if we recall how Aristotle constituted the relation of justice (*dikaisynē*) and friendship (*philia*). Justice is the overall minimal structure required for any interhuman relationship worthy of its human members.[14] Friendship is the actual content of such relationships at the direct personal level. But, whereas the most basic forms of justice might be taken as universal, the highest form of friendship, which for Aristotle is when two persons share qualities they both regard as good, depends to a large extent on what their own culture specifically values as good.[15] Whatever law could contribute to this positive state of human affairs would have to be based on the lawgiver's vision of the specific goals of the culture in which he or she lives.[16]

In the first way of thinking, the locus of concern in natural law theory is with the question of *good*, that is, the positive state of affairs for which humans are to ultimately act. In the second way of thinking, however, the locus of concern is with the question of *truth*, which, in its critical function, is primarily a negation of the arrogant pretensions of humans acting as if they themselves were infinite. Therefore, it stands to reason that the first, more positive view of natural law will assign a more maximal role to it in Judaism, whereas the second, more negative view will assign a more minimal role to it.

Although teleology is necessarily connected to natural law theory, and we shall return to it in the latter half of this chapter, the more minimal view of natural law that I propose requires that we first look at the more negative rather than the more

---

[14] *Ibid.*, 1155a25ff. That is why Aristotle admits the possibility of at least some universal standards of justice (*ibid.*, 1134b20ff.).

[15] See *ibid.*, 1156b8ff.; also *Politics*, 1280a25ff. Following this last reference, one could say that if for Aristotle "friendship is the highest form of justice" (*Nicomachean Ethics*, 1155a28), then that justice is the more specific distributive justice rather than the more general rectifying justice (see *ibid.*, 1130b30).

[16] See *ibid.*, 1155a22, where Aristotle recognizes the universality of the need for friendship (*philia*), but then, more specifically, concentrates on the lawgivers of the *polis*. But their criteria of *philia* would certainly be different from that of the lawgivers of other societies and cultures, who have other values. Let it be remembered that the *polis* is a uniquely Greek form of polity. Aristotle's constitution of *philia* presupposes the reality of the *polis*. See Alasdair MacIntyre, *Whose Justice? Which Rationality?* (Notre Dame, 1988), 103ff.

positive character of Noahide law. And here I think that the data from the rabbinic sources are more supportive of this view than of the more teleological views. Also, this view seems to have more in common with modern "rights-talk" than does more metaphysically constituted natural law theory. That is important because this commonality enables Jewish insights into law and morality to be more easily introduced into current normative discourse, in which the language of rights seems to supply some of its most indispensable vocabulary.[17] That is, unless, of course, dogmatic secularism and the atheism it presupposes are also required for one's views to receive a hearing in the secular sphere – a question we examined in the first chapter.[18]

As even our cursory presentation of the Noahide laws above indicates, six are negative and only one positive. Moreover, the positive one, namely, the requirement to establish a judicial system, is actually for the sake of the adjudication of cases involving the other six, negative precepts. In other words, it is a procedure that functions as a means to the actual social enforcement of the six others.[19] Therefore, it is reasonable to inquire into the essentially negative character of this whole doctrine. And this has a close connection to one of the main features of modern rights-talk.

NOAHIDE LAW AND RIGHTS

It is accepted by most scholars that the impetus to modern theories of rights, especially their minimalism, is the impasse created by the religious wars that began in the sixteenth century in Europe. These wars seemed to have been based on competing claims about what is totally good for human beings, especially in their political arrangements. Civil society was being torn apart, with no end in sight, by the passions these incommensurate views of total human good elicited. Europeans concerned about the peace and welfare of their

---

[17] See Charles Taylor, *Sources of the Self* (Cambridge, Mass., 1989), 11ff.
[18] Above, pp. 12ff.
[19] See H. L. A. Hart, *The Concept of Law* (Oxford, 1961), 94ff.

societies, which were becoming increasingly complex both culturally and religiously, were becoming quite sick of this continuing state of war. They were very much ready for a more radical solution than the *status quo ante.* The emphasis of human rights over natural (and supernatural) goods was the way that was theoretically suggested to get out of this intolerable political conundrum.

The notion of basic human rights, enunciated by philosophers from John Locke to John Rawls, has usually been argued as follows. Since secular society is more and more composed of the members of different subgroups (what we called "communities" in the first chapter), there cannot be agreement on what the common good is to be. The incommensurate claims of each respective view of human good do not lend themselves to any higher criterion that could judge which is true and which is false. Ultimately, of course, competing claims about human good are competing claims about what the final ends of human existence truly are.

Because of this, a seemingly more modest tack has been suggested, namely, to bracket all questions of fundamental human good and concentrate on those minimal conditions that enable otherwise differing persons to at least live in peace together and to pursue their own respective visions of what the good is *for them.*[20] That was to be done basically *by themselves,* that is, in some sort of private space. The minimal public, social requirement to be contracted was that no one person or group of persons (that is, a community) dedicated to its singular vision of final human good be allowed to prevent any other similar group from pursuing its own vision of that final good. Rights are the criteria by which social peace is to be maintained by respecting the private space of every person and group. As such, it seems to be radically pluralistic.

Moreover, as we saw in the first chapter, many Jews took this as the necessary rationale for the constitution of a secular society in which they could become full members without a detour through somebody else's religion, especially Christianity.

[20] See John Rawls, *A Theory of Justice* (Cambridge, Mass., 1971), 31, 396ff.

In such a society tolerance was to be extended to anyone who was respectful of basic human rights and the minimal law enacted to protect these rights. Hence a minority no longer had to bargain or beg to be "tolerated" by a capricious majority.[21]

It is unfortunate that too many people believe that the acceptance of a rights-based society requires for its proper theory the dogmatic secularism and even the atheism that seem to characterize its most prominent proponents. But this is not the time and the place to argue an alternative view of rights; that I hope to do in a future work. What I want to do here and now is suggest at least that the doctrine of Noahide law, when constituted by a Jewish theory of natural law, has many of the strengths of this rights-based approach. That is so precisely because of its minimalism and its pluralism, something quite different from the metaphysically constituted teleologies that characterize the other two basic theories of natural law in the Jewish tradition.

THE NOAHIDE

We have seen that a theory of natural law requires the two dimensions we saw in the thinking of the later Roman jurisprudents about *ius gentium*. These two dimensions are the comparative and the ontological.

In the comparative dimension, certain basic commonalities between one's own system of law and that of others are discovered. This commonality, when recognized, can become the basis for officially constructing a sphere of truly reciprocal, moral relations between communities. And these moral, reciprocal relations are to be sharply distinguished from the more usual relations between communities, relations of dominance and subservience, which is the stuff of war and conquest.

This aspect of natural law thinking became the foundation of the development of modern international law, as seen in the pioneering work of the seventeenth-century Dutch Calvinist jurist and legal theorist Hugo Grotius. And, as several Jewish

---

[21] Above, pp. 1ff.

scholars have been proud to point out, Grotius saw the doctrine of Noahide law as a precedent for his own theorizing about international law.[22] However, his assumption was that this natural law theory could be totally separated from theology, as evidenced by his assertion that one could adhere to natural law "even if we were to say there is no God" (*etiamsi daremus non esse Deum*).[23] Unfortunately, this limited his ability to see the ontological dimension of natural law thinking. For in that dimension, the cosmic relation of nature and law, where neither term is a metaphor, ultimately requires the affirmation of a cosmic lawgiver, who is simultaneously the creator of nature.[24] To a large extent, then, Grotius and those who have followed him have become fixated in the comparative dimension of natural law thinking. So, even though Jews might be flattered by his early recognition of our natural law tradition, we cannot learn all that much from him in our development of it, a development that I would argue can only be a theological enterprise.

It is only in the ontological dimension, which is the order of things or *nature*, where this commonality is to be discovered. And, considering my critique of the natural law thinking of Saadiah and that of Maimonides in the last chapter, precisely because of their respective teleological metaphysics, I must reiterate at this point in our inquiry the distinction between "metaphysics" and "ontology" made earlier. They are not identical and, therefore, they are not synonyms for me.[25] "Metaphysics," in my use of the term, is only one type of ontology, one that makes certain assumptions about universal teleology. It is basically wed to the thinking of Plato and, especially, Aristotle.[26] This can be done in various ways, as we have seen in the differences between the teleology of Saadiah

---

[22] See e.g. Hermann Cohen, *Religion of Reason out of the Sources of Judaism*, trans. S. Kaplan (New York, 1972), 124.
[23] *De Jure Belli et Pacis*, prol., 11. Nevertheless, Grotius himself was certainly no atheist. See Anton-Hermann Chroust, "Hugo Grotius and the Scholastic Natural Law Tradition," *The New Scholasticism* 17 (1943), 126ff.
[24] See above, pp. 123f.   [25] Above, p. 26, n. 44.
[26] See Martin Heidegger, *Being and Time*, sec. 6, trans. J. Stambaugh (Albany, N.Y., 1996), 17ff.

and that of Maimonides. But metaphysics is not the only way to constitute the ontological foundation needed by a sufficient natural law theory. The ontology that I think best serves a Jewish natural law theory is a theology of creation, and one that is not teleological like that of Saadiah. (As for Maimonides, how distinct his metaphysical affirmation of creation is from a neo-Platonic theory of emanation is a point to seriously ponder.[27])

The idea of the Noahide, the subject of Noahide law, an idea which we find invoked in a number of ways in rabbinic texts, partakes of both the comparative and the ontological dimensions of natural law thinking in its constitution. For the Noahide can be termed both "co-Judaic man" and "pre-Judaic man."[28] That is, the term "Noahide" (*ben Noah*) designates two separate but related statuses.

First, comparatively speaking, it designates the non-Jew actually standing before Jews here and now. The Noahide is the "other" with whom Jews desire to discover some significant commonality without, however, sacrificing the singularity which is theirs because of the covenant or the singularity of the "others" because of their singular cultures. Second, ontologically speaking, the Noahide is the non-Jew, situated in the natural order of creation itself, who the Jews themselves had been before being chosen by God and given his Torah. Indeed, Noahide standards are what first had to be fulfilled in order for Israel to be able to accept revelation and its law with cogency.

Each dimension is necessary for the full understanding of the Noahide as the subject of Noahide, that is, natural, law. For operating within the comparative dimension alone, we are either left with merely descriptive generalities, or we have a superficial, poorly grounded *modus operandi*, one that is like too much of intercommunal "dialogue" today. And thinking within the ontological dimension alone, we tend to constitute natural law from "the top down," so to speak, that is, we require theoretical unanimity on first principles, a complete agreement about the grounds (*ratio essendi*) of the law. That is something

---

[27] See D. Novak, *The Election of Israel* (Cambridge, 1995), 202, n. 6.
[28] See Novak, *The Image of the Non-Jew in Judaism*, xiiiff.

most persons in a pluralistic society are rightly suspicious of. For to insist on a strictly ontological approach to natural law robs us of the opportunity to more immediately appropriate its more modest, but more practically effective, function, which is constituted by employing similarities learned from comparative study of different cultures. Thus the comparative dimension offers natural law more practical strengths; the ontological dimension offers it more theoretical strengths. Since law, certainly Jewish law, combines both strengths in its full operation, a Jewish constitution of natural law must clearly do likewise.

The essential difference between the two basic approaches to natural law in Judaism that we have been examining is in the order of its constitution. That is, should the theoretical dimension be constituted before the practical dimension, or vice versa? In terms of the Noahide, that question becomes: Do we begin exploring the Noahide as pre-Judaic man first and then proceed to exploring the Noahide as co-Judaic man, or vice versa? It is clear that the relation to co-Judaic man is essentially a practical one because he or she is a real person before us. The relation to pre-Judaic man, though, is essentially theoretical because he or she is not a real presence but an abstract idea. As we have seen, there is a fundamental difference between regarding natural law as a sufficient foundation *of* positive law and regarding natural law as an abstraction *from* positive law.[29] The former approach is based on the priority of *theōria* over *praxis*; it is metaphysical. The latter approach is based in the priority of *praxis* over *theōria*. As such, it is ontological but decidedly not metaphysical. As creation theory, it attempts to understand God's founding *praxis*.[30]

To see how the dual character of the Noahide operates, let us look at a rather famous, but often misinterpreted, rabbinic text.

---

[29] See above, pp. 19f.

[30] At this point, I am influenced by Hermann Cohen's assertion that "Praxis ist nicht Theorie. Die Theorie der Praxis aber ist die Philosophie" ("Spinoza über Staat und Religion, Judentum und Christentum," *Jüdische Schriften* III, ed. B. Strauss [Berlin, 1924], 302). I am influenced by its logic, but not by its ontology. Cohen is speaking about the only *praxis* he can accept: *praxis* originally human, but I am speaking about *praxis* originally divine. See above, pp. 113ff.

"'And he said that the Lord came forth from Sinai . . .'
(Deuteronomy 33:2) – When the Holy-One-blessed-be-He ap-
peared (*nigleh*) to give the Torah to Israel, he did not appear to
Israel alone but to all the nations."[31]

The text is frequently misinterpreted as meaning that Israel's
election was contingent on her accepting the Torah from God
freely. However, that meaning has two problematic implications. First, it implies that Israel like the nations of the world
had the real option of either accepting or rejecting the
covenant and its law, and that the existence of the covenant
and the authority of its law depended on that choice. But it
would seem that the great preponderance of scriptural and
rabbinic teaching is that Israel had no such choice.[32] Instead,
she could accept the covenant and develop its life together with
God, or she could reject the covenant and have it imposed
upon her by God anyway. Secondly, it implies that the nations
of the world had the real option of accepting or rejecting the
Torah before it was actually given to Israel. Now while there
are some rabbinic texts that indicate that the gentiles knew
about the Sinai revelation, these same texts also assume that
their knowledge of that revelation was after the Torah had
already been given to Israel.[33] Thus, in effect, they had to learn
it from Israel. Furthermore, whereas Israel could not have
rejected the Torah with impunity or have nullified the covenant
either at Sinai or any other time, it seems that the other nations
do have the option of rejecting the covenant with impunity.
Hence there is no norm that makes conversion to Judaism a
requirement, which is a point that well explains the fact that
the acceptance of converts does not entail for Jews any legal
obligation, or even for most Jews any theological impetus, to
proselytize non-Jews.[34]

This misinterpretation of the seminal rabbinic text about the
giving and acceptance of the Torah at Sinai needs to be

[31] *Sifre*: Devarim, no. 343, ed. Finkelstein, 396f. See Novak, *The Image of the Non-Jew in Judaism*, 257ff.
[32] See Jon D. Levenson, *Creation and the Persistence of Evil* (San Francisco, 1988), 141.
[33] See B. Kiddushin 31a re Ps. 138:4. Also see T. Sotah 8.6 and B. Sotah 35b re Deut. 27:8; Zevahim 116a re Exod. 18:1 (the view of R. Eleazar ha-Modaee).
[34] See Novak, *The Election of Israel*, 158ff.

explicitly cleared away because it represents so much of the confusion liberal Jewish thinkers have created by their over-emphasis of voluntarism in Judaism and their conflation of the content of revelation with the rational structure of natural law. By clearing away this misinterpretation, we can better see the role natural law plays in Judaism and its proper relation to revelation.

So, if the misinterpretation of the text assumes that Israel has more freedom than she in truth has, and that the nations of the world have more obligation than they in truth have, what is the correct interpretation of all of this? And what does it teach us about natural law in Judaism?

If the text were really talking about the covenant as a matter of a take-it-or-leave-it choice, then it would have made more sense to have the gentiles asking about the specifically Jewish content of the Torah, like the Sabbath and Festivals and like the dietary and clothing prohibitions and like the various kinship arrangements, so that they could make an intelligent choice about becoming something different from what they had been theretofore.[35] Instead, though, the text continues with the Edomites refusing the Torah when they hear that it prohibits murder. The Ammonites and Moabites refuse it because it prohibits incest. And the Ishmaelites refuse it because it prohibits theft. As such, they are not asking about the specifically Jewish content of the Torah but, rather, they are asking about the content of the Noahide laws and, specifically, those of the Noahide laws that govern interhuman relations.[36] Hence, their immediate concern is neither with what is specific-ally Jewish nor with what is essentially theological. Their concern is with morality, especially with the moral norms they find incompatible with their own respective cultures. Even more general questions of theology (like the prohibition of idolatry, which the Rabbis assumed in principle to be universal) are less immediately evident in the constitution of natural law than questions of interhuman morality *per se*.

At this point, we can better understand the question of

[35] See B. Yevamot 47a–b; also Meiri, *Bet ha-Behirah*, thereon, ed. Dickman, 189.
[36] *Sifre*: Devarim, no. 343.

voluntarism that I raised when discussing the misinterpretation
of this rabbinic text. There I pointed out that in the misinterpretation, Israel is attributed more freedom in the covenant
than she in truth has and that the gentiles are attributed more
obligation to the covenant than they in truth have. However,
when it comes to the Noahide laws, especially those that are
immediately moral in their intent, the freedom Israel has and
the obligation the gentiles have essentially coincide. For both
Israel and the gentiles have the free choice to accept or reject
natural law. Without that choice, natural law would not be law
inasmuch as law presupposes persons who are free enough to
either accept it or reject it.[37] But neither Israel nor the gentiles
can reject natural law with impunity. That is why the "acceptance" (*qabbalah*) of Noahide law which the Rabbis mention
when speaking of the gentiles is similar to the "acceptance" of
the Torah by Israel: neither "acceptance" creates the obligation to follow the law.[38] Unlike a contract, such acceptance
only confirms a prior normative order already in place.

The rejection of natural law by a community means that its
law and culture are fundamentally unworthy of the human
persons to whom they are addressed. Such a community is
fundamentally flawed and it suffers accordingly. Being in
violation of *natural* law, that suffering is akin to the suffering of
any natural entity denied the basic conditions it requires for
living well or living at all.

Here we can see the force of the rabbinic text in its
presentation of the basic choice about God's law being given to
the gentiles before it is given to Israel. It is given to the gentiles
before being given to Israel because Israel herself is one of

---

[37] See Maimonides, *Mishneh Torah*: Teshuvah, 5.1ff.
[38] See B. Shabbat 88a re Est. 9:27. The acceptance of the obligation to obey the
Noahide laws by a gentile does ground his or her becoming a resident-alien (*ger
toshav*) in the fully Jewish land of Israel (B. Avodah Zarah 64b; Maimonides, *Mishneh
Torah*: Isurei Bi'ah, 14.7–8; see T. Demai 2.2ff.; Bekhorot 30b; Arakhin 29a). It is
very much like the acceptance of certain responsiblities (*ahr'ayut*) in a contract in
return for certain privileges (see e.g. B. Ketubot 56b and Tos., s.v. "aval"). However,
aside from becoming a resident-alien in the land of Israel, a gentile is obligated to
obey the Noahide laws even if he or she never accepts any such responsibility. The
option is whether to live in this Jewish polity or not, not whether to obey the
Noahide laws or not. Only in the former case is *qabbalah* to be interpreted literally.

these Noahides before she enters the unique covenant with God.[39] Indeed, the acceptance of the Noahide laws is the very precondition for Israel's entrance into the covenant. The nations of the world are thus not condemned for their rejection of the covenant, but they are condemned for their rejection of that which would make the acceptance of any covenant, any true relationship with either other humans or God, possible. So the rabbinic text concludes:

Not only did they not accept it [the Torah], but even the seven commandments which the Noahides accepted upon themselves they were unable to persevere in them, finally casting them off altogether. When the Holy-One-blessed-be-He saw this he therefore gave them to Israel . . . so Israel accepted the Torah with all its ramifications and details, plus (*af*) those seven commandments in which the Noahides were unable to persevere and which they cast off. Israel came and accepted them.[40]

As another version of this legend puts it: "If the seven commandments which the Noahides were commanded and accepted upon themselves, they were unable to persevere in them, how much more so (*qal ve-homer*) could they not persevere in the commandments of the Torah!"[41]

From all of this we learn five main points: (1) Israel's acceptance of the Torah in history presupposes her acceptance of natural law as a requirement of human nature. (2) That human nature and its normative requirement are something she has in common with all the other nations of the world. (3) That commonality is most immediately evident in certain basic moral norms held in common. (4) The commonality of those moral norms means that there are other real historical communities which have accepted these norms for themselves. Not all the nations of the world are viewed by the Jews as being on the same submoral level as are the nations mentioned in the rabbinic text, who were culturally unable to accept even the natural Torah let alone the specifically revealed one.[42] Hence

---

[39] See M. Nedarim 3.11 and B. Nedarim 31a.
[40] *Sifre*: Devarim, no. 343, p. 397.
[41] *Mekhilta*: Yitro, ed. Horovitz-Rabin, 221f.
[42] See e.g. B. Sanhedrin 39a re Ezek. 5:7; 11:12.

the constitution of natural law initially has a ready comparative dimension. (5) Because Israel has so completely accepted the natural law and included it as a standard for guiding her own unique conventual law, she is in a special position to teach the world about natural law.

HUMAN PERSONHOOD

From all that we have been considering so far, one cannot say that Jewish natural law thinking in and of itself produces any independent norms. It functions at the level of principles, not at the level of specific rules themselves. Actual law is always positive law at work with authority in a specific, concrete human community in history.[43] What natural law does is to provide certain general criteria in the form of a *conditio sine qua non* for the formulation of this positive law so that it can have truth value in the world. Thus it is the limit of the law, not its content and not its *telos*.[44] That is why I have been insisting that what is being presented here is a *minimal* natural law theory.

This would seem to imply that we are not at all interested in the question of teleology. However, that would be unacceptable inasmuch as natural law pertains to rational human action as distinct from mere behavior. The distinction between the two is that only rational action requires the acting person to be ever aware of its end when choosing to act or not to act in any specific situation. Thus the limits on human action proposed by natural law must have some connection to the ends proposed by positive law. If not, there is no way of telling whether the content of the positive law will destroy the limits natural law has placed upon it. In other words, to use Hegelian language, natural law must not be *aufgehoben* by positive law. It must not be so transformed by it that it eventually loses its former identity altogether.[45]

So, it seems to me that the best mediating concept for this interrelation is a concept of human personhood inasmuch as

---

[43] Along these lines, see Jacques Ellul, *The Theological Foundation of Law*, trans. M. Wieser (Garden City, N.Y., 1960), 21.

[44] See D. Novak, *Jewish Social Ethics*, 74ff.   [45] See B. Yevamot 22a.

human persons are the subject of both natural law and positive law. To assume that positive law, specifically the positive law of revelation, makes its addressees a new species (rather than members of a new culture) would make any notion of natural law irrelevant to a tradition like Judaism that bases itself on such a revelation. Thus the mediating concept must be a concept of human personhood in which the subject of natural law and the subject of positive law, even positive divine law, retain enough in common to still be considered human persons in a real sense, that is, members of the same species. And that is to be the case despite whatever differences subsequently inter-vene between Israel and the nations of the world in history. Accordingly, history presupposes nature; it does not consume it, however.

The questions now before us in our inquiry into natural law in Judaism are as follows: (1) How does a Jewish idea of human personhood become a matter of teleology? (2) How does a Jewish idea of human personhood intend revelation without being strictly derived from it, a point which alone could make it relevant to natural law and for all those concerned with it?

When we understand the term *end* or *telos* as that which is intended (and thus it is more than a mere spatial or temporal limit), it can have two very different meanings. On the one hand, it can mean a state of being, as when Aristotle says that the end of human life is happiness (*eudaimonia*), which he explains to mean a state of present human activity that requires no external justification.[46] On the other hand, *end* can mean a person, as when Kant says that morality is treating other persons as ends-in-themselves (*Zweck an sich selbst*), which is to say that a person is not to be treated as a means to some*thing* else. That would be the case, though, in any activity in which the personal dignity of any man or woman as a rational, self-legislating being is violated or even ignored.[47]

Here we learn something extremely helpful from Kant, who after all has always been the favorite philosopher of the most modern Jewish thinkers. This requires further inquiry into

---

[46] *Nicomachean Ethics*, 1102a1–4.
[47] *Groundwork of the Metaphysic of Morals*, trans. H. J. Paton (New York, 1964), 101.

what it means to identify the human person as an end of our action.

There is, of course, the need to reject Kant's ethical theory on theological grounds because of its insistence that the rational human subject is the source of its own law (*autonomy*). For that basically contradicts natural law and revealed law, both of which speak of a real, trans-human grounding of the law.[48] Nevertheless, if we shift his specific denotation of person as end-in-itself from the human *subject* of moral action to the human *object* of moral action, something quite helpful emerges for us theologically.

In Kant's own view, the other person who is the object of my moral action is constituted *after* I have constituted myself as a moral subject a priori. This other person, then, is essentially an analogue of my own fully conscious moral personhood.[49] Thus our commonality is our mutual autonomies subsequently inter-acting. Authentic human community, what Kant called a "kingdom of ends" (*Reich der Zwecke*), is simply the projection of what each of us has now going into the future, where we plan to exercise it more fully together.[50] It is in many ways an ontological constitution of the "social contract," whose work-ings we examined in the first chapter.

But what if, by a phenomenological constitution of the moral realm (here following some of the insights of Martin Buber and, especially, Emmanuel Levinas), I discover that the object of my moral concern presents himself or herself to me *before* I have constituted myself as a moral subject?[51] We then have a very different idea of human mutuality and interaction. For here both the source and the end of my action are one and the same by the very act of the other person *presenting* himself or herself to me, without my prior permission as it were.

This other person's very existence (qua source) is attractive (qua end) to me. My existence is the same to him or to her. Our

[48] See A. P. d'Entrèves, *Natural Law* (New York, 1965), 101.

[49] See *Groundwork of the Metaphysic of Morals*, 105f.; cf. Aristotle, *Nicomachean Ethics*, 1166a30ff.

[50] *Groundwork*, 105f.

[51] See Buber, *I and Thou*, trans. W. Kaufmann (New York, 1970), 124ff.; Levinas, *Totality and Infinity*, trans. A. Lingis (Pittsburgh, 1969), 289ff.

mutuality is not something that each of us already has; rather, it is something new and unexpected, wherein we coexist, going together into a largely unpredictable future. Each of us, then, to a certain extent, is a revelation to the other. Furthermore, my constitution of myself as a moral person is not initially based on my inner self-projection but, rather, it is my response to the presence of that other person. Minimally, as we shall see, it is my preparation for such a possible personal presentation. Moral action is reaction; it is essentially response. It is making oneself answerable, a truth well expressed by the German phrase *verantwortlich sein*.

THE IMAGE OF GOD

What is it about the other person that I am to find attractive, which minimally entails that I refrain from harming him or her in any way? What is it about the other person that teaches me the most elementary moral law, which is the most basic human right: "Do not harm me"? Are there not many other persons who are decidedly unattractive, not only aesthetically but morally as well? Can that other person's attractiveness be anything more than his or her good character that I perceive before me? Can the range of existential attraction be more than the objects of my *eros* or those who are deemed to be potential friends (*philoi*) of mine? How can it be extended so as to include those who do not act well for me or for anyone else, and even those who cannot act at all for anyone else, even themselves? None of these questions can be answered satisfactorily by any ethics that attempts to constitute an ontology or philosophical anthropology out of its own operations. It inevitably reduces human existence to the level of the immanent action of the world and thereby obscures the transcendent dimension of human existence in the world and the action that intends its truth.[52]

These questions, it seems to me, are better answered by an ontology and theological anthropology that emerges from the

---

[52] See Novak, *Jewish Social Ethics*, 14ff.

doctrine of creation, specifically the creation of the human person as the *image of God*. Human dignity, which is sufficient to ground the minimal right to life and safety of every descendant of the first humans, means that human beings *are* more than they can ever *do* or *make* of themselves. To understand this, though, requires some philosophical commentary on what is actually meant by asserting "man – male and female – is made in the image of God" (Genesis 5:1).

I think that one can conceive of the image of God both positively and negatively. Each conception of it must be carefully nuanced so that wrong implications are not drawn from either of them.

There has been a whole trend in the history of western theology (both Jewish and Christian, where the *tselem elohim* or *imago Dei* doctrine is explicit) to positively conceive of the image of God as consisting of some quality humans share with God by virtue of a divine transfer at the moment of creation. Going back at least as far as Philo in the first century, many theologians have identified the image of God with reason.[53] Just as God is the rational power in the macrocosmos, so man is the rational power in the microcosmos. Creation in the image of God means, then, that reason is what distinguishes humans from the rest of creation by enabling humans to have something substantial in common with God. This view nicely dovetails with philosophical notions, going back at least as far as Plato, and most widely discussed by the Stoics, that reason is what unites humankind and the gods, and that reason is, therefore, what separates humankind from the animals.[54]

However, in Jewish tradition humankind includes all those born of human parents.[55] Accordingly, this Platonic ontology and its philosophical anthropology are insufficient to ground an ethics that embraces all of humankind so defined. For this anthropology essentially identifies humanity *in se* with reason as

---

[53] See Philo, *Legum Allegoria*, 3.31–132.96; *De Opificio Mundi*, 69; also D. Novak, *Halakhah in a Theological Dimension* (Chico, Calif., 1985), 94ff.
[54] See Plato, *Phaedrus*, 248A; *Theatetus*, 176A–B; Aristotle, *Nicomachean Ethics*, 1177b25–1178a8; Epictetus, *Discourses*, 1.9; Cicero, *De Legibus*, 1.7.23.
[55] See e.g. M. Niddah 5.3.

opposed to more modestly seeing reason as an excellence to be developed by humans whenever they can and as much as they can. It provides no way of designating those of human*kind* who are without this property as essentially participating in human community. In our day, especially, when essential humanness is denied by some to those at the edges of human life – the unborn, the permanently and severely retarded, the irrevocably comatose – such an ontology and its anthropology are inconsistent with the whole thrust of the Jewish tradition on the issue of human personhood. The issue now is anything but academic, as it once might have been. Maximally, this anthropology must be rejected because it has been invoked as grounds for dehumanizing those at the edges of human life in order to kill them. Minimally, this anthropology must be rejected because even when its adherents avoid drawing immoral conclusions from it in practice, they are still unable to reject with adequate reason such conclusions when they are drawn by others.[56]

Positively, one can also conceive of the image of God as being the human capacity for relationship with God grounded in revelation. This positive definition avoids the identification of a capacity with any specific quality. A capacity is a participant in a relation, only having meaning when viewed from within that relation. As such, it cannot realize itself; it requires the other participant or participants in that relation for its realization. A quality, by contrast, is a property within a substantial entity, a potential that can have meaning even before it is actualized. Indeed, that is the case because it essentially actualizes itself.[57] Nevertheless, it is hard to make a natural law argument based on this positive concept of the image of God, what might be called "covenantal possibility," inasmuch as it requires some sort of positive affirmation of revelation on the part of those to whom the argument is being addressed. Its constitution of human nature can only be made retroactively from revelation; as such, its logic is like that of a

[56] See D. Novak, *Law and Theology in Judaism* II (New York, 1976), 108ff.
[57] See Novak, *Jewish–Christian Dialogue*, 129ff.

Kantian a priori.[58] At best, it works well in Jewish–Christian dialogue, where a covenantal affirmation can be assumed on both sides of the dialogue.[59] But natural law discourse must be able to include nonbelievers as well. That is why it might be better, for purposes of a natural law argument, to conceive of the idea of the image of God negatively.

To conceive of the idea of the image of God negatively is quite akin to the tradition of *via negativa*, which attempts to determine what God is *not* in order to move up to a knowledge of what God *is*.[60] In our case at hand, the *via negativa* helps us to determine what humankind is not, thereby preparing us to know what humankind is. That positive knowledge, at least for Jews and Christians, can only come from God's revelation, namely, where human identity in relationship *with* God is concretely realized. This *via negativa* can be better appreciated when we look at the etymology of the Hebrew term for the "image of God," which is *tselem elohim*.

A plausible etymology of the word *tselem* is that it might come from the noun *tsel*, which means a "shadow." Now whereas an "image" (Greek *eikōn*; Latin *imago*) positively reflects *what* is being "imaged," a shadow only indicates that *some*thing lies behind the blank form that is cast.[61] A shadow is more primitive than an image since it is more inchoate. Unlike an image that gives us positive knowledge of form (*eidos*), a shadow only gives us negative knowledge. It is a bare outline that simply tells us that something is there (*Dasein*), but not what it is.[62] It is akin to what Spinoza meant by his identification of

---

[58] Thus Kant writes: "In the order of time (*Der Zeit nach*), therefore, we have no knowledge antecedent (*vorher*) to experience, and with experience all our knowledge begins (*fängt alle an*). But though all our knowledge begins (*anhebt*) with experience, it does not follow that all arises out of (*aus*) experience" (*Critique of Pure Reason*, B1, trans. N. Kemp Smith [New York, 1929], 41 = *Kritik der reinen Vernunft*, ed. R. Schmidt [Hamburg, 1956], 38).

[59] See Novak, *Jewish–Christian Dialogue*, 141ff.

[60] See Maimonides, *Guide of the Perplexed*, 1.58.

[61] For example, "Man walks about as a mere shadow (*be-tselem*)" (Ps. 39:7).

[62] Cf. Philo, *Legum Allegoria*, 3.31.96, who employs the etymology of "shadow" (*skia*), but then identifies it with a positive "image" (*eikōn*). Cf. Hebrews 10:1 for the emphasis of *eikōn* as positively transcending *skia*.

determinatio and *negatio*.[63] Minimally, a shadow only indicates that something lies behind it.

This understanding of shadow prevents us from making two erroneous assumptions about human persons. First, it prevents us from assuming that what is there comes from ourselves. It thus reminds us that everything we can possibly say about the shadow is only tentative until the real presence behind it makes itself known. To learn from Karl Jaspers, human existence intends transcendence, and to deny that is to confine human existence to a prison of its own making, to confine it to the epitome of what is unnatural for it.[64] Second, this understanding of shadow prevents us from appropriating the shadow into any of our own schemes. The shadow itself is *nothing* without its connection to what lies behind it. As a shadow of something *else*, it limits what use we can make of the space that it occupies. One can thus see the relation of the shadow to its source as limiting our pretension, both theoretical and practical. It is quite similar in its logic to the way Kant constitutes the relation of phenomena to the mysterious *Ding an sich*, the "thing-in-itself" that lies behind them and is never subsumed in them.[65]

Translating this into a philosophical anthropology, which is the proper juncture of ontology and natural law ethics, is to present a theory of human nature. This enables us to better see how such a *via negativa* works in terms of a minimal, hence most immediately universal, notion of the image of God. For if the human person is the "shadow of God," then even before God presents himself to us in revelation, we still have some apprehension of why the human person cannot be definitely categorized by any category by which we determine the nature of the things of the world. Any such categorization, including the category of *animal rationale*, reduces the human person to a merely worldly entity. It is thus a distortion of humankind's true being, especially when put into human practice. The things of the world, humans can name; their own name, however, can

[63] *Epistola*, no. 50, *Opera* III, ed. J. van Vloten and J. P. N. Land (The Hague, 1914), 173.
[64] See *Philosophy* III, trans. E. B. Ashton (Chicago and London, 1971), 164.
[65] See *Critique of Pure Reason*, B311.

only come from beyond.[66] No matter how much humans might share with the other creatures in the world, they are always *in* the world, but never truly *of* it. Any attempt to reduce human persons to some worldly category is a distortion of truth, and it inevitably leads to acts of great injustice against humans as well.

The force of this negative anthropology, as it were, comes out in the great insight of the first-century Sage Akibah ben Joseph.

Rabbi Akibah used to say that man (*adam*) is beloved being created in the image (*be-tselem*). It is an additional act of love (*hibbah*) that it is made known to him that he is created in the image as Scripture states, "in the image of God (*be-tselem elohim*) He made man" (Genesis 9:6).[67]

Following Rabbi Akibah's line of thought, we could say that even before revelation, humans have some inchoate notion of their special status, and that it is beyond anything one could get from the world. But only in revelation do humans learn the truth from the One who is the source of that worth, which is that these humans are loved by this God. And through positive commandments that give the covenant concrete content, humans are enabled to respond to that love as their desired end.[68] But all of this is preceded by a ground-clearing as it were, a *via negativa*. This is the necessary precondition for being able to receive the positive truth of revelation. Nevertheless, even without revelation, which in Jewish tradition always *precedes* revelation, one can take this essential limitation of human pretense as knowledge that can well inform human action. Only when human finitude has been properly accepted can God's light shine through into the world.

Ultimately, we affirm the worth of every human person because we believe somehow or other that we are all the objects of God's concern. To apprehend that concern and Who is so concerned for us is the desire of all desires. That desire is so powerful, so urgent, that we cannot suppress it to wait for

---

[66] See *Tanhuma*: Pequdei (printed edn), no. 3 re Eccl. 6:10. Cf. *Beresheet Rabbah* 17.4 re Gen. 2:20.
[67] M. Avot 3.14.   [68] See Y. Berakhot 9.5/14d.

confirmation of the reality of its goal, to wait for the truth of the Subject of that concern to be revealed to us. It is, indeed, the greatest proof of our own unique existence as humans. One could well say: "I desire, therefore I am" (*cupio ergo sum*). Without that desire, I am something much less, a disposable thing of the world. It is that desire that enables me to pray even without any real assurance that my prayer is heard. "Towards you (*negdekha*) O' Lord is my whole desire (*kol ta'avati*); let not my cry be hidden from you" (Psalms 38:10).[69]

This desire of all desires is our craving to be known more than it is our aspiration to know. Hence our apprehension of the goal of this desire must always outstrip our comprehension of it. Our existence intends more transcendence than our action does or could do. That is so whether our action be thought or deed. Moreover, to regard any human person as anything less than the object of God's concern is to fundamentally deny the true intention of his or her existence – and our own, even if the goal of that intention is only to be found in our desire of it. "Whoever belittles (*lo'eg*) the poorest one blasphemes his Maker" (Proverbs 17:5).[70] No one can desire God's concern for himself or herself alone without denying the very meaning of that concern. Its very operation can only be apprehended as being for more than one existence. It is the very opposite of the narcissism of wanting "not universal love but to be loved alone," as the poet W. H. Auden once put it.[71] Thus our desire to apprehend this concern is the epitome of our existence as communal beings. Our desire can only be answered in the company of those whose desire is for it with us.

Only in human community can we properly wait for God. That is why natural law is manifest to us as moral law, which orders our interhuman relationships. That is what connects it to the law of God.

---

[69] This follows the interpretation of R. Judah Halevi. See *Selected Poems of Jehudah Halevi*, trans. N. Salaman (Philadelphia, 1924), 87. Cf. Augustine, *Confessions*, 1.1.
[70] See B. Kiddushin 33a; also, Nahmanides, *Torat ha'Adam* in *Kitvei Ramban* II, ed. C. B. Chavel (Jerusalem, 1963), 128.
[71] "September 1, 1939" in *Seven Centuries of Verse*, ed. A. J. M. Smith (New York, 1957), 687.

CHAPTER 7

Conclusion

By way of conclusion, I would like to summarize the preceding chapters and suggest some of their main implications for further discussion. This can best be done by presenting ten propositions about natural law in Judaism that have emerged from the previous chapters. Each is followed by some brief elaboration. They are as follows:

1. Natural law is that which lies at the junction of theology and philosophy.
It has long been a matter of some debate whether natural law is a theological doctrine or a philosophical idea. Theology is a method devised to understand the basic notions of revelation, which can be called "doctrine" (*torah*). Philosophy is a method devised to understand basic notions about the world, which can be called "ideas" (*eidos*). Each version of natural law, the theological or the philosophical, is problematic. Perhaps the best solution possible for these respective problems is to see natural law lying at the junction of theology and philosophy rather than in the court of one or the other exclusively.

If natural law is a theological doctrine, then it seems to be basically a form of apologetics. For one of the central doctrines of Judaism, indeed one so central that it has been legally designated a dogma which may not be denied, is that the Torah is the revealed law of God.[1] Aside from whatever ends one might think the various norms of that law intend respectively, the law itself is to be obeyed because God is God. To

---

[1] M. Sanhedrin 10.1; Maimonides, *Commentary on the Mishnah* thereon, principle no. 8.

174

deny that would be to deny what Maimonides rightly called "the foundation of all foundations."[2] Furthermore, this law is taken to be fully sufficient for every question of human practice and thought.[3] That being the case, natural law would seem to be a rather indirect and partial way of learning what revelation can teach more directly and completely. Therefore, natural law type arguments only seem to be after the fact as it were. At best, they can be taken as useful for deflecting criticism of the revealed law of God, coming from those who have been influenced by worldly wisdom, the most compelling of which being philosophy with its rational persuasiveness.[4] Short of banning the study of this and other forms of worldly wisdom (which has been unsuccessfully tried from time to time in Jewish history), rhetorical deflection seems to be called for when philosophy, especially, rears its critical head.[5] According to this line of theology, natural law in essence says too little about matters on which the Torah can always say much more. It only offers silver when gold is readily at hand.[6] As one passage in the Talmud puts it, "let our complete (*shlemah*) Torah not be like their empty conversation (*seehah betelah*)!"[7]

If natural law is a philosophical idea, it seems to be saying too much. In the realm of ethics, the idea of human nature as some sort of universal datum to which our thoughts can readily correspond has been very difficult to maintain, especially in the face of the growing anthropological evidence, from archaeology diachronically and sociology synchronically, of the vast variety of human political experience and practice. Thus much of modern philosophy of law has tried to deal with discovering the

---

[2] *Mishneh Torah*: Yesodei ha-Torah, 1.1.

[3] See M. Avot 5.22; Y. Peah 1.1/15b re Deut. 32:47.

[4] This type of apologetic theology became known in the Middle Ages as *kalam*. Note Maimonides' characterization of it in *Guide of the Perplexed*, 1.71 (trans. S. Pines, Chicago, 1963, p. 177): "the science of kalam . . . [is] to establish premises that would be useful to them in regard to their belief and to refute those opinions that ruined the foundations of their law." Here he is speaking of *kalam* as it developed in Islam. But he also recognizes that there were versions of it in both Judaism and Christianity. Cf. *Commentary on the Mishnah*: Avot, introduction, sec. 1.

[5] See F. I. Baer, *A History of the Jews in Christian Spain* I, trans. L. Schoffman (Philadelphia, 1978), 236ff., 289ff. Cf. S. D. Luzzatto, *Commentary on the Torah*: Deut. 6:5; also, Bernard Lonergan, *Method in Theology* (New York, 1972), 24f.

[6] See B. Berakhot 33b.   [7] Menahot 65b.

necessary procedures of systems of law rather than with any overarching ontological scheme into which these systems must fit in order to be valid *per se*.[8] To do any more than that seems to be a surreptitious claim of universality for what often turns out to be some principles that a particular human culture considers to be normatively indispensable.[9] Indeed, to then assume ready universality for such a particular normative outlook can often be exposed as a form of cultural imperialism. That would seem to be the case even in the attempt of some modern, western, philosophers to postulate (rather than discover) certain natural rights as the necessary requirement of any normative order.[10] Furthermore, because when one goes down deep enough in any historical culture, one finds some god or other, many philosophers have always been suspicious that natural law is really a theological intrusion into philosophy's realm. That suspicion is encouraged by the fact that many of the great natural law thinkers in history happen to have been theologians as well. That is why natural law qua law seems to require the assumption of a universal divine lawgiver. And that is something most philosophers take to be beyond the realm of rational demonstration.[11]

If natural law lies at the junction of theology and philosophy, it must be shown to be able to answer the charges of theologians who reject it because of its defects and philosophers who reject it because of its excesses.

What the proposal of natural law should say to its detractors among the theologians is that it is required for the intelligibility of the theological claim (certainly in Judaism) that God's revelation is of immediate normative import. That can only be accepted by the intended recipients of that revelation when they already have an idea of why God is to be obeyed. God is to be obeyed because law is a necessity of human life in

---

[8] See, e.g., Lon L. Fuller, *The Morality of Law*, rev. edn (New Haven and London, 1969), 96f.; also, R. Dworkin, *Taking Rights Seriously* (Cambridge, Mass., 1978), 16off.

[9] See Alasdair MacIntyre, *Whose Justice? Which Rationality?* (Notre Dame, Ind., 1988), ch. 1.

[10] See, e.g., John Rawls, *A Theory of Justice* (Cambridge, Mass., 1971), 11ff.

[11] See, esp., Kant, *Critique of Pure Reason*, B847; *Critique of Practical Reason*, 1.2.2.5. Cf. Yves Simon, *The Tradition of Natural Law*, ed. V. Kuic (New York, 1992), 62ff.

community. The most basic practical human question is: What am I to do? The most basic theoretical human question is: Why am I to do it? Since human life in community is created *de novo* by God and not by humans themselves, it is God who rules *ab initio* for the ordering of that life. Creation itself is the paradigm for all law-giving. All other law-giving is secondary. Minimally, all other law must not contradict the prior law of God; maximally, it must enhance it. If humans could not discover at least some of God's law for themselves before revelation, how could they possibly accept the fuller version of God's law that comes with historical revelation in the covenant? This type of normative revelation would be meaningless if presented to either a lawless mob or a community that had convinced itself that its highest law is something of its own making. That can be seen by the fact that much of the law governing interhuman relationships found in the Torah is law that has been elevated into the covenant, not introduced by it. Much of that law can only be discovered by human reason, of which philosophy is the epitome. Natural law shows that theology cannot simply avoid philosophy without appearing absurd in the process.[12] That absurdity appears in both practice and theory. Theology need only object to the attempt of some philosophers to present natural law as the sufficient ground rather than the necessary condition of the founding of the covenant and the revelation of the Torah that fully governs it.

What the proposal of natural law should say to its detractors among the philosophers is that human cultures can only avoid the question of natural law when they identify themselves alone with humankind *per se* and regard all outsiders as devoid of humanity. But to accept anything like that would ultimately turn philosophy into some sort of national ideology. Accordingly, thinkers in every culture have to speculate about the human nature that enabled their culture as a normative entity to emerge in history. Without an affirmation of that nature as a *sine qua non* of any culture worthy of human beings, no human choice to affirm a culture would be rational. Hence natural law functions

---

[12] See John Courtney Murray, *We Hold These Truths* (New York, 1960), 298.

as a philosophical corrective within a culture, holding it to the conditions that made its very emergence morally possible. And without that affirmation, intercultural relations inevitably become some sort of conquest, spiritual if not physical. Hence natural law functions as the bridge between cultures, preventing any of them from cornering the market on humankind and humanity. The discovery of the basic norms of natural law, then, has to be much more than proposing postulates for any particular system of law and morals. Being much more than a matter of procedure, it requires the quest for an ontological foundation that might be different from that presented by theology, but which cannot falsify theology, nonetheless.

In this way, maximally, theology and philosophy can fructify each other; minimally, they can at least stay out of each other's way when dealing with the question of natural law. The difference between the two is that in theology natural law is constituted from ontology down to ethics, whereas in philosophy it is constituted from ethics up to ontology. They work best in tandem when their respective trajectories cross each other in motion and can tarry for a while together, each recognizing the value of the other.[13] That happens when theology recognizes the ethical value of philosophy, and when philosophy recognizes the ontological value of theology.

2. Natural law is that which makes Jewish moral discourse possible in an intercultural world.

The interest in natural law throughout Jewish history has been in proportion to the worldly involvement of Jews at any particular time and place. Thus in those times and places when Jews have either not been participants in an intercultural world, or have not wanted to participate in one, the interest in natural law has been negligible or dormant. The best and most persistent example of this worldview has been that of almost all the kabbalists. For them, any world outside of Israel and the Torah is unreal or demonic.[14] The converse of this worldview

---

[13] See Leo Strauss, "The Mutual Influence of Theology and Philosophy," *Independent Journal of Philosophy* 3 (1979), 111ff.

[14] See D. Novak, *The Election of Israel* (Cambridge, 1995), 16ff.

has been that type of Jewish theology that has seen affinities between some doctrines from the classical sources of the Jewish tradition and some ideas of western philosophers.

In the Middle Ages, which could be termed the golden age of Jewish philosophical theology (roughly, from Saadiah in the ninth century to Abrabanel in the fifteenth century), the worldliness of Jews in a cultural sense was largely an academic matter. Indeed, it was more a matter of the exchange of thoughts through books than through person-to-person discourse. Thus one can think of Aquinas in thirteenth-century France in his constitution of natural law learning from the writing of Maimonides in twelfth-century Egypt, and of Albo in fifteenth-century Spain in his constitution of natural law learning from the writing of Aquinas in turn. When it came to social contact, however, the vast majority of Jews lived in their own world.

The three great historical events (or, perhaps, periods) that have determined so much of modern Jewish life have, in effect, catapulted Jews personally into an intercultural world, which has been much more than one whose prime activity was the cross-referencing of different writings. As such, they have been thrown into a world of real political interaction. Here natural law has had to play an even greater role in Jewish life than it did when it was more academically confined, although that role has not benefitted nearly enough from the philosophical insights of the medieval Jewish theologians. These three great events have been: (1), the emancipation of West European Jews from being noncitizens of the larger societies in which they lived (the key date being the French Revolution of 1789); (2), the murder of at last half of European Jewry in the Holocaust (the key date being the beginning of the Second World War in 1939); and (3), the establishment of the State of Israel in 1948.

In terms of the political emancipation of the Jews, natural law was at the heart of arguments for the enfranchisement of Jews as individuals in modern, secular, nation-states. Citizenship was to be a human right dependent on the acceptance of a universally valid moral law. The price Jews paid for this rescue from political (and economic) marginality was the loss of the

rights of the semi-autonomous Jewish communities, separated
by religion from the majority religion of host societies.
Although this was the result of historical processes beyond the
power of the choice of the Jews, most Jews welcomed it anyway.
It was only a small minority who hoped that modernity and the
emancipation it brought would somehow or other miraculously
go away and that an *ancien régime* would return instead. Since
that time, all Jewish claims to be free of any kind of discrimina-
tion or persecution have been made in the language of natural
(later human) rights, even when they have been made in a
conceptually obtuse way. What a natural law perspective does
for Jews at this level is to enable them to make rights claims,
but without having to adopt the type of all- embracing
secularism that is antithetical to the covenantal basis of traditional Jewish life and thought.

In terms of the Holocaust, natural law enables Jews to
present the mass murder of European Jewry by the Nazis and
their cohorts as a genuine crime against humanity. The universality inherent in any natural law argument saves the need
many Jews feel to remind the world about the agony of the
Holocaust and its victims from being dismissed as an example
of special pleading. (That in no way diminishes the uniquely
Jewish aspects of the Holocaust; it simply sees those aspects
being more properly the subject of inter-Jewish discourse.) The
only possible reason for the world to take a moral (as distinct
from sensationalistic) interest in the Holocaust is that it is
probably the worst example to date of the violation of the basic
human right to life. Here again, in order to have its full moral
weight, this right must be seen as much more than a mere
postulate of some system of law or morals. It is only a natural
law type understanding of the meaning of mass murder that
can make it a matter of truly universal concern. In fact, those
thinkers who eschew natural law type reasoning when dealing
with the Holocaust are often tempted by or even succumb to
the sort of racist typology that was employed by the very
villains of the Holocaust themselves.

Finally, when it comes to the establishment and development
of a Jewish polity in the ancestral land, which is the State of

Israel, the most fundamental question of all is just what sort of polity it is to be. Heretofore, it has been designated both a Jewish and a democratic state. Yet many have seen an inherent paradox in that dual designation. Some religious thinkers have argued that an authentically Jewish state cannot possibly be the same as a western style democracy, and many secularist Jewish thinkers have argued, conversely, that a democracy cannot be allowed to be hampered by what is, in their eyes, a necessarily anti-democratic, traditional theocracy (which for them turns out to be a dictatorship of clerics). Here a natural law perspective can perhaps begin to solve this paradox and not leave it at its current level of impasse. For the main sticking point between the two divergent views of the Jewish polity of the State of Israel is the question of human rights.

When human rights are merely postulated as being a necessity for a democratic polity, then the whole religious assumption that all valid law is ultimately God's law is bracketed, if not actually denied. On the other hand, when the idea of human rights is simply denied because of an assumption that it necessarily presupposes a totalizing secularism, then the question of what sort of polity a Jewish state is to be in the present is left unanswered. For beginning with the adoption of the admittedly non-Jewish type of polity of monarchy early in the history of ancient Israel, it became clear that a covenantal community who had accepted the law of God for herself could very well live under almost any type of regime.[15] That is because, unlike so much political theory both ancient and modern, in Judaism the authority of the law does not follow from any sort of political sovereignty in the world. Quite the contrary, the legitimacy of any regime is determined by how consistent it is with the law of God.[16] As long as a regime does not explicitly substitute its own authority for that of God and demand total compliance by everyone within its power to that usurpation (idolatry), Jews can live under it in good faith. No

---

[15] For a discussion of various Jewish political options, both ancient and modern, see D. Polish, *Give Us a King* (Hoboken, N.J., 1989).

[16] This point has been recently presented with great power by the Anglican theologian, Oliver O'Donovan in *The Desire of the Nations* (Cambridge, 1996), 65ff., 233ff.

type of polity that Jews have lived under, either as a community or even as individuals, is originally Jewish. Original Jewish polity will only come with the irrefutable arrival of the Messiah. Until that time, when Jews have the chance to actually choose their own type of polity, it would seem that they should choose one that is most respectful of their prior law in lieu of those less respectful of it. The classical Jewish sources as well as the recent experience of the Jewish people in the world should be the guides for that political choice.

For Jews, especially in their own state, to reject western style democracy, with its hallmark of the recognition of human rights, is to opt for either the communist or fascist alternatives available in the world today. The fact that those societies which have been constituted by either of these two ideological options have almost always been antagonistic to both Jews and Judaism, should be good enough reason for Jews to be suspicious of them for themselves and suspicious of Jewish thinkers who seem to be inclined to them in either their thought or their rhetoric. The task for Jewish thinkers, then, is to recover the doctrine of natural law from within the Jewish tradition itself. For here natural law is seen as the law of God, hence it must eschew the secularism that has accompanied so much natural or human rights talk since the Enlightenment. But by seeing at least the earliest and most general installment of God's law as being discoverable by human reason, much of what modern natural or human rights theorists have postulated can be more deeply affirmed by Jews. And it can be critically affirmed in such a way that it rectifies the excessive individualism that has marred so much of the type of liberal natural or human rights talk that has not had an adequate ontology and anthropology behind it.

3. Natural law is the practical thrust of the doctrine of creation.
The doctrine of creation is not primarily an answer to the questions: When did the world begin? or How did the world begin? It is much more an answer to the question: Why does the world exist?[17] For whereas the former two questions can be

---

[17] See Maimonides, *Guide*, 2.19.

confined to the level of theory alone, the question of the world's
purposiveness is one that combines both practice and theory.[18]
Since humans are the only creatures we know who ask
theoretical questions in connection with their practice, the
intelligent question of why the world exists must be seen in the
light of the human question: Why do we exist? The question is
Why do *we* exist? rather than Why do *I* exist? because of the
essentially communal nature of even individual human persons.
Hence all sustained human questions are political, understanding "politics" in the broadest and the deepest sense.

The truest political situation of the Jews is that they are in an
everlasting covenant with God. The fact that this covenant is
finally to include all humankind means that the purpose of
human existence is to be in intimate relationship with God. "If
your presence does not go with us, do not take us up out of this
place" (Exodus 33:15). "Every one called by my name, I have
created for my glory" (Isaiah 43:7). And because that purposeful existence is communal, there has to be some interhuman
understanding of what authentic human sociality means even
before God's revelation of the covenant and its law. In other
words, before the revelation of the concrete realization of the
final end of human existence to Israel, humans have to be
living in a rudimentary communal way with themselves. That
means they can discover by themselves penultimate ends in the
world and their concrete realization. They can learn how to
live in true peace with one another and be ready for the
revelation of the highest end and its realization when it comes.
This involves the discovery of natural law from creation itself,
especially from created human existence in community. Thus
natural law deals with what makes authentic human community possible, both immanently and in its transcendent intention.
Being law, it does so practically. It hears before it sees. And
being intentional action, it calls forth the full measure of
human intelligence operating theoretically. Hearing leads into
seeing.

[18] See R. Jacob ibn Habib, *Ein Yaakov*, introduction re B. Pesahim 54a quoting Prov.
8:22. Cf. *Beresheet Rabbah* 1.1.

4. Natural law is the reason for revealed commandments governing interhuman relationships.

Natural law emerges from the Jewish attempt to discover the "reasons of the commandments" (*ta'amei ha-mitsvot*), especially reasons of the commandments in the area of interaction between humans themselves (*bein adam le-havero*). The discovery of these reasons is a specific pursuit. That is, it deals not just with the fact that the commandments in general come from God and that to be in relationship with God is their ultimate end. Rather, it deals with the more immediate ends these commandments intend. As such, it is part of that strand of the Jewish tradition that sees political philosophy as being a useful "handmaiden" of the Torah (*ancilla theologiae*).[19]

It is no accident that those concerned with the reasons of the commandments, reasons which are universally discernible by ordinary ratiocination, have tended to be those in contact with the philosophers and their ideas. The usual interpretation of this has been that Jewish thinkers have been externally challenged by philosophy and have had to adjust their understanding of Judaism accordingly by a synthesis of sorts.[20] This seems to imply, though, that Judaism is really purer and more authentic when left in its originally pristine isolation from the world. However, one can more profoundly see that the very problematic the Jewish philosophical theologians have concerned themselves with did not come from philosophy but from the Jewish tradition itself, even before it was exposed to philosophy. Exposure to and concern with philosophy have helped Jewish thinkers, especially in the area of political/ethical questions, sharpen and deepen their own development of the Jewish tradition. But they have done so because the world itself lies on Judaism's own horizon and is not, therefore, a foreign invader to be tamed through compromise. The discovery of natural law by means of this inherent Jewish rationalism enables political philosophy to become part of a Jewish search for truth rather than making the search for truth and the affirmation of Judaism to be some sort of antinomy.

[19] See H. A. Wolfson, *Philo* I (Cambridge, Mass., 1947), 145ff.
[20] See, e.g., I. Husik, *A History of Medieval Jewish Philosophy* (Philadelphia, 1940), xix.

Finally, an affirmation of natural law can be a coherent guide for making decisions of Jewish law for those in the State of Israel who are dedicated to bringing Jewish law to bear on what others consider to be purely "secular" matters. The whole movement of *mishpat ivri* (literally, "Hebrew jurisprudence") is an attempt to do that, but it has been hindered heretofore by the lack of an adequate philosophical foundation.[21] Since theological agreement is most improbable at this point in Jewish and Israeli history, perhaps philosophical agreement can be more easily reached. In other words, perhaps in the area of political activity, we Jews might have to become (figuratively, that is) the Noahides we had to be before we could accept the covenant at Sinai with rational integrity.[22]

5. Natural law is the precondition of the covenant.

In recent discussions about natural law in Judaism, especially among more traditionally oriented Jewish thinkers, the debate has been between those who deny there is any Jewish doctrine of natural law and those who affirm it. However, even some of those who affirm it seem to see natural law only as a supplement to the revealed law of Scripture and the traditional law of the Rabbis.[23] It would seem that they are somewhat fearful of ascribing any more fundamental role to natural law in Jewish law and theology because, in principle even if not in actual practice, that would constitute a surrender of revelation to reason. And such a surrender is what they see to be the theological error of all liberal Judaisms. Basically, I think they

---

[21] See D. Novak, "A Critical Review-Essay of Menachem Elon's *Jewish Law*," *Vera Lex* 14 (1994), 51ff. Elon's magisterial work is the greatest example of *mishpat ivri*.

[22] See R. Solomon ibn Adret, *Teshuvot ha-Rashba* III, no. 393; R. Asher ben Yehiel, *Teshuvot ha- Rosh*, 17.8; R. Joseph Karo, *Bet Yosef* on *Tur: Hoshen Mishpat*, II, s.v. "ve-katav ha-Rashba." Also, see D. Novak, *The Image of the Non-Jew in Judaism* (New York and Toronto, 1983), 66ff.

[23] See, e.g., J. D. Bleich, "Judaism and Natural Law," *Jewish Law Annual* 7 (1988), 5ff. For a traditionalist view that seems to be ascribing more centrality to natural law in Judaism, however, see Aharon Lichtenstein, "Does Jewish Tradition Recognize an Ethic Independent of Halakha?" in *Modern Jewish Ethics*, ed. M. Fox (Columbus, Ohio, 1975), 62ff. For the most famous traditionalist argument against natural law in Judaism in recent years, see Marvin Fox, "Maimonides and Aquinas on Natural Law," *Dine Israel* 3 (1972), v and ff. For a critique of Fox *et al.* on this point, see D. Novak, *Jewish Social Ethics* (New York, 1992), 24ff.

have been traumatized by the philosophical power of Hermann Cohen's constitution of Judaism, which did just that, very persuasively. (That is the case with even those who either do not understand Cohen or have never even read him. They have been traumatized by those who did understand him, or whose basic point of view was better thought out by Cohen than by themselves.) Cohen did Jewish natural law thinking brilliantly, but his way is not the only way (or even the best one, I think).[24]

For natural law thinking to develop again among Jewish thinkers, the defects of fideism and the excesses of modern rationalism will have to be avoided. That can be done best when natural law is seen as the precondition of the covenant. By "precondition," I mean something quite similar to what Kant meant by the term *Bedingung* (literally, "what enables a thing to be").[25] That *enabling*, though, does not function as a cause or a ground of what comes to be. What it does is make an opening in the world as we can experience it for an entity to appear in it. But because such a precondition is in place does not mean there is any necessity for that entity to appear. (The confusion of the condition of revelation with its ground is the error – and what an exalted error it is – of Hermann Cohen and all the lesser modern Jewish rationalists.[26]) If that appearance is personal – and surely God's appearance reported by Scripture, epitomized by the theophany at Sinai, is personal: God speaks – then his appearance can only be freely given and freely accepted as an interpersonal event. The careful analysis of the meaning of natural law as this kind of precondition for revelation and its law, and the location of this precondition at specific points within the Halakhah itself, gives it a heuristic role richer than its more circumspect proponents can admit, but not as exaggerated as some of its enthusiasts would have us

---

[24] Jewish thinkers were not the only ones who seem to have thought that natural law could only be done Cohen's neo-Kantian way. Thus Karl Barth, who himself had been Cohen's student at the University of Marburg, seems also to have been so seduced. See *Church Dogmatics* 2/2, trans. G. W. Bromiley *et al.* (Edinburgh, 1957), 514.

[25] See *Critique of Pure Reason*, B72; also, D. Novak, *Jewish–Christian Dialogue* (New York, 1989), 136ff.

[26] See Novak, *The Election of Israel*, 72ff.

believe. As the Talmud puts it, "when one grasps too much, one grasps nothing; when one grasps something less (*mu'at*), something is indeed grasped."[27] A true precondition always accompanies what it has enabled to appear; it can never be left behind as finished.

6. Natural law is the criterion for human legislation of interhuman relationships.

One of the things most of the opponents of natural law in Judaism forget is that Jewish law pertaining to interhuman relationships, especially Jewish civil and criminal law, is an area where, as the Mishnah puts it, "there is little from Scripture and much more from traditional law (*halakhot merubbot*)."[28] Now one can see much of the "traditional law" that was developed by the Rabbis and recorded in the Talmud as being based on ancient, inherited, traditions, believed to go back to the time Moses was also receiving the parallel Written Torah from God. However, most of the literary evidence suggests otherwise. It presents much of this civil and criminal law as the development of human legislation by the Rabbis themselves. This point was best constituted theoretically by Maimonides. In his view, aside from those very few traditional laws, indisputably designated by the Rabbis as "Mosaic" (*halakhah le-Mosheh mi-Sinai*), all the rest are clearly devised by human minds. But did the Rabbis simply exercise their legislative authority arbitrarily as some sort of expression of their own political power? Was not their political power, instead, to be justified by some objective criterion? In other words, did not the justification of their legal power have to be by persuasion? And can persuasion be anything but rational?[29]

What Maimonides showed so well in his interpretation (aided but not inspired by his use of Aristotelian type teleology) of Jewish civil and criminal law is that it is based on what the Rabbis discerned as universal standards of justice. There being so little in this area specifically from Scripture itself, the reasoning of the Rabbis had to be far more conceptual than

[27] B. Rosh Hashanah 4b and parallels.   [28] M. Hagigah 1.8.
[29] See B. Gittin 14a; B. Avodah Zarah 35a.

exegetical. Here is where the philosophical idea of natural law is needed for the coherent development of that type of conceptual reasoning in matters of human experience and practice that can hardly be taken as singularly Jewish. The two Jewish terms for this type of criterion seem to be *derekh erets* (literally, "the way of the earth") and *tiqqun ha'olam* (literally, "the rectification of the world").[30] They seem to more or less correspond to the philosophical concept of the "common good" (*bonum commune*). When this line of thinking is followed, one can learn much from the whole philosophical tradition of seeing natural law as a limit and corrective of positive law made by humans (*lex humana*).

7. *Natural law is a cultural construct.*

Perhaps the greatest vulnerability of natural law theory, both in ancient and modern times, is its seeming oblivion to and disrespect of cultural diversity, especially in normative matters. Natural law is taken as what is to be universal. But from where does one begin to constitute this universe? Those who take their natural law inspiration from Plato and Aristotle must also become aware of the fact that they were speaking Greek to Greeks. It would seem that they mostly followed the assumption of their culture that non-Greeks, or at least non-Greek speakers, are really subhuman "barbarians."[31] Consequently, they were, in effect, attempting to conceptualize what was regarded in their own culture as optimal human standards, when being "Greek" and being "human" were taken to be identical. (The Greek conquests of large numbers of barbarians during the time of Alexander the Great were an attempt to Hellenize their captives both physically and culturally.[32]) Moreover, the Roman concept of the "law of nations" (*ius gentium*), without which their concept of *ius naturale* cannot be understood, was originally an institution of Roman imperialism conceived for the rule over certain non-Romans living under

---

[30] Re *derekh erets*, see *Vayiqra Rabbah* 3.9 re Gen. 3:24. Re *tiqqun ha'olam*, see M. Gittin 4.5 re Is. 45:18.

[31] See Aristotle, *Politics*, 1252b5–15; also Plato, *Republic*, 469B–C.

[32] See I Macc., ch. 1.

Rome. And natural law as most famously conceived by Roman Catholic theorists is part of the teaching of a church that explicitly attempts to include all humankind within herself. Jews too must admit that much of what could be termed "Jewish universalism" is the hope of a kind of "judaizing" of the world, as it were.[33] All of this leads to a considerable credibility problem for a "universality" that is not, in effect, a reduction of the many particularities to one particularity, which only becomes universal by a process of elimination.[34]

The problem is not only the moral one raised above, but there is also an epistemological problem. Universal thinking by very particularly formed persons seems to be an imaginative attempt to constitute a world that *would be the case if I were not part of the singular culture in which I now have been living concretely.* But does this world actually correspond to anything we have really experienced? Any attempt to locate some universal moral phenomena is so vaguely general as to be normatively useless. Such attempts to transcend cultural particularity remind me of a judge instructing a jury to "disregard the statement you have just heard," when a lawyer or a witness says something ruled out of order in court. Of course, such a judicial pronouncement is effective in preventing the introduction of such statements from explicitly becoming official points of reference during the actual deliberations of the jury. But it cannot be forgotten (and that is usually why it was made anyway, often with full awareness that a competent judge will most certainly rule it out of order in the trial). It will implicitly influence the thinking of the jurors who heard it, like it or not. Our imagination can tentatively abstract us from our own cultures from time to time, but we cannot transcend them by some nonculturally conceived Archimedean fulcrum in order to either escape them, destroy them, or re-create them.

Instead of an attempt to find some universal phenomenon to ground natural law, it seems more authentic and more useful to see it as the constitution of a universal horizon by a thinker *in* a

---

[33] See Novak, *Jewish–Christian Dialogue*, 57ff.

[34] See Hegel, *Lectures on the Philosophy of Religion*, trans. R. F. Brown *et al.* (Berkeley, Calif., 1988), 202, 371ff.

particular culture *for* his or her own culture. Here is where the doctrine of creation comes in because it does not allow any member of the covenanted community to ignore the world beyond the community facing her. It must be taken with utmost seriousness. (The minimization of that political reality very much correlates with a weak or nonexistent theology of creation.[35]) As we have seen already, that imaginative project is one where one conceives just what sort of a world revelation (the founding event of the culture) requires in order for the One who speaks to present himself in it. The coherence of that imaginative construction makes it plausible. The "construction" here is of the approach to the reality; it is not the reality itself that is constructed. It is like making a telescope, assuming there is something "out there" to be discovered, but which is unlike any object that could be seen by the naked eye. The object to be discovered must be believed to exist, even if there is no other way to see it except through the telescope. (Quantum Theory argues that such "telescopes" themselves are inseparable from the objects they telescope. That is a most useful analogue for natural law theory.) Only that belief, functioning as a regulative principle, saves this type of natural law thinking from becoming, in effect, an elaborate and unconvincing rationalization for a body of positive law (human or revealed) that is better presented authoritatively rather than by argument.

8. Natural law requires comparative law and ethics.
The coherent plausiblity of natural law theory, when it is theoretically good, is complemented by work in comparative law and ethics. The fact is that there are commonalities *between* the universal normative constructions of a number of different cultures. That is especially the case when one looks at Jewish, Christian, Islamic, Greek, and Roman ways of thinking about natural law. These commonalities certainly do not verify natural law. They are themselves too general to do that, and their abstract speculation can never reach the level of the type

---

[35] See Novak, *The Election of Israel*, 16ff.

of transcendental viewpoint Kant attempted to constitute for universal morality.[36] They do not themselves directly correspond to a reality readily apprehended. But they do have correspondences among themselves, what some have called "overlappings."

Despite the minimal character of these overlappings, they do admit of further development, especially in a multicultural context, where enough people want it to be intercultural as well. (That is without, however, the proposal that it must become supercultural, which means one culture swallowing up all the rest.) And if this represents a desire on the part of people and communities to discover criteria for living together in mutual justice and peace, then perhaps this type of natural law theory will have some sort of correspondence with the lives of the human subjects of natural law. In order for this type of correspondence to be valid, however, the test of its universality will be the extent to which it is able to be interculturally inclusive. Perhaps natural law thinking can save "multiculturalism" from the moral dead-end of relativism; and perhaps multiculturalism can save natural law thinking from its all too frequent myopia.

9. *Natural law is Noahide law.*

To say that natural law is Noahide law is not to identify natural law with a concept constructed within the Jewish tradition. For natural law to be "natural," namely, inherently *universal*, it must be recognized and developed throughout the world. If only Jews had thought it, that itself would falsify it. Instead, we should say that with the concept of Noahide law, Jewish thinkers have an authentically Jewish way to engage in thinking natural law. And they can offer their thinking both within and without their own community, although the latter requires the additional intellectual work of translation.

That Noahide law is the Jewish way of thinking natural law is, of course, a highly disputed point, both in ancient, medieval, and modern Judaism. But it is enough for any Jewish thinker to

---

[36] Cf. Kant, *Critique of Practical Reason*, preface.

be able to connect himself or herself with a sustained subtradition within the overall tradition itself, even if that subtradition
has a counter subtradition.[37] Thinking within the context of a
tradition is always an essentially normative pursuit, whether it
advocates "do this" practically or "say this" theoretically. The
direct implication, whether stated or only inferred, is always
"don't do that" or "don't say that." In the case of speech, there
is more legal latitude than in the case of action. The coherence
of communal life requires more conformity in behavior, the
visible aspect of action, than it does in thought, the invisible
aspect of speech.[38] Anything normative is always selective,
which is the only appropriate method (both as *modus operandi*
and as *modus cognescendi*) for anything finite and temporal and
conscious of it – like human creatures aware of their own
condition. We are always here and not there, now and not
then. Eternity is not a humanly attainable perspective. All
human judgment is within history, even when made in relation
to God who can transcend history.[39] Finite normative selection
is not only between what is just and unjust, between right and
wrong in the practical sense, it is also a selection between what
seems wise and unwise at the moment. The intelligent requirement of Jewish thinkers to think natural law as Noahide law has
enough traditional precedent to make it more than idiosyn-
cratic. Moreover, it is a practical requirement for dealing with
the new multicultural political setting most Jews now find
themselves in; and it is a theoretical requirement for the
development of philosophy within Judaism at a time when the
most pressing philosophical questions seem to be those of
political thought.

10. Natural law intends the unique dignity of humanness.
Natural law thinking seems to be best inspired by a sense of
urgency about assaults on the inherent dignity of people and of
human community. In Greek culture, it is best seen in Anti-
gione's protest against the tyrannical abuse of human person-

---

[37] See T. Yevamot 1.12.
[38] See B. Kiddushin 40a re Ps. 66:18 and *ibid.*, 49b and parallels.
[39] See Novak, *The Election of Israel*, 200ff., 262f.

hood by Creon's refusal to allow her dead brother Polynices decent burial.[40] In Scripture, it is best seen in the cry to God from the innocent victims of the injustice of Sodom and Gomorrah.[41] It is a most urgent human need when one is confronted by abuses of political power by those who hold it. And those abuses are a temptation both for those who hold secular power and for those who hold religious power. "Those who hold the Torah do not know Me" (Jeremiah 2:8). It is also a most urgent human need when "every man does what is right in his own eyes" (Deuteronomy 12:8). In other words, we need it when people are abused by communities, and we need it when people abuse human community. Natural law seems to be the best corrective for both the excesses of collectivism and the defects of individualism. It comes from the search for ourselves as the reflection of someone greater than anything we ourselves could make or of anything already in our world. It is truly a perennial need. By whatever name it happens to be called at any one time, it cannot be suppressed, like anything else that is natural.

Natural law, then, is the necessary and perpetual critique needed by all culture and all positive law, even by that culture whose adherents are still conscious of its origin in revelation. Natural law is the essential limit on the pretensions of human action for the sake of human existence and its transcendent intention. It operates best when its rightful role is understood, when neither too much nor too little is expected of it. Whatever it has been called at various points in Jewish history, it has been functioning from the very beginnings of Judaism. But when natural law has been ignored, Judaism has often become distorted in the process, either by understating or overstating its own worldly dimension.

---

[40] See Sophocles, *Antigone*, 20–38.
[41] See Gen. 18:20.

Bibliography

CLASSICAL JUDAIC TEXTS

Abrabanel, Isaac, *Commentary on the Torah*. Warsaw, 1862

Albo, Joseph, *Iqqarim*, 5 vols., ed. and trans. I. Husik. Philadelphia, 1929–30

Alfasi (Rif) in *Talmud Bavli*

Apocrypha and Pseudepigrapha of the Old Testament, 2 vols., ed. R. H. Charles. Oxford, 1913

Asher ben Yehiel (Rosh) in *Talmud Bavli*
    Teshuvot ha-Rosh. Zalkva, 1803

Avot de-Rabbi Nathan, ed. S. Schechter (reprint). New York, 1967

Bahya ben Asher, *Commentary on the Torah*, 3 vols., ed. C. B. Chavel. Jerusalem, 1982

Beresheet Rabbah, 3 vols., ed. J. Theodor and C. Albeck (reprint). Jerusalem, 1965

Bet ha-Midrash, 2 vols., ed. A. Jellinek. Leipzig, 1855

Biblia Hebraica, 7th edn, R. Kittel (ed.). Stuttgart, 1951

David ibn Abi Zimra, *Teshuvot ha-Radbaz*, 2 vols. Warsaw, 1882

Edels, Samuel (Mahrasha), *Hiddushei Aggadot* in *Talmud Bavli*

Eliezer ben Joel ha-Levi, *Sefer Ravyah*, 4 vols., ed. V. Aptowitzer (reprint). Brooklyn, N.Y., 1983

Gersonides, (Ralbag), *Commentary on the Torah*. Venice, 1547
    Wars of the Lord. Riva di Trento, 1560

Halakhot Gedolot, 2 vols., ed. E. Hildesheimer (reprint). Jerusalem, 1971

Halevi, Judah, *Kuzari*, trans. Y. Even-Shmuel. Tel Aviv, 1972
    Selected Poems, trans. N. Salaman. Philadelphia, 1924

Hizquni, *Commentary on the Torah*, ed. C. B. Chavel. Jerusalem, 1982

Jacob ben Asher, *Tur*, 7 vols. (reprint). Jerusalem, 1969

Jacob ibn Habib, *Ein Yaaqov*, 3 vols. (reprint). New York, 1953

Karo, Joseph, *Shulhan Arukh*, 7 vols. Lemberg, 1873

Maharam me-Rothenburg, *Teshuvot, Pesaqim u-Minhagim*, ed. I. Z. Kahana. Jerusalem, 1957

Maimonides, Moses, *Dalalat al-ha'irin*, ed. S. Munk. Jerusalem, 1931
  Guide of the Perplexed, trans. S. Pines. Chicago, 1963
  Commentary on the Mishnah, 3 vols., trans. Y. Kafih. Jerusalem,
    1964–67
  Iggeret Teman, trans. B. Cohen. New York, 1952
  Millot ha-Higayon, ed. L. Roth. Jerusalem, 1965
  Mishneh Torah, 5 vols. (reprint). New York, 1957
  Moreh Nevukhim, trans. Samuel ibn Tibbon (reprint). New York,
    1946
  Sefer ha-Mitsvot, ed. C. Heller. Jerusalem, 1946
  Sefer ha-Mitsvot with Notes of Nahmanides, ed. C. B. Chavel. Jerusalem,
    1981
  Teshuvot ha-Rambam, 3 vols., ed. Y. Blau. Jerusalem, 1960
Mekhilta de-Rabbi Ishmael, ed. H. S. Horovitz and I. A. Rabin (reprint).
  Jerusalem, 1960
Menahem ha-Meiri, *Bet ha-Behirah*: Baba Kama, ed. K. Schlesinger.
  Jerusalem, 1967
Midrash ha-Gadol: Beresheet, ed. M. Margulies. Jerusalem, 1947
Midrash Leqah Tov, 2 vols., ed. S. Buber. Vilna, 1884
Midrash Rabbah, 2 vols. (reprint). New York, 1957
Mishnah, 6 vols., ed. C. Albeck. Tel Aviv, 1957
Mishnah, 12 vols. (reprint). New York, 1969
Nahmanides, Moses, *Commentary on the Torah*, 2 vols., ed. C. B. Chavel.
  Jerusalem, 1959–63
  Kitvei Ramban, 2 vols., ed. C. B. Chavel. Jerusalem, 1963
Nissim Gerondi (Ran) in *Talmud Bavli*
Philo, *Legum Allegoria*, trans. F. H. Colson and G. H. Whitaker.
  Cambridge, Mass., 1929
  De Migratione Abrahami, trans. F. H. Colson and G. H. Whitaker.
    Cambridge, Mass., 1932
  De Opficio Mundi, trans. F. H. Colson and G. H. Whitaker.
    Cambridge, Mass., 1929
Rashbam, *Commentary on the Torah*, ed. A. Bromberg. Jerusalem, 1969
Rashi, *Commentary on the Torah*, ed. C. B. Chavel. Jerusalem, 1982
Saadiah Gaon, *The Book of Theodicy: Commentary on the Book of Job*,
  trans. L. E. Goodman. New Haven and London, 1988
  Book of Beliefs and Opinions, trans. S. Rosenblatt. New Haven, 1948
  Emunot ve-Deot. Jerusalem, 1993
Semahot (Evel Rabbati), ed. D. Zlotnick. New Haven, 1966
Sifra, ed. I. H. Weiss. Vienna, 1862
Sifre: Bemidbar, ed. H. S. Horovitz. Leipzig, 1917
Sifre: Devarim, ed. Louis Finkelstein. New York, 1969
Solomon ibn Adret, *Hiddushei ha-Rashba*, 3 vols. Warsaw, 1902

Teshuvot ha-Rashba, 5 vols. (reprint). B'nai B'rak, 1958
Talmud Bavli, 20 vols. Vilna, 1898
Talmud Yerushalmi, 7 vols., ed. Pietrkov (reprint). Jerusalem, 1959
    ed. Venice/Krotoschin (reprint). New York, 1948
Tanhuma. Jerusalem, 1962
Tosefta: Berakhot-Baba Batra, 5 vols., ed. Saul Lieberman. New York,
    1955–88
Tosefta, ed. M. S. Zuckermandl (reprint). Jerusalem, 1937
Vayiqra Rabbah, 4 vols., ed. M. Margulies. Jerusalem, 1953
Yalqut Shimoni, 2 vols. (reprint). New York, 1944
Yom Tov ben Abraham Ishbili, *Hiddushei ha-Ritva*, 3 vols. Warsaw,
    1902
Zohar, 3 vols., ed. R. Margaliot. Jerusalem, 1984

MODERN JUDAIC TEXTS

Altmann, Alexander, *Essays in Jewish Intellectual History.* Hanover,
    N.H., 1981
    Moses Mendelssohn. University, Ala., 1973
Atlas, Samuel, *Netivim be-Mishpat ha'Ivri.* New York, 1978
Baeck, Leo, *Judaism and Christianity*, trans. and ed. W. Kaufmann.
    Philadelphia, 1958
Baer, F. I., *A History of the Jews in Christian Spain*, 2 vols., trans. L.
    Schoffman. Philadelphia, 1978
Bauer, Yehuda, *The Jewish Emergence from Powerlessness.* Toronto, 1979
Bleich, J. David, *Contemporary Halakhic Problems*, New York, 1977
    "Judaism and Natural Law," *Jewish Law Annual* 7 (1988)
Brown, F., Driver, S. R., and Briggs, C. A., *A Hebrew and English
    Lexicon of the Old Testament.* Oxford, 1952
Buber, Martin, *I and Thou*, trans. W. Kaufmann. New York, 1970
Buber, Martin and Rosenzweig, Franz, *On Jewish Learning*, trans.
    W. Wolf, ed. N. N. Glatzer. New York, 1955
    Die Fünf Bücher der Weisung. Cologne and Olten, 1954
Chajes, Zvi Hirsch, *Kol Kitvei Maharats Chajes*, 2 vols. Jerusalem, 1958
Cohen, Boaz, *Jewish and Roman Law*, 2 vols. New York, 1966
Cohen, Hermann, *Der Begriff der Religion im System der Philosophie.*
    Giessen, 1915
    Ethik des reinen Willens, 4th edn. Berlin, 1923
    Jüdische Schriften, 3 vols., ed. B. Strauss. Berlin, 1924
    Logik der reinen Erkenntnis, 3rd edn. Berlin, 1922
    Religion of Reason out of the Sources of Judaism, trans. S. Kaplan. New
    York, 1972

Religion der Vernunft aus den Quellen des Judentums, 2nd edn. Darmstadt, 1966

Diesendruck, Zvi, "Die Teleologie bei Maimonides," *Hebrew Union College Annual* 4 (1928)

Efros, Israel, *Studies in Medieval Jewish Philosophy*. New York, 1974

Elon, Menachem, *Jewish Law*, 4 vols., trans. B. Auerbach and M. J. Sykes. Philadelphia and Jerusalem, 1994

Encyclopedia Talmudit, 21 vols. Jerusalem, 1955–93

Faur, J., *Iyunim be-Mishneh Torah le-ha-Rambam*. Jerusalem, 1978

Fox, Marvin, "Maimonides and Aquinas on Natural Law," *Dinē Israel* 3 (1972)

Fraade, Steven D., "Navigating the Anomolous: Non-Jews at the Intersection of Early Rabbinic Law and Narrative," *The Other in Jewish Thought and History*, ed. L. J. Silberstein and R. L. Cohn. New York and London, 1995

Frank, D. H., "The End of the Guide: Maimonides on the Best Life for Man," *Judaism* 34 (1985)

Ginzberg, Louis, *The Legends of the Jews*, 7 vols., trans. S. Szold. Philadelphia, 1909–38

Glatzer, Nahum, *Franz Rosenzweig*, 2nd ed.. New York, 1961

Goodman, L. E., *God of Abraham*. New York, 1996

On Justice. New Haven, 1991

Greenwald, Y. Y., *Kol Bo al Avelut*. New York, 1965

Guttmann, Julius, *Philosophies of Judaism*, trans. D. W. Silverman. New York, 1964

Halivni, David Weiss, *Meqorot u-Mesorot*, 5 vols. Tel Aviv and Jerusalem, 1968–93

Midrash, Mishnah, and Gemara. Cambridge, Mass., 1986

Peshat and Derash. New York, 1991

Harris, J. M., *How Do We Know This?* Albany, N.Y., 1995

Hartman, David, *Maimonides*. Philadelphia, 1976

Heinemann, Isaak, *Taamei ha-Mitsvot be-Sifrut Yisrael*, 2 vols. Jerusalem, 1949

Herberg, Will, *Judaism and Modern Man*. New York, 1951

Heschel, Abraham Joshua, *God in Search of Man*. New York, 1955

Torah min ha-Shamayim b'Ispaqlaryah shel ha-Dorot, 2 vols. London, 1962

Husik, I., *A History of Medieval Jewish Philosophy*. Philadelphia, 1940

Jewish Law Annual 6 (1987) and 7 (1988)

Kasher, M. M., *Torah Shlemah*, 11 vols. (reprint). Jerusalem, 1992

Katz, Jacob, *Tradition and Crisis*. New York, 1971

Landau, Ezekiel, *Teshuvot Noda bi-Yehudah*, 2 vols. Vilna, 1904

Levenson, Jon D., *Creation and the Persistance of Evil*. San Francisco, 1988

Lichtenstein, Aharon, "Does Jewish Tradition Recognize an Ethic Independent of Halakha?," *Modern Jewish Ethics*, ed. M. Fox. Columbus, Ohio, 1975

Lieberman, Saul, *Tosefta Kifshuta*, 11 vols. New York, 1955–88

Liebman, C. S. and Don-Yehiya, E., *Civil Religion in Israel*. Berkeley, Calif., 1983

Luzzatto, Samuel David, *Commentary on the Torah*, ed. P. Schlesinger. Tel Aviv, 1965

Mendelssohn, Moses, *Jerusalem*, trans. A. Arkush. Hanover, N.H., and London, 1983

Neusner, Jacob, *Meaning and Method in Ancient Judaism*. Chico, Calif., 1979

Novak, David, "Are Philosophical Proofs of the Existence of God Theologically Meaningful?," *God in the Teachings of Conservative Judaism*, ed. S. Siegel and E. B. Gertel. New York, 1985

"A Critical Review-Essay of Menachem Elon's *Jewish Law*," *Vera Lex* 14 (1994)

The Election of Israel. Cambridge, 1995

Halakhah in a Theological Dimension. Chico, Calif., 1985

The Image of the Non-Jew in Judaism. New York and Toronto, 1983

Jewish–Christian Dialogue. New York, 1989

Jewish Social Ethics. New York, 1992

Law and Theology in Judaism, 2 vols. New York, 1974–76

"Philosophy and the Possibility of Revelation: A Theological Response to the Challenge of Leo Strauss," *Leo Strauss and Judaism*, ed. D. Novak. Lanham, Md., 1996

"The Self-Contraction of the Godhead in Kabbalistic Theology," *Neoplatonism and Jewish Thought*, ed. L. E. Goodman. Albany, N.Y., 1992

The Theology of Nahmanides Systematically Presented. Atlanta, 1992

"The Treatment of Islam and Muslims in the Legal Writings of Maimonides," *Studies in Islamic and Judaic Traditions*, ed. W. M. Brinner and S. D. Ricks. Atlanta, 1986

Polish, D., *Give Us a King*. Hoboken, N.J., 1989

Rosenzweig, Franz, *The Star of Redemption*, trans. W. W. Hallo. New York, 1970

Rosner, F. and Bleich, J. D. (eds.), *Jewish Bioethics*. New York, 1979

Roth, Cecil, *A History of the Marranos*. Philadelphia, 1932

Sarna, N. M., *Exploring Exodus*. New York, 1986

Schechter, Solomon, *Some Aspects of Rabbinic Theology*. New York, 1909

Schepansky, I., *Ha-Taqqanot be-Yisrael*, 4 vols. Jerusalem, 1991–93

Schwarzschild, Steven, "Moral Radicalness and 'Middlingness' in the Ethics of Maimonides," *Studies in Medieval Culture* 11 (1977)

Seeskin, Kenneth, *Jewish Philosophy in a Secular Age*. Albany, N.Y., 1990

"The Positive Contribution of Negative Theology," *Proceedings of the Academy for Jewish Philosophy: 1986–1987*, ed. N. M. Samuelson. Lanham, Md., 1987

Soloveitchik, Joseph B., "Ish ha-Halakhah," *Talpioth* 3–4 (1944)

Stanislawski, M., *For Whom Do I Toil? Judah Leib Gordon and the Crisis of Russian Jewry*, New York and Oxford, 1988

Twerski, Isadore, *Introduction to the Code of Maimonides*. New Haven, 1980

Urbach, E. E., *Halakhah*. Jerusalem, 1984

Hazal. Jerusalem, 1971

Wegner, J. R., "Islamic and Talmudic Jurisprudence: The Four Roots of Islamic Law and Their Talmudic Counterparts," *American Journal of Legal History* 26 (1982)

Wolfson, H. A., *Philo*, 2 vols. Cambridge, Mass., 1947

Yehoshua, A. B., *Between Right and Right*, trans. A. Schwartz. Garden City, N.Y., 1981

GENERAL TEXTS

Abbott, W. M. (ed.), *The Documents of Vatican II*, trans. J. Gallagher *et al.* London and Dublin, 1966

Arendt, Hannah, *Eichmann in Jerusalem*, rev. edn New York, 1965

The Human Condition. Garden City, N.Y., 1959

The Life of the Mind, 2 vols. New York, 1978

Aristotle, *Metaphysics*, 2 vols., trans. H. Tredennick. Cambridge, Mass., 1933

Nicomachean Ethics, trans. H. Rackham. Cambridge, Mass., 1926

Politics, trans. H. Rackham. Cambridge, Mass., 1932

Posterior Analytics, trans. H. Tredennick. Cambridge, Mass., 1960

Topica, trans. E. S. Forster. Cambridge, Mass., 1960

Augustine, *Basic Writings*, 2 vols., ed. W. J. Oates. New York, 1948

Barth, Karl, *Church Dogmatics*, II.2, trans. G. W. Bromiley *et al.* Edinburgh, 1957

Barton, J. "Natural Law and Poetic Justice in the Old Testament," *Journal of Theological Studies* 30 (1979)

Burrell, David B., *Knowing the Unknowable God*. Notre Dame, Ind., 1986

Calvin, John, *Institutes of the Christian Religion*, 2 vols., trans. F. L. Battles. Philadelphia, 1960

Carnap, Rudolf, *The Logical Structure of the World*, trans. R. A. George. Berkeley and Los Angeles, 1967

Cassirer, Ernst, *The Logic of the Humanities*, trans. C. S. Howe. New Haven, 1961

Chroust, Anton-Hermann, "Hugo Grotius and the Scholastic Natural Law Tradition," *The New Scholasticism* 17 (1943)

Cicero, *De Legibus*, trans. C. W. Keyes. Cambridge, Mass., 1928

Cohen, R. A., *Elevations*. Chicago, 1994

"God in Levinas," *Journal of Jewish Thought and Philosophy* 1 (1992)

Daube, David, "The Peregrine Praetor," *Journal of Roman Studies* 41 (1951)

Davies, W. D., *Paul and Rabbinic Judaism*, 2nd edn. London, 1955

d'Entrèves, A. P., *Natural Law*. New York, 1965

Dewey, John, *A Common Faith*. New Haven, 1934

Dilthey, Wilhelm, *Introduction to the Human Sciences*, trans. R. J. Betanzos. Detroit, 1988

Dworkin, Ronald, *Taking Rights Seriously*. Cambridge, Mass., 1978

Eliade, Mircea, *The Sacred and the Profane*, trans. W. R. Trask. New York, 1961

Eliot, T. S., *The Idea of a Christian Society*, 2nd edn. London, 1982

Ellul, Jacques, *The Technological System*, trans. J. Neugroschel. New York, 1980

The Theological Foundation of Law, trans. M. Wieser. Garden City, N.Y., 1960

Epictetus, *Discourses*, 2 vols., trans. W. A. Oldfather. Cambridge, Mass., 1925

Finnis, John, *Natural Law and Natural Rights*. Oxford, 1980

Freud, Sigmund, *Civilization and Its Discontents*, trans. J. Riviere. Garden City, N.Y., 1958

Fuller, Lon L., *The Morality of Law*, rev edn. New Haven and London, 1969

Gadamer, Hans-Georg, *Truth and Method*, trans. G. Barden and J. Cumming. New York, 1982

Geertz, Clifford, *The Interpretation of Cultures*. New York, 1973

Gilson, Etienne, *God and Philosophy*. New Haven, 1941

Grisez, Germain, "The First Principle of Practical Reason," *Natural Law Forum* 10 (1965)

Grotius, Hugo, *De Jure Belli et Pacis*. Cambridge, 1953

On the Law of War and Peace, trans. F. W. Kelsey *et al.* Oxford, 1925

Habermas, Jürgen, *Communication and the Evolution of Society*, trans. T. McCarthy. Boston, 1979

Moral Consciousness and Communicative Action, trans. C. Lenhardt and S. W. Nicholsen. Cambridge, Mass., 1990

Hart, H. L. A., *The Concept of Law*. Oxford, 1961

Hegel, Georg Wilhelm Friedrich, *Lectures on the Philosophy of Religion*, trans. R. F. Brown *et al.* Berkeley, Calif., 1988

Phänomenologie des Geistes, ed. J. Hofmeister. Hamburg, 1952
Phenomenology of Spirit, trans. A. V. Miller. Oxford, 1977
Heidegger, Martin, *Being and Time*, trans. J. Stambaugh. Albany, N.Y.,
   1996
Horst, F., *Gottes Recht*. Munich, 1961
Husserl, Edmund, *The Crisis of European Sciences and Transcendental
   Phenomenology*, trans. D. Carr. Evanston, Ill., 1970
Ideas, trans. W. R. Boyce Gibson. New York, 1962
Jackson, Timothy P., "Love in a Liberal Society: A Response to Paul
   J. Weitham," *Journal of Religious Ethics* 22 (1994)
Jaspers, Karl, *Philosophy*, 3 vols., trans. E. B. Ashton. Chicago and
   London, 1971
Jolowicz, H. J. and Nicholas, B., *Historical Introduction to the Study of
   Roman Law*, 3rd edn. Cambridge, 1972
Kant, Immanuel, *Critique of Practical Reason*, trans. L. W. Beck.
   Indianapolis, 1956
Critique of Pure Reason, trans. N. Kemp Smith. New York, 1929
Groundwork of the Metaphysic of Morals, trans. H. J. Paton. New York,
   1964
Kritik der praktischen Vernunft, ed. K. Vorlander. Hamburg, 1929
Kritik der reinen Vernunft, ed. R. Schmidt. Hamburg, 1956
Religion within the Limits of Reason Alone, trans. T. M. Greene and
   H. H. Hudson. New York, 1960
Kelsen, Hans, *The Pure Theory of Law*, trans. M. Knight. Berkeley,
   Calif., 1967
Koester, Helmut, "NOMOS PHUSEOS: The Concept of Natural
   Law in Greek Thought," *Religions in Antiquity*, ed. J. Neusner.
   Leiden, 1968
Levinas, Emmanuel, *Collected Philosophical Papers*, ed. and trans.
   A. Lingis. Dordrecht, 1987
Difficile Liberté. Paris, 1976
"Ideology and Idealism," trans. S. Ames and A. Lesley, in *The
   Levinas Reader*
In the Time of the Nations, trans. M. B. Smith. Bloomington, Ind.,
   1994
The Levinas Reader, ed. S. Hand. Oxford, 1989
Otherwise Than Being or Beyond Essence, trans. A. Lingis. The Hague,
   1981
Totality and Infinity, trans. A. Lingis. Pittsburgh, 1969
Levy, E., *Gesammelte Schriften*, 2 vols. Cologne, 1963
Locke, John, *Second Treatise of Government*, ed. G. B. Macpherson.
   Indianapolis, 1980
Lonergan, Bernard, *Method in Theology*. New York, 1972

Löwith, Karl, "M. Heidegger and F. Rosenzweig or Temporality and Eternity," *Philosophy and Phenomenological Research* 3 (1942)

MacIntyre, Alasdair, *After Virtue.* Notre Dame, Ind., 1981
    Whose Justice? Which Rationality? Notre Dame, Ind., 1988

Maine, Sir Henry, *Ancient Law.* Oxford, 1931

Murray, John Courtney, *We Hold These Truths.* New York, 1960

Nagel, Thomas, *The View from Nowhere.* New York, 1986

Niebuhr, Reinhold, *The Nature and Destiny of Man,* 2 vols. New York, 1941

Novak, David, *Suicide and Morality.* New York, 1975

Novum Testamentum Graece, 24th edn. ed. E. Nestle Stuttgart, 1960

O'Donovan, Oliver, *The Desire of the Nations.* Cambridge, 1996

Orwell, George, *1984.* London, 1987

Owens, Joseph, *The Doctrine of Being in the Aristotelian Metaphysics,* 3rd rev. edn. Toronto, 1978

Plato, *Crito,* trans. H. N. Fowler. Cambridge, Mass., 1914
    Euthyphro, trans. H. N. Fowler. Cambridge, Mass., 1914
    Phaedo, trans. H. N. Fowler. Cambridge, Mass., 1914
    Phaedrus, trans. H. N. Fowler. Cambridge, Mass., 1914
    Republic, 2 vols., trans. P. Shorey. Cambridge, Mass., 1930
    Statesman, trans. H. N. Fowler. Cambridge, Mass., 1925
    Theatetus, trans. H. N. Fowler. Cambridge, Mass., 1921
    Timaeus, trans. R. G. Bury. Cambridge, Mass., 1929

Quine, W. V., *From a Logical Point of View,* 2nd rev. edn. New York and Evanston, 1963

Quran, trans. N. J. Dawood. Baltimore, 1968

Rawls, John, *Political Liberalism.* New York, 1993
    A Theory of Justice. Cambridge, Mass., 1971

Rhees, R., "Can There Be a Private Language?," *Wittgenstein the Philosophical Investigations,* ed. G. Pitcher. Garden City, N.Y., 1966

Rockefeller, S. C., *John Dewey.* New York, 1991

Rorty, Richard, "Religion as Conversation-Stopper," *Common Knowledge* 3 (1994)

Seven Centuries of Verse, ed. A. J. M. Smith. New York, 1957

Shaw, George Bernard, *Saint Joan.* Baltimore, 1951

Simon, Yves, *The Tradition of Natural Law,* ed. V. Kuic. New York, 1992

Sophocles, *Antigone,* trans. H. Lloyd-Jones. Cambridge, Mass., 1994

Spinoza, Baruch, *Opera,* 3 vols., ed. J. van Vloten and J. P. N. Land. The Hague, 1914
    Tractatus Theologico-Politicus, trans. S. Shirley. Leiden and New York, 1989

Stanlis, P. J., *Edmund Burke and the Natural Law.* Ann Arbor, Mich., 1965

Strauss, Leo, "The Mutual Influence of Theology and Philosophy,"
    Independent Journal of Philosophy 3 (1979)
    Natural Right and History. Chicago, 1953
    Philosophy and Law, trans. E. Adler. Albany, N.Y., 1995
Taylor, Charles, *Sources of the Self.* Cambridge, Mass., 1989
Thomas Aquinas, *Basic Writings*, 2 vols., Eng. trans., ed. A. Pegis. New
    York, 1945
Tönnies, Ferdinand, *Community and Society,* ed. and trans. C. P. Loomis.
    East Lansing, Mich., 1957
Ulpian, *The Institutes of Gaius and Rules of Ulpian*, trans. W. Studemund
    and J. Muirhead. Edinburgh, 1880
van Beeck, Frans Jozef, *Loving the Torah More Than God?* Chicago, 1989
Walzer, Michael, *Thick and Thin.* Notre Dame, Ind., 1994
Weithman, Paul J., "Rawlsian Liberalism and the Privatization of
    Religion: Three Theological Objections Considered," *Journal of
    Religious Ethics* 22 (1994)
Wittgenstein, Ludwig, *Philosophical Investigations*, 2nd edn, trans.
    G. E. M. Anscombe. New York, 1958
    Tractatus Logico-Philosophicus, trans. D. F. Pears and B. F. McGuiness.
    London, 1961

Index